Roland Barthes

THE FASHION
SYSTEM

Translated from the French by
Matthew Ward and Richard Howard

JONATHAN CAPE
THIRTY BEDFORD SQUARE LONDON

First published in Great Britain 1985
Translation copyright © 1983 by Farrar, Straus and Giroux, Inc.
Originally published in French as *Système de la Mode*
Copyright © 1967 by Editions du Seuil

Jonathan Cape Ltd, 30 Bedford Square, London WC1B 3EL

British Library Cataloguing in Publication Data
Barthes, Roland
The fashion system
1. Clothing and dress – Terminology
2. Clothing and dress – Social aspects
3. Sociolinguistics
I. Title   II. Systeme de la mode.   *English*
391'.0014   GT521

ISBN 0-224-02984-3

Printed in Great Britain by Ebenezer Baylis and Son Ltd
The Trinity Press, Worcester and London

THE FASHION
SYSTEM

Contents

Foreword

A method functions from the first word; now, this is a book of method; it must therefore stand on its own. Nonetheless, before beginning his journey, the author would like to account for the origin and the direction of his inquiry.

The object of this inquiry is the structural analysis of women's clothing as currently described by Fashion magazines; its method was originally inspired by the general science of signs postulated by Saussure under the name *semiology*. Begun in 1957, this work was finished in 1963: when the author undertook it and first conceived its expository form, linguistics was not yet the model it has since become in the eyes of some investigators. Aside from a few studies which existed here and there, semiology was still an entirely prospective discipline; given its elementary methods and uncertain results, any work of applied semiology would then naturally take the form of a discovery, or more precisely of an exploration. Faced with a specific object (in this case the garment of Fashion), equipped with only a few working concepts, the apprentice semiologist ventured forth.

This venture, it must be admitted, is already dated. While writing his book, the author was unacquainted with certain important works that have appeared subsequently; participating in a world where reflection on meaning develops, deepens, and divides very rapidly in several directions at once, benefiting from all the speculation surrounding him, the author himself has changed. Does this mean that at the time of publishing this work—belatedly—he cannot acknowledge it as his own? Not at all (if so, he would not publish it); but beyond a literal response, what is proposed here is *already* a certain history of semiology; in relation to the new intellectual art now being sketched out, this book forms a kind of slightly naïve window through which may be discerned, I hope, not the certainties of a doctrine, nor even the unvarying conclusions of an investigation, but rather the beliefs, the temptations, and the trials of an apprenticeship: wherein its meaning; hence, perhaps, its use.

My main intention has been to reconstitute step by step a system of meaning, in a more or less immediate manner, that is, with the least possible recourse to external concepts, even to those of linguistics, whose use here is admittedly frequent but always elementary. Along the way, the author has encountered many obstacles, several of which, he knows, have not been removed (at least he has not attempted to disguise these failures). What is more, the semiological project itself has altered en route; whereas initially my project was to reconstitute the semantics of actual Fashion (apprehended in clothing as worn or at least as photographed), I very soon realized that a choice had to be made between the analysis of the real (or visual) system and that of the written system. The second course was chosen, for reasons that will be given later, for they are part of the method itself. The analysis which follows deals only with the written system of Fashion. This is a choice that may well disappoint: it would have been more agreeable to analyze a system of real Fashion (an institution which has always held a lively interest for sociologists) and apparently more useful in establishing the semiology of an independent object, one in no way related to articulated language.

Yet, by working not on real Fashion but on written (or more exactly on *described*) Fashion, the author believes he has ultimately respected a certain complexity and a certain order of the semiological project. Though the object of study consists entirely of verbal utterances, of "sentences," the analysis is by no means concerned with only one segment of the French language. For what is governed here by words is not just any collection of real objects, but vestimentary features already constituted (at least ideally) into a system of signification. The object of analysis is therefore not a simple nomenclature; it is a true code, even though it is always only "spoken." Hence, this study actually addresses neither clothing nor language but the "translation," so to speak, of one into the other, insofar as the former is already a system of signs: an ambiguous goal, for it does not correspond to the customary distinction which puts the real on one side and language on the other; thus, it escapes both linguistics, the science of verbal signs, and semiology, the science of object-signs.

Doubtless, this is an uncomfortable situation for a study stemming from the Saussurean postulate that the semiologic "over-
flows" the linguistic; but this discomfort is perhaps ultimately an
indication of a certain truth: Is there any system of objects, a
system of some magnitude, which can dispense with articulated
language? Is not speech the inevitable relay of any signifying
order? If we go beyond a few rudimentary signs (eccentricity,
classicism, dandyism, sport, ceremony), can clothing signify without recourse to the speech that describes it, comments upon it,
and provides it with signifiers and signifieds abundant enough to
constitute a system of meaning? Man is doomed to articulated
language, and no semiological undertaking can ignore this fact.
Perhaps we must invert Saussure's formulation and assert that
semiology is a part of linguistics: this work's essential function is
to suggest that in a society like ours, where myths and rite have
assumed the form of a *reason*, i.e., ultimately of a discourse,
human language is not only the model of meaning but its very
foundation. Thus, as soon as we observe Fashion, we discover
that writing appears constitutive (to the point where it seemed
useless to specify in the title of this work that it addressed *written
Fashion*): the system of actual clothing is always the natural
horizon which Fashion assumes in order to constitute its significations: without discourse there is no total Fashion, no essential
Fashion. It thus seemed unreasonable to place the reality of
clothing *before* the discourse of Fashion: true reason would in
fact have us proceed from the instituting discourse to the reality
which it constitutes.

This unavoidable presence of human speech is clearly not an
innocent one. Why does Fashion utter clothing so abundantly?
Why does it interpose, between the object and its user, such a
luxury of words (not to mention images), such a network of
meaning? The reason is, of course, an economic one. Calculating,
industrial society is obliged to form consumers who don't cal-
culate; if clothing's producers and consumers had the same consciousness, clothing would be bought (and produced) only at the
very slow rate of its dilapidation; Fashion, like all fashions, depends on a disparity of two consciousnesses, each foreign to the
other. In order to blunt the buyer's calculating consciousness, a
veil must be drawn around the object—a veil of images, of reasons, of meanings; a mediate substance of an aperitive order must

be elaborated; in short, a simulacrum of the real object must be created, substituting for the slow time of wear a sovereign time free to destroy itself by an act of annual potlatch. Thus, the commercial origin of our collective image-system (always subject to fashion, not merely in the case of clothing) cannot be a mystery to anyone. Yet no sooner has it altered than this universe detaches itself from its origin (moreover, how could it *copy* that origin?): its structure obeys certain universal constraints, those of any system of signs. But what is remarkable about this image-system constituted with desire as its goal (and, it is hoped, semiological analysis will make this sufficiently clear) is that its substance is essentially *intelligible:* it is not the object but the name that creates desire; it is not the dream but the meaning that sells. If this is so, the countless objects that inhabit and comprise the image-system of our time will increasingly derive from a semantics, and, given certain developments, linguistics will become, by a second birth, the science of every imagined universe.

Introduction

METHOD

GRAPHIC SYMBOLS USED

∫ : Function
≡ : Relation of equivalence
)(: Relation of double implication or solidarity
• : Relation of simple combination
≠ : Different from . . .
/ : Pertinent or significant opposition
/. . ./ : The word as signifier
". . ." : The word as signified
[. . .] : Implicit term
[——] : Normal
Sr : Signifier
Sd : Signified

References to the text consist of two numbers: the first designates the chapter, the second designates the paragraph group if it is a Roman numeral, or the paragraph if it is an Arabic numeral.

1

Written Clothing

"A leather belt, with a rose stuck in it, worn above the waist, on a soft shetland dress."

I. The Three Garments

1.1. *Image-clothing and written clothing*

I open a fashion magazine; I see that two different garments are being dealt with here. The first is the one presented to me as photographed or drawn—it is image-clothing. The second is the same garment, but described, transformed into language; this dress, photographed on the right, becomes on the left: *a leather belt, with a rose stuck in it, worn above the waist, on a soft shetland dress;* this is a written garment. In principle these two garments refer to the same reality (this dress worn on this day by this woman), and yet they do not have the same structure,[1] because they are not made of the same substances and because, consequently, these substances do not have the same relations with each other: in one the substances are forms, lines, surfaces, colors, and the relation is spatial; in the other, the substance is words, and the relation is, if not logical, at least syntactic; the first structure is plastic, the second verbal. Is this to say that each of these structures is indistinguishable from the general system from which it derives—image-clothing from photography, written

---

[1] It would be preferable to have only objects to define and not words; but since so much is expected today from the word *structure*, we will assign it here the meaning it has in linguistics: "an autonomous entity of internal dependencies" (L. Hjelmslev, *Essays in Linguistics*, 1959).

clothing from language? Not at all: the Fashion photograph is not just any photograph, it bears little relation to the news photograph or to the snapshot, for example; it has its own units and rules; within photographic communication, it forms a specific language which no doubt has its own lexicon and syntax, its own banned or approved "turns of phrase."[2] Similarly, the structure of written clothing cannot be identified with the structure of a sentence; for if clothing coincided with discourse, changing a term in the discourse would suffice to alter, at the same time, the identity of the described clothing; but this is not the case; a magazine can state: "Wear shantung in summer" as easily as "Shantung goes with summer," without fundamentally affecting the information transmitted to its readership. Written clothing is carried by language, but also resists it, and is created by this interplay. So we are dealing with two original structures, albeit derived from more general systems, in the one case language, in the other the image.

1.2. *Real clothing*

At the least we might suppose that these two garments recover a single identity at the level of the real garment they are supposed to represent, that the described dress and the photographed dress are united in the actual dress they both refer to. Equivalent, no doubt, but not identical; for just as between image-clothing and written clothing there is a difference in substances and relations, and thus a difference of structure, in the same way, from these two garments to the real one there is a transition to other substances and other relations; thus, the real garment forms a third structure, different from the first two, even if it serves them as model, or more exactly, even if the model which guides the information transmitted by the first two garments belongs to this third structure. We have seen that the units of image-clothing are located at the level of forms, those of written clothing at the level of words; as for the units of real clothing, they cannot exist

---

[2] We touch here on the paradox of photographic communication: being in principle purely analogical, the photograph can be defined as *a message without a code;* yet there is actually no photograph without signification. So we must postulate a photographic code which obviously operates only on a second level which we shall later call the level of connotation. (Cf. "Le message photographique," *Communications,* no. 1, 1961, pp. 127–38, and "La rhétorique de l'image," *Communications,* no. 4, 1964, pp. 40–51.) In the case of Fashion illustration, the question is simpler, since the *style* of a drawing refers to an openly cultural code.

at the level of language, for, as we know, language is not a tracing of reality;[3] nor can we locate them, although here the temptation is great, at the level of forms, for "seeing" a real garment, even under privileged conditions of presentation, cannot exhaust its reality, still less its structure; we never see more than part of a garment, a personal and circumstantial usage, a particular way of wearing it; in order to analyze the real garment in systematic terms, i.e., in terms sufficiently formal to account for all analogous garments, we should no doubt have to work our way back to the actions which governed its manufacture. In other words, given the plastic structure of image-clothing and the verbal structure of written clothing, the structure of real clothing can only be technological. The units of this structure can only be the various traces of the actions of manufacture, their materialized and accomplished goals: a seam is what has been sewn, the cut of a coat is what has been cut;[4] there is then a structure which is constituted at the level of substance and its transformations, not of its representations or significations; and here ethnology might provide relatively simple structural models.[5]

II. Shifters

1.3. *Translation of structures*

There are, then, for any particular object (a dress, a tailored suit, a belt) three different structures, one technological, another iconic, the third verbal. These three structures do not have the same circulation pattern. The technological structure appears as a mother tongue of which the real garments derived from it are only instances of "speech." The two other structures (iconic and verbal) are also languages, but if we believe Fashion magazines, which always claim to discuss a primary real garment, these are derived languages, "translated" from the mother tongue; they intervene as circulation relays between this mother tongue and its

---

[3] Cf. A Martinet, *Elements of General Linguistics,* 1.6.

[4] Provided, of course, these terms are given in a technological context as, for example, in a program of manufacture; otherwise, these terms of technological origin have a different value (cf., below, 1.5).

[5] For example, A. Leroi-Gourhan differentiates clothing that hangs straight with parallel edges, clothing which is cut and open, cut and closed, cut and double-breasted, etc. (*Milieu et techniques,* Paris, Albin-Michel, 1945, p. 208).

instances of "speech" (the real garments). In our society, the circulation of Fashion thus relies in large part on an activity of *transformation:* there is a transition (at least according to the order invoked by Fashion magazines) from the technological structure to the iconic and verbal structures. Yet this transition, as in all structures, can only be discontinuous: the real garment can only be *transformed* into "representation" by means of certain operators which we might call *shifters,* since they serve to transpose one structure into another, to pass, if you will, from one code to another code.[6]

1.4. *The three shifters*

Since we are dealing with three structures, we must have three kinds of shifters at our disposal: from the real to the image, from the real to language, and from the image to language. For the first translation, from the technological garment to the iconic garment, the principal shifter is the sewing pattern, whose (schematic) design analytically reproduces the stages of the garment's manufacture; to which should be added the processes, graphic or photographic, intended to reveal the technical substratum of a look or an "effect": accentuation of a movement, enlargement of a detail, angle of vision. For the second translation, from the technological garment to the written garment, the basic shifter is what might be called the sewing program or formula: it is generally a text quite apart from the literature of Fashion; its goal is to outline not what is but what is *going to be* done; the sewing program, moreover, is not given in the same kind of writing as the Fashion commentary; it contains almost no nouns or adjectives, but mostly verbs and measurements.[7] As a shifter, it constitutes a transitional language, situated midway between the making of the garment and its being, between its origin and its form, its technology and its signification. We might be tempted to include within this basic shifter all Fashion terms of clearly technological origin (*a seam, a cut*), and to consider them as so

---

[6] Jakobson reserves the term *shifter* for the elements intermediary between the code and the message (*Essais de linguistique générale*, Paris, Editions de Minuit, 1963, chap. 9). We have broadened the sense of the term here.

[7] For example: "*Place all the pieces on the lining you are cutting and baste. Baste a vertical fold three cm. wide on each side, one cm. from the ends of the shoulders.*" This is a transitive language.

many translators from the real to the spoken; but this would ignore the fact that the value of a word is not found in its origin but in its place in the language system; once these terms pass into a descriptive structure, they are simultaneously detached from their origin (what has been, at some point, sewn, cut) and their goal (to contribute to an assemblage, to stand out in an ensemble); in them the creative act is not perceptible, they no longer belong to the technological structure and we cannot consider them as *shifters*.[8] There remains a third translation, one which allows the transition from the iconic structure to the spoken structure, from the representation of the garment to its description. Since Fashion magazines take advantage of the ability to deliver *simultaneously* messages derived from these two structures—here a dress photographed, there the same dress described—they can take a notable shortcut by using elliptical *shifters:* these are no longer pattern drawings or the texts of the sewing pattern, but simply the anaphorics of language, given either at the maximum degree (*"this" tailored suit, "the" shetland dress*) or at degree zero (*"a rose stuck into a belt"*).[9] Thus, by the very fact that the three structures have well-defined translation-operators at their disposal, they remain perfectly distinct.

III. THE TERMINOLOGICAL RULE

1.5. *Choice of the oral structure*

To study the garment of Fashion would first be to study each of these three structures separately and exhaustively, for a structure cannot be defined apart from the substantial identity of the units which constitute it: we must study either acts, or images, or words, but not all these substances at once, even if the structures which they form combine to constitute a generic object

---

[8] We might regard the catalogue garment as a shifter, since it is intended to effect an actual purchase by means of the relay of language. In fact, however, the catalogue garment obeys the norms of Fashion description altogether: it seeks not so much to account for the garment as to persuade us that it is in Fashion.

[9] Anaphora, according to L. Tesnières (*Eléments de syntaxe structurale*, Paris, Klincksieck, 1959, p. 85), is "a supplementary semantic connection without a corresponding structural one." There is no structural link between the demonstrative "this" and the photographed skirt, but rather, so to speak, a pure and simple collision of two structures.

which, for convenience' sake, we call the garment of Fashion. Each of these structures calls for an original analysis, and we must choose. The study of the garment "represented" (by image and text), i.e., the garment dealt with by the Fashion magazine, affords an immediate methodological advantage over the analysis of real clothing.[10] Clothing "in print" provides the analyst what human languages deny the linguist: a pure synchrony; the synchrony of Fashion changes abruptly each year, but during the year it is absolutely stable; by studying the clothing in magazines, it is possible to study a state of Fashion without having to cut it artificially, as a linguist must cut the tangled continuum of messages. The choice remains between image-clothing and written (or, more precisely, described) clothing. Here again, from the methodological point of view, it is the structural "purity" of the object which influences the choice.[11] "Real" clothing is burdened with practical considerations (protection, modesty, adornment); these finalities disappear from "represented" clothing, which no longer serves to protect, to cover, or to adorn, but at most to signify protection, modesty, or adornment; but image-clothing retains one set of values which risks complicating its analysis considerably, i.e., its plastic quality; only written clothing has no practical or aesthetic function: it is entirely constituted with a view to a signification: if the magazine describes a certain article of clothing verbally, it does so solely to convey a message whose content is: *Fashion;* we might say, then, that the being of the written garment resides completely in its meaning, it is there that we stand the greatest chance of discovering the semantic pertinence in all its purity; written clothing is unencumbered by any parasitic function and entails no vague temporality: for these reasons, we have chosen to explore the verbal structure. This does not mean that we will simply be analyzing the language of Fashion; it is true that the nomenclature under study is a specialized part of the main territory of (the French) language; this part, however, will not be studied from the point of view of language, but only from the point of view of the structure of the

---

[10] Troubetskoy postulated the possibility of the semantic analysis of real clothing in his *Principles of Phonology,* 1949.

[11] These are reasons contingent upon operational method; the fundamental reasons, concerning the essentially *spoken* nature of Fashion, were given in the foreword.

clothing it alludes to; it is not a part of a subcode of (the French) language which is the object of the analysis, but rather of the "supercode" which words impose on the real garment, for words, as we shall see,[12] take over an object, the garment, which itself is already a system of signification.

1.6. *Semiology and sociology*

Although the choice of oral structure corresponds to reasons immanent in its object, it finds some reinforcement from sociology; first of all because the propagation of Fashion by magazines (i.e., in particular by the text) has become so vast; half of all French-women read magazines at least partially devoted to Fashion on a regular basis; the description of the garment of Fashion (and no longer its production) is therefore a social fact, so that even if the garment of Fashion remained purely imaginary (without affecting real clothing), it would constitute an incontestable element of mass culture, like pulp fiction, comics, and movies; second, the structural analysis of written clothing can also effectively pave the way for the inventory of real clothing that sociology will require for its eventual study of the circuits and circulation-rhythms of real Fashion. Nonetheless, the objectives of sociology and semiology are, in the present case, entirely different: the sociology of Fashion (even if it remains to be constituted[13]) starts from a *model* of imagined origin (the garment conceived of by the *fashion group*) and follows (or should follow) its actualization through a series of real garments (this is the problem of the circulation of models); it therefore seeks to systematize certain actions and to relate them to social conditions, standards of living, and roles. Semiology does not follow the same path at all; it describes a garment which from beginning to end remains imaginary, or, if one prefers, purely intellective; it leads us to

---

[12] Cf., below, chap. 3.

[13] As early as Herbert Spencer, Fashion became a privileged sociological object; first of all, it constitutes "a collective phenomenon which shows us with particular immediacy . . . what is social about our own behavior" (J. Stoetzel, *La psychologie sociale*, Paris, Flammarion, 1963, p. 245); it then presents a dialectic of conformity and change which can only be explained sociologically; finally, its transmission seems to depend on those relay systems studied by P. Lazarsfeld and E. Katz (*Personal Influence: The Part Played by People in the Flow of Mass-Communications*, Glencoe, Illinois, The Free Press, 1955). Nonetheless, the actual circulation of models has not yet been the object of a complete sociological study.

recognize not practices but images. The sociology of Fashion is entirely directed toward real clothing; the semiology of Fashion is directed toward a set of collective representations. The choice of oral structure therefore leads not to sociology but rather to that *sociologics* postulated by Durkheim and Mauss;[14] the function of the description of Fashion is not only to propose a model which is a copy of reality but also and especially to circulate Fashion broadly as a *meaning*.

1.7. *The corpus*

Once the oral structure has been decided upon, what corpus should be chosen for study?[15] Thus far, we have referred only to Fashion magazines; this is because, on the one hand, descriptions from literature proper, although important in a number of great authors (Balzac, Michelet, Proust), are too fragmentary, too variable historically to be of use; and on the other, descriptions from department-store catalogues can be easily assimilated into the descriptions of Fashion; Fashion magazines thus constitute the best corpus. All Fashion magazines? By no means. Two limiting factors can intervene here, justified by the goal intended, which is not to describe a concrete Fashion but to reconstitute a formal system. The first selection concerns time; seeking to constitute a structure, it would be most useful to limit one's work to a state of Fashion, i.e., a synchrony. Now, as has been stated, the synchrony of Fashion is established by Fashion itself: the Fashion of a year.[16] We have chosen to work here on magazines from the year 1958–59 (from June to June), but this date obviously has no methodological importance; one could choose any other year, for we are not attempting to describe some Fashion in particular but Fashion in general. As soon as it is gathered, extracted from its year, the raw material (the utterance) must take its place in a purely formal system of functions;[17] hence, no

---

[14] "Essai sur quelques formes primitives de classification," *Année Sociologique*, vol. 6, 1901–2, pp. 1–72.

[15] Corpus: "intangible synchronic collection of statements on which one works" (Martinet, *Elements*).

[16] There are seasonal Fashions within the year, but here the seasons constitute less a diachronic series than a table of different signifieds within the lexicon of a year. The synchronic unit is indeed the "line," which is annual.

[17] On occasion, we have even drawn on other synchronies for a control or an interesting example.

indication will be given here as to any contingent Fashion, and a fortiori no history of Fashion: we have not sought to deal with any particular substance of Fashion, but only with the structure of its written signs.[18] Similarly (and this will be the second limit imposed on the corpus), it would be of interest to study all the magazines of a single year only if one were concerned with the substantial differences among them (ideological, aesthetic, or social); from a sociological viewpoint, this would be an important problem, since each magazine refers both to a socially defined public and to a specific body of representations, but this differential sociology of magazines, readerships, and ideologies is not the declared object of this inquiry, which aims only at finding the (written) "language" of Fashion. Thus, we have exhaustively studied only two magazines (*Elle* and *Le Jardin des Modes*), with a few forays into other publications (notably, *Vogue* and *L'Echo de la Mode*)[19] as well as the weekly Fashion page to be found in some of the daily papers. The semiological project requires the constitution of a corpus reasonably saturated with all the possible *differences* in clothing signs. On the other hand, it matters far less that these differences are more or less often repeated, for it is difference that makes meaning, not repetition. Structurally, a rare feature of Fashion is as important as a common one, a gardenia as important as a long skirt; the objective here is to *distinguish* units, not to count them.[20] Last, we have further eliminated, within this reduced corpus, any notations which might imply a finality other than signification: advertisements, even when they claim to account for Fashion, and technical instructions for the manufacture of clothing. We have considered neither hairstyles nor makeup, since these elements contain their own particular variants which would have encumbered the inventory of clothing proper.[21]

---

[18] This does not rule out, of course, a general reflection on the diachrony of Fashion (cf., below, Appendix I).

[19] This choice is not altogether arbitrary, however. *Elle* and *L'Echo de la Mode* seem to have a more "popular" appeal than *Vogue* and *Le Jardin des Modes*.

[20] Disparity of frequencies is of sociologic but not of systematic importance; it informs us about the "tastes" (the obsessions) of a magazine (and thus of a readership), not about the general structure of the object; the frequency of signifying units is relevant only for the comparison of magazines with one another.

[21] The statements of Fashion will be quoted without sources, like examples from grammar.

1.8. *The terminological rule*

We will thus be dealing here with written clothing exclusively. The preliminary rule that determines the constitution of the corpus to be analyzed is *to retain no other raw material for study than the language provided by the Fashion magazines*. No doubt, this considerably limits the material for analysis; on the one hand it rules out any recourse to related documents (such as dictionary definitions), and on the other it deprives us of the rich resources of photography; in short, it treats the Fashion magazine only marginally, where it seems to duplicate the image. But this impoverishment of the raw material, aside from being methodologically inevitable, has perhaps its own rewards: to reduce the garment to its oral version is thereby to encounter a new problem which can be formulated thus: *What happens when an object, whether real or imaginary, is converted into language?* or rather, *when an object encounters language?* If the garment of Fashion appears to be a paltry thing in the face of so broad a question, we would do well to keep in mind that the same relation is established between literature and the world: isn't literature the institution which seems to convert the real into language and place its being in that conversion, just like our written garment? Moreover, isn't written Fashion a literature?

IV. DESCRIPTION

1.9. *Literary description and Fashion description*

Fashion and literature in fact utilize a common technique whose end is seemingly to transform an object into language: it is *description*. This technique, however, is used quite differently in each case. In literature, description is brought to bear upon a hidden object (whether real or imaginary): it must make that object exist. In Fashion the described object is actualized, given separately in its plastic form (if not its real form, since it is nothing other than a photograph). The functions of Fashion description are thus reduced, but also, thereby, original: since it need not render the object itself, the information which language communicates, unless it is pleonastic, is by definition the very information which photography or drawing cannot transmit. The importance of the written garment confirms the fact that specific language-functions exist which the image, whatever its development in contemporary society may be, could not possibly assume. For the written garment in particular, what then are the specific functions of language in relation to the image?

1.10. *Immobilization of levels of perception*

The primary function of speech is to immobilize perception at a certain level of intelligibility (or, as the theoreticians of information would say, of prehensibility). We know in fact that an image inevitably involves several levels of perception, and that the reader of images has at his disposal a certain amount of freedom in his choice of the level (even if he is not aware of this freedom): this choice is of course not without limits: there are *optimum* levels: precisely those where the intelligibility of the message is highest; but from the grain of the paper to this tip of the collar, then from this collar to the whole dress, every glance cast at an image inevitably implies a decision; i.e., the meaning of an image is never certain.[22] Language eliminates this freedom, but also this uncertainty; it conveys a choice and imposes it, it requires the perception of this dress to stop here (i.e., neither before nor beyond), it arrests the level of reading at its fabric, at its belt, at the accessory which adorns it. Thus, every written word has a function of authority insofar as *it* chooses—by proxy, so to speak—instead of the eye. The image freezes an endless number of possibilities; words determine a single certainty.[23]

1.11. *Function of knowledge*

The second function of speech is a function of knowledge. Language makes it possible to deliver information which photography delivers poorly or not at all: the color of a fabric (if the photograph is black and white), the nature of a detail inaccessible to view (*decorative button, pearl stitch*), the existence of an element hidden because of the two-dimensional character of the image

---

[22] As we know from Ombredanne's experiment with the perception of the film image (cf. E. Morin, *Le cinéma ou l'homme imaginaire*, Editions de Minuit, 1956, p. 115).

[23] That is why all news photographs are captioned.

(the back of a garment); in a general way, what language adds to the image is *knowledge*.[24] And since Fashion is a phenomenon of initiation, speech naturally fulfills a didactic function: the Fashion text represents as it were the authoritative voice of someone who knows all there is behind the jumbled or incomplete appearance of the visible forms; thus, it constitutes a technique of opening the invisible, where one could almost rediscover, in secular form, the sacred halo of divinatory texts; especially since the knowledge of Fashion is not without its price: those who exclude themselves from it suffer a sanction: the stigma of being *unfashionable*.[25] Such a function of knowledge is obviously possible only because language, which sustains it, constitutes in itself a system of abstraction; not that the language of Fashion intellectualizes the garment; on the contrary, in many cases it helps to grasp it much more concretely than the photograph, restoring to such notation all the compactness of a gesture (*with a rose stuck in it*); but because it permits dealing with discrete concepts (*whiteness, suppleness, velvetiness*), and not with physically complete objects; by its abstract character, language permits isolating certain functions (in the mathematical sense of the term), it endows the garment with a system of functional oppositions (for example, fantasy/classic), which the real or photographed garment is not able to manifest in as clear a manner.[26]

1.12. *Function of emphasis*

It also happens—and frequently—that speech seems to duplicate elements of a garment which are clearly visible in the photograph: *the large collar, the absence of buttons, the flared line of the skirt*, etc. This is because speech also has an emphatic function; the photograph presents a garment no part of which is privileged and which is consumed as an immediate whole; but from this ensemble the commentary can single out certain ele-

---

[24] From the photograph to the drawing, from the drawing to the diagram, from the diagram to language, there is a progressive investment of knowledge (cf. J.-P. Sartre, *L'imaginaire*, Paris, Gallimard, 1947).

[25] Cf., below, 2.3; 15.3.

[26] In relation to photography, language has a role somewhat analogous to that of phonology in relation to phonetics, since it permits isolating the phenomenon "as an abstraction drawn from sound, or as groups of functional characteristics of a sound" (N. S. Troubetskoy, quoted by E. Buyssens, "La nature du signe linguistique," *Acta Linguistica*, II: 2, 1941, 82–86).

ments in order to stress their value: this is the explicit *note* (*Note: the neckline cut on the bias, etc.*[27]). This emphasis obviously rests upon an intrinsic quality of language: its discontinuity; the described garment is a fragmentary garment; in relation to the photograph, it is the result of a series of choices, of amputations; in *the soft shetland dress with a belt worn high and with a rose stuck in it,* we are told certain parts (the material, the belt, the detail) and spared others (the sleeves, the collar, the shape, the color), as if the woman wearing this garment went about dressed only in a rose and softness. This is because, in fact, the limits of written clothing are no longer material limits, but limits of value: if the magazine tells us that this belt is made of leather, it is be-cause its leather has an absolute value (and not its shape, for example); if it tells us of a rose on a dress, it is because the rose is worth as much as the dress; a neckline, a pleat, if put into words, become clothing with full status, with the same "standing" as a whole coat. Applied to clothing, the order of language decides between the essential and the accessory; but it is a Spartan order: it relegates the accessory to the nothingness of the unnamed.[28] This emphasis of language involves two functions. On the one hand, it permits reviving the general information conveyed by the photograph when the latter, like all informative entities, tends to wear out: the more photographed dresses I see, the more banal becomes the information I receive; verbalized notation helps to reinvigorate the information; furthermore, when it is explicit (*note* . . .) it generally does not deal with eccentric details whose very novelty guarantees its informative power, but with elements so commonly offered in the variations of Fashion (collars, trim, pockets)[29] that it is necessary to recharge the message they con-tain; here Fashion behaves like language itself, for which the novelty of a turn of phrase or of a word always constitutes an emphasis destined to repair the wear in its system.[30] On the other hand, the emphasis language places on certain vestimentary fea-tures by naming them remains perfectly functional; description

---

[27] In fact, all Fashion commentary is an implicit *note;* cf., below, 3.9.

[28] By antiphrasis, what is called the *accessory*, in Fashion, is very often the essential, the spoken system having precisely the task of making the *almost noth-ing* signify. *Accessory* is a term derived from the real, economic structure.

[29] These are the vestimentary genera which best lend themselves to the signifi-cant variation (cf., below, 12.7).

[30] Cf. Martinet, *Elements,* 6.17.

does not aim at isolating certain elements in order to praise their aesthetic value, but simply to render intelligible in an analytical way precisely those reasons which make an organized whole out of a collection of details: description here is an instrument of structuration; in particular, it permits orienting the perception of the image: in itself, a photographed dress does not begin or end anywhere; none of its limits is privileged; it can be looked at indefinitely or in the blink of an eye; the look we give it has no duration because it has no regular itinerary;[31] whereas, when described, this same dress (we saw only it) begins at its belt, continues on to a rose and ends in shetland; the dress itself is barely mentioned. Thus, by introducing an organized duration into the representation of the Fashion garment, description institutes, so to speak, a protocol of unveiling: the garment is unveiled according to a certain order, and this order inevitably implies certain goals.

1.13. *Finality of description*

Which goals? It must be understood that from a practical point of view, the description of a Fashion garment serves no purpose; we could not make a garment by relying solely on its Fashion description. The goal of a sewing pattern is transitive: it involves making something; the goal of a written garment seems purely reflexive: the garment seems to *speak itself*, to refer to itself, enclosed in a sort of tautology. The functions of description, whether they are fixation, exploration, or emphasis, aim only at manifesting a certain state of being for the garment of Fashion, and this being can only coincide with Fashion itself; image-clothing can most certainly be *fashionable* (it is so by its very definition), but it cannot be *Fashion* directly; its materiality, its very totality, its evidence, so to speak, make the Fashion it represents an attribute and not a being; *this* dress, which is represented to me (and not described), may well be something other than fashionable; it may be warm, strange, attractive, modest,

---

[31] A dubious experiment conducted in the United States by a clothing firm (cited by A. Rothstein, *Photo-journalism*, New York, Photographic Book Publishing Co., 1956, pp. 85, 99) nonetheless tried to discover the itinerary of the look that "reads" the representation of a human silhouette: the privileged zone of reading, what the look most often returns to, is apparently the neck—in vestimentary terms, the collar: it is true that the firm in question sold shirts.

protective, etc., *before* being fashionable; on the contrary, this same dress, described, can only be Fashion itself; no function, no accident succeeds in barring the evidence of its existence, since functions and accidents themselves, if they are noted, proceed from a declared intention of Fashion.[32] In short, the proper aim of description is to direct the immediate and diffuse knowledge of image-clothing through a mediate and specific knowledge of Fashion. Here we find once again the considerable difference, of an anthropological order, which opposes looking to reading: we look at image-clothing, we read a described garment, and it is probable that two different audiences correspond to these two activities; the image makes the purchase unnecessary, it re-places it; we can intoxicate ourselves on images, identify ourselves oneirically with the model, and, in reality, follow Fashion merely by purchasing a few boutique accessories; speech, on the con-trary, rids the garment of all corporal actuality; being no more than a system of impersonal objects whose mere assemblage creates Fashion, the described garment encourages the purchase. The image provokes a fascination, speech an appropriation; the image is complete, it is a saturated system; speech is fragmentary, it is an open system: when combined, the latter serves to *dis-appoint* the former.

1.14. *Language and speech, clothing and dress*

We will gain a still better understanding of the relation between image-clothing and written clothing, between the represented object and the described object, by referring to a conceptual opposition which has become classic since Saussure:[33] that of language and speech. Language is an institution, an abstract body of constraints; speech is the momentary part of this institu-tion which the individual extracts and actualizes for purposes of communication; language issues from the mass of spoken words, and yet all speech is itself drawn from language; in history this is a dialectic between the structure and the event, and in com-

---

[32] The functionalization of the Fashion garment (a dance skirt) is a phenom-enon of connotation; hence, it is entirely a part of the Fashion system (cf., below, 19.II).
[33] F. de Saussure, *Cours de linguistique générale*, Paris, Payot, 4th ed., 1949, chap. III.

munication theory between the code and the message.[34] Now, in relation to image-clothing, written clothing has a structural purity which is more or less that of language in relation to speech: description is, in a necessary and sufficient manner, based on the manifestation of institutional constraints which make *this* garment, represented here, fashionable; it is in no way concerned with the manner in which the garment is worn by a particular individual, even if that person is "institutional," as, for example, a cover girl.[35] Here is an important difference, and, when necessary, we might agree to call the structural, institutional form of what is worn *clothing* (that which corresponds to language), and this same form when actualized, individualized, worn, *dress* (that which corresponds to speech). Undoubtedly, described clothing is not entirely general, it remains *chosen;* it is, if you will, an example of grammar, it is not grammar itself; but at least, in order to speak an informative language, it produces no *static,* i.e., nothing that disturbs the pure meaning it transmits: it is entirely *meaning:* description is speech without static. However, this opposition is valuable only at the level of the vestimentary system; for at the level of the linguistic system, it is evident that description itself is sustained by particular instances of speech (the one in *this* magazine, on *this* page); description is, if you will, an abstract garment entrusted to a concrete speech; written clothing is at once institution ("language") on the level of clothing, and action ("speech") on the level of language. This paradoxical status is important: it will govern the entire structural analysis of written clothing.

---

[34] Martinet, *Elements*, 1.18.—The identity of the code and of the language, of the message and of speech, has been discussed by P. Guiraud, "La mécanique de l'analyse quantitative en linguistique," in *Etudes de linguistique appliquée,* no. 2, Didier, 1963, p. 37.

[35] On the cover girl, cf., below, 18.11.

2

The Relation of Meaning

"A soft canezou for a festive lunch at Deauville."

I. FIELDS WITH CONCOMITANT VARIATIONS OR COMMUTATIVE CLASSES

2.1. *The commutation test*

With written clothing, we confront an infinite communication whose units and functions remain unknown to us, for although its structure is oral, it does not coincide exactly with that of language.[1] How is this communication to be structured? Linguistics offers an operating model which we shall try to take advantage of, *the commutation test*. Suppose we have a structure given in its entirety. The commutation test consists of artificially varying one term[2] of this structure and observing whether this variation introduces a change in the reading or the usage of the given structure; thus, by successive approximations, we can hope on the one hand to determine the smallest fragments of substance responsible for a change in reading or in usage, and consequently to define these fragments as structural units; on the other hand, by observing which variations occur in conjunction, we are able to draw up a general inventory of concomitant variations, and

---

[1] Cf., above, 1.1.
[2] We must remember Saussure's remark here: "As soon as we say 'term' instead of 'word,' the idea of system is evoked" (R. Godel: *Les sources manuscrites du cours de linguistique générale de F. de Saussure*, Geneva, Droz, Paris, Minard, 1957, pp. 90, 220).

consequently to determine a certain number of commutative classes in the ensemble of a given structure.

2.2. *Commutative classes: clothing and the world*

Magazines greatly facilitate the commutation test by openly employing it in certain privileged cases. For instance, if we are told that *this long cardigan is discreet when unlined and amusing when reversible,* we see right away that there are two concomitant variations: a variation in clothing (from *absence of lining* to *reversible*) produces a variation in character (transition from *discreet* to *amusing*); conversely, the variation in character necessitates a variation in clothing. By combining all utterances which manifest such a structure, we are led to posit the existence (on the level of written clothing) of two large commutative classes: in one are found all the vestimentary features, and in the other all the character features (*discreet, amusing,* etc.) or the circumstantial features (*evening, weekend, shopping,* etc.); on one side, forms, fabrics, colors, and on the other, situations, occupations, states, moods; or, to simplify still further, on one side, clothing, and on the other, the world. But this is not all. If, setting aside the examination of these privileged cases, we turn to that of simple utterances apparently lacking this double concomitant variation, we encounter just as often, made explicit by the language, terms derived from our two commutative classes, the garment and the world; if the magazine tells us that *prints are winning at the races,* we can attempt to make the commutation artificially, and, referring to other utterances in the corpus, state for instance that the transition from prints to solid colors involves (elsewhere) a transition from the Races to garden parties; in short, that a variation in clothing is inevitably accompanied by a variation in the world and vice versa.[3] These two commutative classes, the world and the garment, encompass a great many Fashion utterances: all those where magazines assign to clothing a certain function, or more generally, a certain suitability: *Accessories make the spring. —Pleats are a must in the after-*

---

[3] Unless of course the magazine itself explicitly neutralizes the variations of the world (*"This sweater for city or country"*) or those of the garment (*"For summer nights, mousseline or taffeta"*). Cf., below, 11.III and 14.II.

noon. —This hat is young because it shows the forehead. —These shoes are ideal for walking, etc. Of course, by giving a title ("world," "garment") to the two classes we have just identified, by "filling" them with a certain content which is never actually acknowledged by the language of the magazine itself (it never mentions the "world" or the "garment"), the analyst has interposed his own language, i.e., a metalanguage; strictly speaking, we should limit ourselves to calling these two classes X and Y, for ultimately their basis is entirely a formal one. Nonetheless, it might be useful at this point to mark the disparity of the substances (here vestimentary, there worldly[4]) engaged in each of these two classes, and above all to note that in the examples cited here, the two classes are made equally actual or, if you prefer, explicit: neither garment nor world is ever deprived of a verbal expression.[5]

2.3. *Commutative classes: clothing and Fashion*

The two classes of *clothing* and *world* are far from exhausting the whole corpus being studied; in many utterances, the magazine simply describes the garment without correlating it to characteristics or worldly circumstances; here we have *a waist-length bolero for a turquoise shetland suit cut high at the neck, elbow-length sleeves, and two fob pockets on the skirt;* there we have *a halter top buttoned down the back, its collar tied like a little scarf,* etc.; we shall only say that in this sort of example we have only one class at our disposal, the clothing, and that consequently these utterances lack the correlative term without which the commutation test, and hence the structure of written clothing, cannot occur. In the first case, a variation in clothing entailed a variation in the world (and vice versa), but for clothing to continue to constitute a commutative class, even when purely and simply described, changing a term in the description would have to determine a concomitant change *elsewhere.* Now, it must be recalled that every description of a garment serves a specific

---

[4] We shall use "worldly" here not in a purely social sense but in the sense of *that which belongs to the world, intra-worldly.*

[5] We shall see (below, 17.4) that certain worldly terms can become vestimentary terms when they are signifieds solidified into signifiers (a sports shirt).

purpose, which is to manifest, or better still, to *transmit* Fashion: any clothing that is noted coincides with the being of Fashion. It follows that a variation in certain elements of the described garment would determine a concomitant variation in Fashion; and since Fashion is a normative whole, a law without degrees, to change Fashion is to depart from it; changing an utterance of Fashion (at least in its terminology),[6] imagining, for example, a halter buttoned *in front,* and no longer *down the back,* is to shift correlatively from Fashion to the unfashionable. Of course, the class *Fashion* contains only this single variation (*Fashion/ unfashionable*); but this is enough to validate it, since this variation, poor as it is, permits the commutation test. In all cases where clothing is not related to the world, we therefore find ourselves confronted with a new pair of commutative classes, constituted this time by clothing and Fashion. However, unlike the first pair (*Clothing ʃ World*), the terms derived from the second pair (*Clothing ʃ Fashion*) are actualized, or made explicit, unequally: the *fashionable* is almost never enunciated: it remains implicit, exactly like the signified of a word.[7]

2.4. *Set A and set B*

To sum up, we may now be certain that any utterance provided by the corpus being studied consists of two terms, derived from two commutative classes. Sometimes these two terms are explicit (*Clothing ʃ World*), sometimes one is explicit (*Clothing*) and the other is implicit (*Fashion*). But whatever the pair of classes being dealt with, one term is always uttered, and consequently the class to which it belongs is actualized: *Clothing.*[8] This explains why commutation always takes place either between cloth-

---

[6] We shall see later (cf., below, 4.9 and 5.10) that the utterance of Fashion can include insignificant variations, insofar as the structure of even the written garment does not coincide exactly with that of language.

[7] Without referring to its linguistic meaning, we shall here call *isology* the substantial coincidence of signifier and signified in the sign, including the implicit character of the signified (cf., below, 20.1).

[8] Examples: I.   *prints*   ʃ *the races*
                      accessory   ʃ *spring*
                      this hat   ʃ *youth*
                      these shoes ʃ *walking*
              II. *halter top, buttoned . . .* ʃ [*Fashion*]
                      waist-length bolero . . . ʃ [*Fashion*]

ing and the world or between clothing and Fashion, but never directly between the world and Fashion, or even between worldly clothing and Fashion:[9] even though we have three main categories at our disposal, we are dealing with two commutative ensembles: *set A* (*Clothing ʃ World*) and *set B* (*Clothing ʃ* [*Fashion*]). Thus, the corpus will be exhausted by locating all utterances belonging to set A and all utterances belonging to set B.

II. THE SIGNIFYING RELATION

2.5. *Equivalence*

We might compare the commutative classes to reservoirs from which the magazine draws on each occasion a certain number of features which constitute the utterance of Fashion. These features or groups of features always come in pairs (of necessity, for commutation). But what is the nature of the relation that unites these features or groups of features? In the case of set A, the relation of the two classes appears at first sight quite varied; it is sometimes purposive (*These shoes are made for walking*), sometimes causal (*This hat is young because it shows the forehead*), at other times transitive (*Accessories make the spring*), and at others circumstantial (*One sees prints at the races. Pleats are for the afternoon*); it would seem that, for Fashion magazines, clothing and the world can enter into any sort of relation. This means that, from a certain point of view, the content of this relation is a matter of indifference to the magazine; the relation being constant and its content varied, we see that the structure of written clothing is concerned with the constancy of the relation, not its content;[10] such contents may very well be fallacious (for instance, accessories in no way make the spring), without destroying the correlation between clothing and the world; in a way this correlation is empty: structurally, it is nothing but an

---

[9] There is a relation between the worldly garment and Fashion, but this relation is indirect, accounted for by a second system of relation (cf., below, 3.9 and 3.11).

[10] Strictly speaking, the content of the relation is a matter of indifference on a certain structural level (the one which concerns us for the moment), but not on all levels; for the written functions of clothing belong to the level of connotation, they belong to the Fashion system (cf., below, 19.11).

equivalence:[11] accessories are *good for* the spring, these shoes are *good for* walking, prints are *good for* the races. In other words, when we try to reduce the diversity of the garment's reasons to a function general enough to contain them all (which is the proper task of structural analysis), we find that the functional precision of the utterance is simply a variation of a much more neutral relation, that of simple equivalence. The "empty" character of the relation appears still more clearly in the case of set B (*Clothing* ∫ [*Fashion*]); on the one hand, since the second term of this set is almost always implicit,[12] the relation cannot be varied; on the other, Fashion being pure value, it cannot produce clothing or constitute one of its uses; we can grant that a raincoat protects from the rain and that for this reason there is, at least originally or partially, an authentic transitive relation between the world (the rain) and the garment (the raincoat);[13] but when a dress is described because it honors the value of Fashion, there cannot be any relation between this dress and Fashion other than a purely conventional conformity, not a functional one; it is really the magazine and no longer the use which institutes the equivalence of clothing and Fashion. Hence, the relation of equivalence between the two commutative classes is always certain: in set B because it is declared, in set A because it is constant through the variety of figures the magazine gives it.

2.6. *Orientation*

This is not all. The equivalence of the garment and the world, of the garment and Fashion, is an oriented equivalence; insofar as the two terms which compose it are not of the same substance, they cannot be manipulated in the same manner. The marks of worldliness are infinite (without precise limits), innumerable, and abstract; the classes of the world and Fashion are immaterial; contrariwise, that of clothing is constituted by a finite collection

---

[11] *Equivalence* and not *identity:* clothing is not the world. We can see this clearly in the following example, which is obviously noted as a paradox: *Garden style for the garden.* Henceforth the graphic symbol ≡ will be used to designate the relation of equivalence (and not = which is the symbol of identity). It will be written: *Clothing* ≡ *World* and *Clothing* ≡ *Fashion.*

[12] Almost always: *almost,* because magazines sometimes say: *Blue is the Fashion.*

[13] Moreover, this would be to raise the problem prejudicially, for, as we shall see (below, 19.2), every function is also a sign.

of material objects; it is thus inevitable that when they are confronted in a relation of equivalence, world and Fashion on one side and clothing on the other become terms of a relation of manifestation: not only does the vestimentary feature become the worldly feature or the assertion of Fashion,[14] but it manifests them as well. In other words, by establishing equivalence between the visible and the invisible, the relation between the garment and the world or the garment and Fashion observes only one use, which is a certain *reading*. This reading is not to be confused with the immediate reading of the utterance which aims at establishing the relations between the words as letters and the words as meaning; in fact, this verbal utterance serves a second level of *reading*, the equivalence of clothing to the world or to Fashion. Every utterance in the magazine, beyond the words that make it up, constitutes a system of significations consisting of a signifier whose terms are discrete, material, numerable, and visible: the garment; and an immaterial signified, which is, depending on the case, the world or Fashion; conforming to Saussure's nomenclature, we can call that correlation of two terms, the vestimentary signifier and the worldly signified or the signified of Fashion, a *sign*.[15] For example, the entire phrase *Prints win at the races* becomes a sign in which *prints* are the (vestimentary) signifier and *the races* the (worldly) signified; *a halter buttoned down the back, its collar tied like a little scarf* becomes the signifier of an implicit signified [fashionable], and also, as a consequence, a complete sign, like a word in a language.

2.7. *Directions of analysis: depth and breadth*

We can henceforth assign two complementary directions to the analysis of written clothing. On the one hand, since every utterance, as we have seen, consists of at least two readings, that of the words themselves and that of the relation signifying world [Fashion] ≡ clothing, or, if one prefers, since the reading of the vestimentary sign is given through a discourse which transforms it into a function (this garment serves this worldly use) or an

---

[14] Assertion and not feature, because the class "Fashion" has only one variation: Fashion/non-Fashion.

[15] Sign, in Saussure's sense, is the union of the signifier and the signified, and not the signifier alone, as is commonly believed (Martinet, *Elements*).

assertion of value (this garment is in Fashion), we can henceforth be sure that written clothing consists of at least two types of signifying relation; we should thus proceed to an analysis in depth which attempts to disengage the signifying elements from the Fashion utterance they form. On the other hand, since it would appear that all vestimentary signs are organized according to a system of differences, we will seek to uncover the presence of a *vestimentary code* in written clothing, in which a class of signifiers (the garment) will *stand for* a class of signifieds (the world or Fashion) even more than the sign itself.[16] Thus it is that the manner in which vestimentary signifiers are organized among themselves,[17] that is to say their range, will become the object of study; for a system of signs is not founded on the relation of a signifier to a signified (this relation can be the basis for a symbol, but not necessarily for a sign), but on the relation among the signifiers themselves: the *depth* of a sign adds nothing to its determination; it is its breadth which counts, the role it plays in relation to other signs, the systematic fashion in which it resembles them or differs from them: every sign takes its being from its surroundings, not from its roots. Hence, the semantic analysis of written clothing must be pursued in depth when it attempts to "unravel" the systems, and in breadth when it attempts to analyze the succession of signs, at each level of these systems. We shall begin by clarifying as distinctly as possible the imbrication of systems whose existence we have just begun to suspect.

---

[16] The sign of Fashion will be analyzed in chapter 5.

[17] This is the most important part of the Fashion system, dealt with in chapters 5 through 12.

3

Between Things and Words

"A little braid gives elegance."

I. SIMULTANEOUS SYSTEMS: PRINCIPLES AND EXAMPLES

3.1. *Principle of simultaneous systems: connotation and metalanguage*

We have seen that a Fashion utterance involves at least two systems of information: a specifically linguistic system, which is a language (such as French or English), and a "vestimentary" system, according to which the garment (*prints, accessories, a pleated skirt, a halter top,* etc.) signifies either the world (the races, springtime, maturity) or Fashion. These two systems are not separate: the vestimentary system seems to be taken over by the linguistic system. The problem posed by the coincidence of two semantic systems in a single utterance has been addressed principally by Hjelmslev.[1] We know that linguistics distinguishes a level of expression (E) and a level of content (C); these two levels are linked by a relation (R), and the ensembles of levels and their relations form a system (ERC); the system thus constituted can itself become the simple element of a second system which consequently extends it. The two systems can be separated from one another at two different points of articulation; in the first case, the primary system constitutes the level of expression for the secondary system: (ERC) R C: system 1 thus corresponds to the level of *denotation*, system 2 to the level of *connotation;*

---

[1] *Essays.*

in the second case, the primary system (ERC) constitutes the level of content for the secondary system: E R (ERC); system 1 then corresponds to the level of *object language,* system 2 to the level of *metalanguage.* Connotation and metalanguage are mirror opposites of each other, depending on the place of the first system in the second. A rough diagram (for, in fact, expression and content are often conflated within language) will show these two symmetrical realignments:

2	E	C		E	C
1	E	C		E	C

According to Hjelmslev, metalanguages are *operations,* they form the majority of scientific languages, whose role is to provide a real system, grasped as signified, out of an ensemble of original signifiers, of a descriptive nature. As opposed to metalanguages, connotations pervade languages which are primarily social, in which a first, literal message serves as a support for a second meaning, of a generally affective or ideological order;[2] the phenomena of connotation are certainly of great though as yet unrecognized importance in all the languages of culture and in literature in particular.

3.2. *Three-system ensembles: articulation points*

For there to be connotation or metalanguage, two systems are sufficient. Nothing, however, prevents us from conceiving of three-system ensembles; but since the messages of articulated language are normally saturated by two systems (as in the most widely socialized case, that of denotation-connotation, which will be our main concern here), the third system of these tripartite ensembles is naturally made up of an extra-linguistic code, whose substance is the object or the image; for example, a linguistic ensemble that is denotative-connotative can incorporate a primary signifying system of objects; the ensemble presents two different articulations: one shifts from the real code (of objects) to the denotative system of language; the other from the denotative system of language to its connotative system. The opposition of metalanguage and connotation corresponds to this difference in

---

[2] *Mythologies,* Seuil, 1957, p. 213.

substances: when linguistic denotation preempts the real code, it acts as a metalanguage, for the code becomes the signified of a nomenclature, or, if one prefers, of a purely *terminological* system; this double system is then taken as the signifier of the final connotation, which is integrated into the third and final system, which one could call rhetoric:

3. *Articulated language: rhetorical system*

2. *Articulated language: terminological system*

1. *Real code*

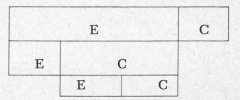

System 3 is pure connotation; system 2, which is intermediary, is simultaneously denotation (in relation to system 3) and metalanguage (in relation to system 1). The dissymmetry of the articulation points (here the signifier, there the signified) stems from the disparity of substances; as systems 2 and 3 are both linguistic, their signifiers are homogeneous (they are words, phrases, phonic forms); to the contrary, systems 1 and 2 are mixed, one real and the other linguistic, so their signifiers cannot communicate directly with one another; the substance of the real code cannot supply the substance of the verbal code without a relay; hence, in this motion of realignment, the real code is preempted by the insubstantial and conceptual part of the linguistic system, i.e., by its signified. Here an example is necessary; we shall take one from the highway code *as taught,* that is to say *as spoken.*[3]

3.3. *The highway code as taught*

I have in front of me three different-colored lights (red, green, yellow). I have no need of language to understand that each of these signals has a different meaning (stop, go, caution[4]): I simply need an apprenticeship period so that the meaning will come to me directly in situations where the sign is used: by re-

---

[3] Since Buyssens, of course (*Les langages et les discours,* Brussels, J. Lebegue, 1943), the highway code has served as a basic example for semiological reflection; it is a useful example as long as it is remembered that the highway code is a very "poor" code.

[4] It will be noted that in this elementary code the signifieds organize themselves into structured opposition: there are two polar terms (*stop/go*) and a mixed term (*stop + go = caution*).

peatedly associating the green with going and the red with stopping, I will learn to decipher the semantic relation; I am definitely dealing with a code, and this code is real, non-linguistic, composed of visual signifiers which the deaf-and-dumb could use quite easily. But if I learn the meaning of these signals from an instructor, his speech relays the real code; and since speech itself is a signifying system, I am faced with a binary, heterogeneous ensemble, half real, half linguistic; in the first system (or the highway code proper), a certain color (perceived, but at no point named) signifies a certain situation; in my instructor's speech, this semantic equivalence is reduplicated in a second semantic system, making a verbal structure (*a sentence*) into the signifier for a certain concept (*a proposition*). At this point in the analysis, I have two shifted systems which can be diagramed like this:[5]

2. *Spoken code:*	Sr /Red is a sign for stopping/: Sentence		Sd "Red is a sign for stopping": Proposition	
1. *Real code:*		Sr Perception of red		Sd Means stop

We must stop here for a moment. For even if my teacher were objective enough to say to me, literally and in a neutral tone of voice, "Red is the sign for stopping," in short, even if his words attained a rigorously denoted state of the real (which is rather utopian), language never relays a primary system of significations with impunity. If I learn the highway code in an empirical (extra-linguistic) manner, I perceive differences, not qualities: red, green, and yellow have (for me) no reality other than their relation, the play of their oppositions;[6] the linguistic relay has, no

---

[5] The obvious imperfection of this diagram has to do with the nature of language, which substantially confuses its signifiers and signifieds, so that every extension of semantic equivalence (its spatialization) is a deformation. —*Concept* is a notion from Saussure's theory which is open to discussion; it is used here as a reminder, without reopening any such discussion.

[6] Here, in fact, is a utopian situation; as an acculturated individual, even without language, I can only have a mythical idea of "red."

doubt, one advantage, it dispenses with the need for a table of functions; but also, by isolating and distancing the sign, it allows one to "forget" the virtual opposition of the primary signifiers; we might say that language solidifies the equivalence of red with stopping: red becomes the "natural" color of interdiction; the color is transformed from sign to symbol; the meaning is no longer a form, it takes on substance. When applied to another semantic system, language tends to neutralize it: the most social of institutions is this very power which allows man to produce the "natural." But this is not all. My teacher's speech is, so to speak, never neutral; at the very moment when he seems simply to be telling me that red signals an interdiction, he is telling me other things as well: his mood, his character, the "role" he wishes to assume in my eyes, our relation as student and teacher; these new signifieds are not entrusted to the words of the code being taught, but to other forms of discourse ("values," turns of phrase, intonation, everything that makes up the instructor's rhetoric and phraseology). In other words, another semantic system almost inevitably builds itself on the instructor's speech, i.e., the system of connotation. Ultimately, we are dealing here with a ternary system, consisting of a real code, a terminological or denotative system, and a rhetorical or connotative system according to the theoretical framework already sketched and which we are now able to fill in:

3. *Rhetorical system*	*Sr* Phraseology of the instructor		*Sd* "Role" of the instructor
2. *Terminological system*	*Sr* /Red is the sign for stopping/ (Sentence)	*Sd* "Red is the sign for stopping" (Proposition)	
1. *Real highway code*		*Sr* Perception of red	*Sd* Situation of interdiction

This schema elicits two remarks.

3.4. *Dissociation of systems*

First of all, since the two lower systems are entirely present in the upper system, it is at the level of rhetoric that the whole is directly taken in; I no doubt receive an objective message: *Red is the sign of interdiction* (the proof of this lies in the conformity of my behavior), but what I actually experience is the speech of my teacher, his phraseology; if, for example, this phraseology is intimidating, the meaning of red will inevitably include a certain terror: in the rapid process (as experienced) of the message, I cannot put the signifier of the terminological system to one side, and the signified of the rhetorical system to the other, dissociating red from terror. The dissociation of the two systems can only be theoretical or experimental: it does not correspond to any real situation; for it is quite rare that in the face of intimidating speech (which is always connotative), one would be able to separate *in petto* the denoted message (the content of the discourse) from the connoted message (intimidation); quite to the contrary, the second message at times impregnates the first to the point of substituting for it and obstructing its intelligibility: a menacing tone can be so upsetting as to obscure the given order altogether; inversely, the dissociation of the two systems would be a way of distancing the message from the second system and, consequently, of "objectifying" its signified (for instance, tyranny): this is no doubt what a doctor does with abusive language from his patient; he does not allow himself to confuse the actual signified of the aggressive discourse with the neurotic symbol which it constitutes; but if this same doctor were not in an experimental situation and were to receive the same discourse in a real situation, the dissociation would be much more difficult.

3.5. *Hierarchy of systems*

This leads us to the second remark. Supposing one were able to dissociate them, the three systems would not imply the same manner of communication. The real code presupposes a practical communication based on apprenticeship and thus on a certain duration; in general it is a matter of a simple and narrow communication (for example, road signs or landing signals used on aircraft carriers, etc.). The terminological system implies an immediate communication (it does not need time to develop, the word economizes the duration of apprenticeship) but one that is conceptual; it is a "pure" communication. The communication set in motion by the rhetorical system is in a sense larger, because it opens the message to the social, affective, ideological world: if we define the real by the social, it is the rhetorical system that is more real, while the terminological system, since it is more formal, akin to a logic, would be less real; but also, this denoted code is more "select," it is the one which best gives evidence of a pure human effort: a dog can understand the first code (signals) and the last (the intonations of the master), it cannot understand the denoted message, which is accessible to man alone. If the three systems must be put into a hierarchy from an anthropological point of view, in measuring man against the powers of an animal, we could say that the animal can receive and emit signals (first system); that it can only receive the third;[7] and that it can neither receive nor emit the second; man, however, has the ability to make objects into signs and to transform these signs into articulated language and the literal message into a connoted message.

II. The Systems of Written Clothing

3.6. *Breakdown of the systems*

The general remarks which have been made regarding simultaneous systems now permit a description of what could be called the "geology" of written clothing and the specification of the number and the nature of the systems it mobilizes. How can we enumerate these systems? Through a series of controlled commutation tests: we need only apply this test to different levels of the utterance and to observe whether it indicates specifically different signs; these signs then necessarily refer to systems which are themselves different. For example, the commutation test can

[7] A dog cannot make use of the signals it emits in order to build a second system of reasons and of masks.

designate the word as simply a part of the linguistic system (*pars orationis*); this same word (or phrase, or even sentence) can be an element of vestimentary signification; again, it can be a signifier of Fashion; and finally it can be a stylistic signifier: it is the multiplicity of the levels of commutation which attests to the plurality of simultaneous systems. This point deserves emphasis, for the entire semiological analysis being proposed here rests upon a distinction between language and the written vestimentary code which may scandalize but which owes its validity to the fact that language and description do not have the same level of commutation. Since there are two sorts of equivalences or two pairs of commutative classes in written clothing (set A: *clothing* ≡ *world*; set B: *clothing* ≡ *Fashion*) we shall first analyze those utterances with explicit signifieds (set A), and then utterances with implicit signifieds (set B), in order to examine subsequently the relations between these two sets.

3.7. *Systems of set A*

Let there be an utterance with an explicit (worldly) signified: *Prints win at the races.* I already know that I have at least two signifying systems here. The first is located, in principle, in reality: if I were to go (at least that year) to Auteuil, I would *see*, without needing to have recourse to language, that there is equivalence between the number of prints and the festivity of the races; this equivalence is obviously the basis for every utterance of Fashion, since it is experience as anterior to language and its elements are supposedly real, not spoken; it clearly places a real garment in relation to an empirical circumstance in the world; its typical sign is: *real garment* ≡ *real world*, and it is for this reason that it will henceforth be called: the real vestimentary code. Nonetheless, here, i.e., within the limits of written clothing (which we are committed to respect in deference to the terminological rule), the reality (the racetrack at Auteuil, prints as a specific fabric) is never anything but a reference: I see neither the prints nor the track; one and the other are represented to me through a verbal element that is borrowed from the French (or English) language; thus, in this utterance, language constitutes a second system of information, which I shall call the written vestimentary code or the terminological system,[8] for it does nothing other than denote in a crude manner the reality of the world and of the garment, in the form of a nomenclature; if I were to stop the elaboration of the written garment at this level, I would end up with an utterance of this sort: *This year, prints are the sign of the races.* In this system, the signifier is no longer *prints* (as in system 1), but rather the ensemble of phonic (here: graphic) substances required for the utterance, which is called the sentence; the signified is no longer *the races,* but rather the set of concepts,[9] actualized by the sentence, which is called the *proposition.*[10] The relation between these two systems obeys the principle of metalanguages: the sign of the real vestimentary code becomes the simple signified (proposition) of the written vestimentary code; this second signified is in turn provided with an autonomous signifier: the sentence.

System 2 or terminological	Sr Sentence	Sd Proposition	
System 1 or vestimentary code		Sr Real clothing	Sd Real world

But this is not all. There remain other typical signs (other equivalences) in my utterance, and hence, other systems. First of all, it is certain that the equivalence between *prints* and *races,* between the garment and the world, is given (written) only insofar as it indicates (signifies) Fashion; in other words, wearing prints at the races becomes in its turn the signifier of a new signified: Fashion; but since this signified is only actualized insofar as the equivalence between the world and the garment is *written,* it is the notation of this equivalence itself which becomes the signifier of system 3, whose signified is Fashion: by what is simply *noted,* Fashion connotes the signifying relation between prints and the

---

[8] We cannot call it the linguistic system, for the following systems are also linguistic (p. 45).

[9] In Saussure's sense, even if this term is questionable.

[10] The distinction between sentence and proposition comes from logic.

races, merely denoted at the level of system 2. This third system (*prints* ≡ *the races* ≡ [*Fashion*]) is important since it allows all the worldly utterances of set A to signify Fashion (it is true in a less direct manner than the utterances of set B[11]); but since it is, despite everything, quite a reduced system, its typical sign having in and for everything only one binary variation (noted/non-noted, in-Fashion/out-of-Fashion), we will simply call it the connotation of Fashion. Following the principle of realigned systems, it is the sign of system 2 that becomes the simple signifier of system 3: by the act of notation alone, the terminological utterance signifies Fashion in a supplementary way. Finally, the set of all three systems identified thus far includes one last original signified, and hence one last typical sign: when the magazine states that *prints win at the races*, it is not only saying that prints signify the races (systems 1 and 2) and that the correlation between the two signifies Fashion (system 3), but it also masks this correlation in the dramatic form of a competition (*win at*); thus we are faced with a new typical sign, whose signifier is the Fashion utterance in its complete form, and whose signified is the representation which the magazine makes or wants to give of the world and Fashion; as in the teaching of road signs, the magazine's phraseology constitutes a connotative message, aimed at transmitting a certain vision of the world; so we shall call this fourth and final system the rhetorical system. Such are, in strict form, the four signifying systems one should find in every utterance with an explicit (worldly)[12] signified: (1) the real vestimentary code; (2) the written vestimentary code or the terminological system; (3) the connotation of Fashion; and (4) the rhetorical system. The order in which these four systems are read is, obviously, the opposite of their theoretical elaboration; the first two are part of the level of denotation, the last two of the level of connotation: these two levels may constitute, as we shall see, the levels of analysis for the general system.[13]

---

[11] The difference between the two sets, which is due to the fact that Fashion is denoted in set B and connoted in set A, is crucial for the system's general economy, and notably for what we could call its ethics (cf., below, 3.10 and chap. 20).

[12] In speaking of an *explicit signified,* we are obviously referring to the second or terminological system.

[13] Cf., below, 4.10.

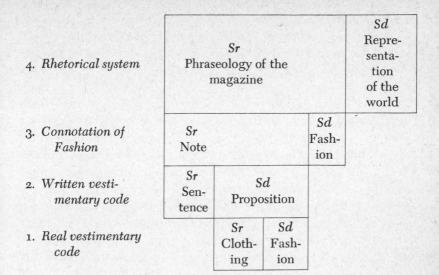

	Sr Phraseology of the magazine			Sd Repre- senta- tion of the world
4. *Rhetorical system*				
3. *Connotation of* *Fashion*	Sr Note		Sd Fash- ion	
2. *Written vesti-* *mentary code*	Sr Sen- tence	Sd Proposition		
1. *Real vestimentary* *code*		Sr Cloth- ing	Sd Fash- ion	

3.8. *Systems of set B*

What becomes of each of these systems in the utterances of set B, that is, when written clothing is the direct signifier of the implicit signified *Fashion?* Take the following utterance: *Women will shorten skirts to the knee, adopt pastel checks, and wear two-toned pumps.* We can conceive of a real situation in which each of these vestimentary traits (none of which refers to a worldly signified) would be immediately understood as a general sign of Fashion by all women who were to see such clothing; clearly, we are dealing here with a primary code both real and vestimentary, analogous to that of set A, the difference being that the signified is no longer the world, but in an immediate manner (and no longer indirectly), Fashion. Yet this real code exists in the magazine only as the referant for a written vestimentary code; here again, the architecture of the utterances of set A is identical to that of the utterances of set B, except, to note once again (for it is at this level that the difference appears), that the signified *Fashion* is always implicit. Now, since Fashion is the signified of system 2, it cannot serve as the connoted signified in system 3, which is unnecessary and which disappears: it is in fact no longer the simple notation of the sign *clothing* ≡ *world* that refers to Fashion, it is the detail of vestimentary features, their organization per se that *immediately* signifies Fashion, exactly as, in the utterances of set A, this same detail and this same organization immediately signify the worldly circumstance (the races): in the utterances of set B, there is no longer any connotation of Fashion. But since the utterance of the garment (*Women will shorten . . .*) takes the form of a legal and almost religious decree (it matters little for this analysis that it is *cum grano salis*), we here discover a system of connotation once again: the rhetorical system; as in the case of the utterances of set A, it transmits the representation of Fashion that the magazine can have or wants to give—or more precisely of Fashion in the world, experienced as a higher and essentially tyrannical authority. Thus, the utterances of set B are comprised of three systems: a real vestimentary code, a written vestimentary code or terminological system, and a rhetorical system; the level of connotation includes only one system instead of two.

3. *Rhetorical system*	*Sr* Phraseology of the magazine		*Sd* (Representation of the world)
2. *Written vestimentary code*	*Sr* Sentence	*Sd* Proposition	
1. *Real vestimentary code*		*Sr* Clothing	*Sd* World

3.9. *Relations of the two sets*

All written clothing is thus divided into two types of sets, the first having four systems, the second having three. What are the relations between these two sets? To begin with, we notice that the two sets have the same typical signifier on the denotative level: the garment, or more exactly, a succession of vestimentary features; it follows that when one wants to study the structure of codes 1 and 2, there is only one signifier to analyze, the garment, whether it is part of an utterance of a set of type A or B, that is, no matter which set it belongs to. After this has been said, the difference between the two sets must be reemphasized. Such a difference comes down to this: that Fashion is a connoted value in set A and a denoted value in set B. At the level of code 2B, the meaning of Fashion does not come from simple notation (the act of noting), but from vestimentary features themselves; more precisely, the notation is immediately absorbed into the detail of the features, it cannot function as a signifier, and Fashion cannot escape its situation as an immediate signified; but by interposing worldly signifieds between the garment and Fashion in set A, the magazine manages to elude Fashion, makes it regress to an implicit or latent state.[14] Fashion is an arbitrary value; in the case of set B, consequently, the general system turns out to be arbitrary, or, if one prefers, openly cultural; on the contrary, in the case of set A, the arbitrariness of Fashion becomes surreptitious and the general system presents itself as natural, since the garment no longer appears as a sign, but rather as a function. To describe *a halter top buttoned down the back,* etc., is to establish a sign;[15] to declare that *prints win at the races* is to mask the sign beneath the appearance of an affinity between the world and the garment, i.e., of a nature.

III. AUTONOMY OF THE SYSTEMS

3.10. *Degree of autonomy of the systems*

In order to analyze the general system of Fashion, it must be possible to deal with each of the systems that comprise it separately; it is thus important to understand the degree to which these systems are autonomous; because if certain systems are indissolubly linked, they must clearly be analyzed together. A system will be (relatively) independent if, after subtracting its signifier from the ensemble, it nonetheless remains possible to deal with the rest of the utterance without in any way altering the respective meaning of the residual systems. Thus, it is by opposing a system to the "remains" of the inferior systems that we will be able to judge its autonomy.

---

[14] On implicit and latent, cf., below, 16.5.
[15] Except that the rhetorical system of set B can transform this sign into a "natural fact" ("Skirts are short") (cf. chap. 19).

3.11. *The rhetorical system*

Compared to the "remainder" of the systems it heads, the rhetorical system is (relatively) independent. Take the following utterance: *A little braid gives elegance* (set A). In this utterance, it is easy to isolate a succession of rhetorical signifiers: first of all, the metaphorical use of the verb *gives* transforms the signified of the terminological code (*elegance*) into a pure product of the signifier (braid);[16] also, the ambiguity of the adjective *little* refers simultaneously to a physical measurement ($\neq$ large) and to an ethical judgment ($=$ humble, modest, appealing);[17] and the shape of the (French) sentence flirts with the form of a distich:

> Un(e) petit(e) ganse
> Fait l'élégance.[18]

Finally, the very isolation of the utterance presents it as a precious proverb. If all these rhetorical signifiers are taken from the utterance, there still remains a verbal utterance of this sort: A braid is a sign of elegance; in its reduced, denoted form, this utterance still condenses systems 1, 2, and 3. Thus it will be legitimate to consider the rhetorical system as an independent object of analysis.

3.12. *The connotation of Fashion*

The connotation of Fashion (system 3 of set A) has no autonomy: notation cannot be separated from the *noted;* this system, then, is entirely parasitical to the written vestimentary code; we have seen elsewhere that in set B the notation of Fashion is identified with the terminological utterance of vestimentary features, for which it becomes the simple denoted signified. Thus, the connotation of Fashion cannot be submitted to an independent analysis.

---

[16] Here and henceforth, when the terms *signifieds* and *signifiers* are used without greater specificity, it is and always will be a matter of the elements of the written vestimentary code or terminological system.

[17] *Little* is one of those rare terms that can straddle both the denotative and the connotative systems. Cf., below, 4.3 and 17.3.

[18] Of course, the English translation does not duplicate the distich form of the French utterance, but there are numerous examples of this process in both languages. [Trans.]

3.13. *Theoretical autonomy of the written vestimentary code and of the real vestimentary code*

This leaves the two lower systems of the set (whether it is set A or B), the terminological system and the real vestimentary code. In principle, these two systems are independent, since they are made up of different substances (here "words," there objects and situations); one is not entitled to identify them with one another, to announce that there is no difference between the real garment and the written garment, between the real world and the world that is named; first, because language is not a tracing of the real, and second, because, in the case of written clothing, the terminological system could not exist if it did not refer to the presumed existence of a *real* equivalence between the world and the garment, between Fashion and the garment; of course, this equivalence is not empirically established; nothing (in the magazine) "proves" that prints actually are good for the races or that a halter top actually stands for Fashion; but this matters little to the distinction between the two systems; for it is enough that one be entitled (and obliged) to distinguish them, that their criteria of validity be different: the validity of the terminological system depends on the general rules of (the French) language; that of the real vestimentary code depends on the magazine: the equivalence of the garment with the world, of the garment with Fashion, must conform to the norms (as obscure as they may be) of the *fashion group*. Hence, there is principled autonomy in the two systems,[19] and the entirety of the general system of Fashion clearly includes three levels theoretically available to analysis: the rhetorical, the terminological, and the real.

---

[19] The distinction is obviously valid here only because the (presumed) real itself constitutes a code.

4

The Endless Garment

"Daytime clothes in town are accented with white."

I. TRANSFORMATIONS AND DIVISIONS

4.1. *Principle and number*

Imagine (if possible) a woman dressed in an endless garment, one that is woven of everything the magazine of Fashion says, for this garment without end is proffered through a text which is itself unending. This total garment must be organized, i.e., cut up and divided into significant units, so that they can be compared with one another and in this way reconstitute the general signification of Fashion.[1] This endless garment has a double dimension: on the one hand, it grows deeper through the different systems which make up its utterance; on the other hand, it extends itself, like all discourse, along the chain of words; here it is made of superimposed blocs (these are the systems or codes), and there it is made of juxtaposed segments (these are the signifiers, the signifieds and their union, i.e., the signs). Thus, in *A little braid gives elegance,* we were able to discern,[2] vertically, four "blocs" or systems (one of which, it is true, is immediately subtracted from the analysis: the connotation of Fashion), and,

---

[1] We understand *signification,* not in the current sense of signified, but in the active sense of process.
[2] Cf., above, chap. 3.

horizontally, at the terminological level, two terms: a signifier (*a little braid*) and a signified (*elegance*). The analysis, then, should be directed both behind (or beneath) the chain of words and simultaneously along this chain. This is tantamount to anticipating, when faced with any Fashion utterance, two types of operations: one of *transformation,* when we shall reduce the systems among themselves; and one of *division,* when we shall seek to isolate the signifying elements and the signified elements. Transformation is aimed at the systems in depth; division is aimed at each system's signs in extent. Transformation or division should be determined under the guarantee of the commutation test: only those elements of the endless garment whose variation entails a variation in the signified should be considered: inversely, any element whose alteration would have no effect on any signified should be declared insignificant. How many analytical operations should we anticipate? Since the connotation of Fashion is entirely parasitical to the written vestimentary code, there are only (in set A as well as in set B) three systems to reduce, and hence, only two transformations: from the rhetorical system to the written vestimentary code, and from the written vestimentary code to the real vestimentary code. As for divisions, not all of them are necessary or even possible. Isolating the connotation of Fashion (system 3 of set A) cannot constitute an autonomous operation, since the signifier (the notation) is spread throughout the entire utterance and because its signified (Fashion) is latent. Dividing up the terminological system (system 2) into significant units has no place here, since it would consist of establishing the system of the French (or English) language, which is, strictly speaking, the task of linguistics itself.[3] Dividing up the rhetorical system into such units is both possible and necessary; as for dividing up the real vestimentary code (system 1), since this code is accessible only through language, dividing it into segments, necessary as that is, demands a certain amount of "preparation" and, so to speak, a certain "compromise"; it nonetheless remains, to sum up, that the endless garment will have to be submitted to two operations of "transformation" and two operations of "division."

---

[3] We might quote K. Togeby, *Structure immanente de la langue française,* Copenhagen, Nordisk Sprog og Kulturforlag, 1951.

II. TRANSFORMATION 1:
FROM THE RHETORICAL TO THE TERMINOLOGICAL

4.2. *Principle*

The first transformation does not pose any original problems, for it is only a matter of divesting the sentence (or the period) of its rhetorical values, in order to reduce it to a single verbal (denoted) utterance of a vestimentary signification. Such values are generally known (even though they have scarcely been studied from the point of view of a semantics of connotation): they consist of metaphors, cadence, word play, and rhymes which one would have no trouble "evaporating" into a simple verbal equivalence between clothing and the world, or between clothing and Fashion. When we read: *Pleated skirts are a must in the afternoon,* or: *Women will wear two-toned pumps,* it suffices to substitute: *Pleated skirts are the sign of afternoon,* or *Two-toned pumps signify Fashion,* in order to arrive immediately at the terminological system or the written vestimentary code which is the aim of this first transformation.

4.3. *Mixed terms: "little"*

The only possible difficulty lies in encountering verbal units which we cannot immediately determine as belonging to the rhetorical system or to the terminological system, insofar as, due to their lexical condition, they carry several values and are in fact part of two systems at the same time; this is the case—as has been suggested—with the adjective "little"; "little" belongs to the denotative system if it refers to a simple appreciation of measure, and to the connotative system if it refers to an idea of modesty, economy, or even affection (caritative nuance);[4] the same is true of adjectives such as "brilliant" or "strict," which can be taken in both a literal and a metaphorical sense at once. Such cases are not insoluble, even setting aside all recourse to a stylistic judgment; it is obvious that in the utterance: *A little braid,* the unit "little" is a vestimentary signifier (belonging to the terminological or denotative system) only insofar as it is possible to

---

[4] Cf., below, 17.3 and 17.6.

encounter "big braids," that is, insofar as it is part of a pertinent opposition *big/little*, whose variation in meaning would be attested to by the Fashion magazine; since this is not the case, we must conclude (in the case of braids) that "little" belongs entirely to the rhetorical system. Thus, it is correct to reduce *A little braid gives elegance* to *A braid is a sign of elegance*.

III. TRANSFORMATION 2:
FROM THE TERMINOLOGICAL TO THE VESTIMENTARY CODE

4.4. *Limits of transformation 2*

We said[5] that in principle the written vestimentary code and the real vestimentary code are autonomous. However, if the terminological system aims at the real code, this code is never reached apart from the words which "translate" it; its autonomy is sufficient to require an original decipherment, one necessarily different from language (not purely linguistic); it is not sufficient to enable us to work on an equivalence between the world and clothing that is separate from language. From a methodological point of view, this paradoxical status is quite perplexing. For if we treat the units of the written garment as verbal units, the only structure we reach in such a garment is that of the French (or English) language; we analyze the meaning of the sentence, not the meaning of the garment; and if we treat them as objects, as real elements of the garment, we cannot make any sense out of their arrangement, since this sense is the "speech" of the magazine which produces it. We stay too near or go too far; in both cases we lack the central relation, which is that of the vestimentary code as actualized by the magazine, i.e., one that is simultaneously real in its aim and written in its substance. When I am told that *daytime clothes in town are accented with white*, even if I reduce this utterance to its terminological state (*White accents on day clothes are a sign of the city*), I cannot, from a structural point of view, find any relations between the accents, white, day clothes, and the city other than syntactic ones: those of subject, verb, complement, etc. In no way do these relations,

---

[5] Cf., above, 3.13.

derived from language, constitute the semantic relations of the garment, which knows neither verbs, subjects, nor complements, but rather materials and colors. Of course, if we were only dealing with a problem of description and not one of signification, we could unhesitatingly "translate" the magazine's utterance into materials and actual uses, since one function of language is that it communicates information about what is real; but we are not dealing here with a "recipe"; if we had to "realize" the magazine's utterance, how many uncertainties there would be (the form, the number, the arrangement of white accents)! In fact, it must be recognized that the meaning of clothing (which is the very point of the utterance) is directly tributary to the verbal level: white accentuation signifies *by its very imprecision:* language is a limit beyond which meaning cannot be realized, and yet the relations of language cannot be identified with those of the real vestimentary code.

4.5. *Autonymy*

This circuit suggests that of an equivocal form of writing which would confuse the *usage* and the *mention* of a term, constantly blending the objectivity of language with its autonymy, simultaneously designating the word as both object and word. *Mus rodit caseum, mus est syllaba, ergo . . . ;*[6] writing of this sort, which plays with what is real, capturing it, then eluding it, somewhat resembles an ambiguous logic which would manage to treat *mus* as both a syllable and a rat, and to "disappoint" the rat beneath the syllable at the very moment it would reinflate the syllable with all the reality of the rat.

4.6. *Toward a pseudo-syntax*

Analysis can only be the perpetual prisoner of this ambiguity unless it decides to inhabit and exploit it. Indeed, without departing from the same chain of words (which guarantees the meaning of the garment), we can attempt to replace the grammatical relations (which themselves are charged with no vestimentary signification) with a *pseudo-syntax,* whose articula-

---

6 "*Job est indeclinabile, Caesar est dissyllabum: verba accepta sunt materialiter.*"

tions, freed from grammar, would have as their sole aim the manifestation of a vestimentary meaning, not the intelligibility of the discourse. Thus, beginning with a terminological utterance like *White accents on daytime clothes are a sign of the city*, we can "evaporate," as it were, the syntactical relations of the phrase and replace them with functions that are sufficiently formal, i.e., sufficiently empty, to prepare for the shift from the linguistic to the semiological,[7] from the terminological system to the last vestimentary code that we can reasonably hope to attain. For the moment, these functions will be *equivalence* ($\equiv$), which we have already used, and *combination* ($\bullet$); we do not yet know if such combination will take the form of implication, solidarity, or simple conjunction;[8] we thus obtain a half-verbal, half-semiological utterance of the following type:

$$\text{daytime clothes} \bullet \text{accents} \bullet \text{white} \equiv \text{city}$$

4.7. *The mixed or pseudo-real code*

We can now see what the result of transformation 2 will be: it will be a specific code which will take its units from language[9] and its functions from a logic general enough to enable it to preempt certain relations of the real garment; in other words, it will be a mixed code, intermediary between the written vestimentary code and the real vestimentary code. This half-verbal, half-algorithmic utterance we have arrived at (*daytime clothes* • *accents* • *white* = *city*) certainly represents the optimum state of transformation: for, on the one hand, the verbal terms of the equation cannot legitimately be broken down any further: any attempt to break down *daytime clothes* into its component parts (pieces of a garment) would be to go beyond language, resorting, for example, to a technical or visual knowledge of the garment and violating the terminological rule; on the other hand, we are certain that all the terms of the equation (*day clothes, accents, city*) have a significant value (at the level of the vestimentary

---

[7] *Semiological* is understood here as extra-linguistic.

[8] These are the three types of structural relations which Hjelmslev's theory has used when it has tried to "degrammatize" itself (cf. K. Togeby's account in *Structure immanente*, p. 22).

[9] Language gives the pseudo-real vestimentary code its nomenclature, but it also takes away its empty words, which, as we know, represent half the words of a text.

code, and no longer at the level of language), since by modifying any one of them, we change the vestimentary sense of the sentence: we cannot substitute *blue* for *white* without the equivalence between clothes and city being rendered problematic, that is, without altering the entire signification. This, then, is the final code to which the analysis can lead if it is to abide by the terminological rule; we must now rectify (which we were unable to do before) the notion of the real vestimentary code, which we have used up to now: it is in fact a pseudo-real code. If we set aside the connotation of Fashion (system 3A), the entirety of the written garment then comprehends the following systems:

3. Rhetorical: *Daytime clothes in town are accented with white* .
2. Terminological: *White accents on day clothes signify the city*
1. Pseudo-real: *day clothes • accents • white ≡ city*

4.8. *Servitude imposed by transformation 2*

Insofar as transformation 2 is incomplete, since it fails in any exhaustive way to transform the written vestimentary code into a real vestimentary code and is content to produce a code detached from linguistic syntax but still partially written, it imposes certain constraints on the analysis. The general constraint stemming from the terminological rule is that it must not transgress the denominative nature of the garment being analyzed, i.e., must not shift from words to images or techniques. This limitation is particularly important wherever the garment is named according to its kind: *hat, bonnet, toque, cloche, boater, felt hat, bowler, hood,* etc.; it would be quite tempting, in order to structure the differences among these varieties of headwear, to break them down into simple elements perceived at the level of the image or at the level of fabrication; the terminological rule forbids this: the magazine stops its notation at the level of the species or kind, and we can go no further than it goes. This suspension of the analysis is not as gratuitous as might appear: the meaning the magazine gives to the garment does not come from any particular intrinsic qualities of form, but only from particular oppositions of kind: if the *toque* is in Fashion, it is not because it is high and has no brim, it is simply because it is no longer a bonnet and not yet a hood; to go beyond the nomination of species would thus be to "naturalize" the garment and hence to miss the very essence of Fashion: the terminological rule does not require a Byzantine servitude: it serves as the narrow doorway through which the meaning of Fashion passes; for, without its verbal limits, Fashion would be nothing other than an infatuation with certain forms or details, as has always been the case with costume; in no way would it be an ideological elaboration.

4.9. *Freedom afforded by transformation 2*

Nonetheless, the tyranny of language is not absolute (if it were, transformation would be impossible). Not only is it necessary to transcend the syntactical relation furnished by language,[10] but it is still permissible, at the very level of the terminological units, to transgress the letter of the utterance. Within which limits? Clearly, it is the commutation test which determines them: we can freely substitute some words for other words as long as this substitution does not entail a change in the vestimentary signified; if two terms refer to the same signified, their variation is insignificant, and we can replace one with the other without altering the structure of the written garment: *from top to bottom* and *for its whole length* will be considered interchangeable terms if they have the same signified; but, inversely, all that is necessary to ban the substitution is that the magazine attach one variation in vestimentary meaning to two terms whose lexical appearance is quite close or even identical: thus, according to the dictionary, *silken* and *silky* have exactly the same denotative sense (made of silk); if, however, the magazine asserts that this year *silky fabrics take the place of silken fabrics,* Littré (or Webster) notwithstanding, it must be admitted that *silky* and *silken* are distinct signifiers since each refers to a different signified (*last year/this year,* i.e., *fashionable/unfashionable*). Here we see what use can be made of the synonyms of language: linguistic synonymy does not necessarily coincide with vestimentary synonymy, for the reference level of the vestimentary code (pseudo-real) is not language, but rather the equivalence between the garment and

---

[10] For example, vestimentary (and no longer linguistic) syntax cannot know the opposition of active and passive voice (cf., below, 9.5).

Fashion or the world: only what disturbs this equivalence indicates the locus of a significant phenomenon; but since this phenomenon is *written,* everything that upsets or displaces it is the prisoner of a certain nomenclature. We are held in check by language to the extent that the meaning of the garment (*braid* ≡ *elegance*) is supported solely by a notion which in one way or another receives its validation from language itself; but we are free of language to the extent that the linguistic *values* of this notion have no effect on the vestimentary code.

4.10. *Reductions and amplifications*

What good is this freedom? It must be remembered that what we are seeking to establish is a general structure, capable of accounting for all the utterances of Fashion, whatever their content; for it to be universal, this structure must be as formal as possible. The transformation from the terminological to the vestimentary (which henceforth will be called the pseudo-real code) is effective only if it is guided by the search for simple functions, common to the largest possible number of utterances: it would be interesting to *cast*, so to speak, the utterances of the pseudo-real vestimentary code, even the reduced ones, into a small number of models each time we can do so without modifying the vestimentary meaning. This explains why transformation 2 is not in the least guided by a concern for economy, as would be the case of a *reduction* proper, but rather by a concern for generalization: hence, the amplitude of the second transformation will vary; most often, of course, it will actually be a reduction: the vestimentary utterance will find itself to be more exiguous than its terminological version: we have seen that *day clothes* • *accents* • *white* ≡ *city* constitutes a narrower utterance than *Daytime clothes in town are accented with white;* but it might be useful, conversely, to enlarge the terminological utterance in order to make it assume a broad form to whose generality the rest of the system attests; thus, *a linen dress* should be developed into *a dress whose fabric is linen,*[11] or better still: *dress* • *fabric* • *linen,* because an infinitude of other cases demonstrate the structural utility of a relay (fabric) between the linen-type and the dress.

---

[11] *Fabric* will belong to the genus *material.*

Therefore, transformation 2 is at times a reduction, and at other times an amplification.

IV. THE LEVELS OF ANALYSIS

4.11. *Machine for making Fashion*

Such are the two transformations according to which we must proceed in the interest of extremely varied utterances. If we want to get an idea of their operational role, think for a moment of the magazine as a machine that makes Fashion. Strictly speaking, the machine's work would involve the residue of the second transformation, i.e., the pseudo-real vestimentary code; this residue must be formal, general, and capable of providing alternatives and routines; the first transformation, that which goes from the rhetorical to the terminological, is merely the pre-edition (as we say when speaking of translating machines) of the text which we would ideally like to convert into clothing. Moreover, this double-stage transformation is also to be found in logic, which converts *The sky is blue* into *There is blue sky*, before submitting this second utterance to a final algorithmic treatment.[12]

4.12. *The two levels of analysis*

We have seen that in every utterance of Fashion there are three principal systems: the rhetorical, the terminological, and the pseudo-real; in principle, we should now proceed to three inventories; but the inventory of the terminological system would be confused with that of language, because it would consist of exploring the relations of the signifier and the signified within the linguistic sign (of the "word," for instance). In fact, there are only two structures which directly concern the written garment: the rhetorical level and the pseudo-real vestimentary code; the role of both transformation 1 and transformation 2 is to lead to the pseudo-real code; and since this code constitutes the infrastructure of the rhetorical system, we shall begin our analysis of written clothing with it; we shall proceed then, in all, to two

---

[12] Cf. R. Blanché, *Introduction à la logique contemporaine*, Paris, A. Colin, 1957, p. 128.

inventories: one for the pseudo-real vestimentary code, or more simply, the vestimentary code (Part I), and one for the rhetorical system (Part II).

V: FIRST DIVISION:
THE UTTERANCE OF THE SIGNIFICATION

4.13. *Case of set A*

Reduced in depth, that is, taken to the level of the pseudo-real code, the endless garment must still be divided up into units of signification, i.e., in extent. In set A (*Clothing ≡ World*) it is easy to isolate the utterances of signification, because the signifieds in them are explicit, preempted by language (*the races, elegance, autumn evenings in the country,* etc.). In such utterances, there is a reciprocal designation between the signifier and the signified, and it is sufficient to organize the magazine's discourse around the vestimentary meanings that the magazine itself has taken care to formulate:[13] any sentence saturated, like the two arguments of a function, by two objects, one worldly (W) and the other vestimentary (V), whatever detours the writing might take, will constitute a semantic equation of the type V ≡ W, and hence an utterance of signification: *Prints win at the races. Accessories make it spring. These shoes are ideal for walking*—all these sentences, given here in their rhetorical forms, constitute so many utterances of signification, because each one of them is entirely saturated by a signifier and a signified:

$$prints ≡ races$$
$$accessories ≡ spring$$
$$these\ shoes ≡ walking$$

Naturally, all homogeneous features must be shifted to the same side of the equation, without any regard for their rhetorical dispersal throughout the sentence; if, for example, the magazine fragments the signifier, if it presents a worldly signified in the

---

[13] The magazine itself sometimes goes so far as to undertake a semantic analysis of the signification: "*Dissect her well-dressed look: it comes from the collar, the bare arms, the delicate tones,*" etc. It is obvious here that this analysis is a "game," it "shows off" its technical knowledge: it is a signifier of connotation.

middle of its vestimentary signifieds, we should be able to reestablish their separate domains; reading *a youthful hat because
it reveals the forehead,* we shall reduce it, without risk of altering
the vestimentary meaning, to *a hat revealing the forehead* ≡
youthful. We should no longer be disturbed by the length or
complexity of any utterance. We can encounter an utterance that
is quite long: *a solitary promenade along the docks of Calais;
dressed in a reversible raincoat, raw cotton gabardine and bottle-
green loden cloth, broad shoulders,* etc.; this does not prevent
it from being constituted as a single unit of signification, for we
have only two domains, that of the promenade and that of the
reversible, united by a single relation. All the utterances we
have cited are simple (even if they are long or "broken"), because in each of them the signification mobilizes only one signifier
and one signified. But there are more complicated cases. The
magazine may very well give two signifieds for one signifier
within the limits of a single verbal phrase (*a linen overcoat for
mid-season or cool summer evenings*), or two signifiers for one
signified (*for cocktails, mousseline or taffeta*),[14] or even two
signifiers and two signifieds, linked in a double concomitant variation (*striped flannel or polka-dot twill, depending on whether for
morning or evening*). If we keep to the terminological level, we
should see only one utterance of signification in these examples,
since at this level the sentence assumes only one relation of meaning; but if we want to grasp the vestimentary code, we must always
try to attain the smallest fragment productive of meaning; from
an operational point of view, it is preferable to count as many
utterances of signification as there are unions of signifier and
signified, even if one of these terms is implicit at the terminological
level; hence, in the examples that have been cited, we have the
following utterances of signification:

> *overcoat • fabric • linen* ≡ *mid-season*
> *overcoat • fabric • linen* ≡ *cool summer evenings*
>
> *fabric • mousseline* ≡ *cocktails*
> *fabric • taffeta* ≡ *cocktails*
>
> *fabric • flannel • striped* ≡ *morning*
> *fabric • twill • polka-dot* ≡ *evening*

---

[14] On the particle *or*, cf., below, 13.8 and 14.3.

Naturally, the verbal form of these complex utterances is not without importance; it can provide information about certain internal equivalences between signifiers (*mousseline* ≡ *taffeta*) or signifieds (*mid-season* ≡ *cool summer evenings*), which recalls cases of synonymy and homonymy in language; and the double concomitant variation (*striped flannel or polka-dot twill, depending on whether for morning or evening*) is even more important, since in it the magazine itself sketches out certain paradigms for signifiers, by actualizing the pertinent, usually virtual opposition between *striped flannel* and *polka-dot twill*.

4.14. *Case of set B*

In sets of type B (*Clothing* ≡ [*Fashion*]), the inventory of utterances cannot employ the same criteria, because the signified is implicit. We might even be tempted to consider the entire mass of vestimentary descriptions of type B as one single and immense signifier, since all these descriptions correspond to the same signified (*Fashion this year*). But just as, in language, distinct signifiers can refer to the same signified (synonyms), in the same way in the written garment of type B, it is correct to anticipate the fragmentation of the signifying mass into units of signification which are not actualized at the same time in the magazine (this could only be done by dispersing them from one page to another) and which therefore constitute distinct units. How are these units to be defined in operational terms? The sentence, in the linguistic sense, cannot constitute a criterion for "division," for it has no structural relation to the vestimentary code;[15] on the other hand, the garment, as a group of features arranged on one person (*an outfit, a suit*, etc.), is no longer a guaranteed unit, for quite often the magazine confines itself to describing smaller details of dress (*a collar knotted like a scarf*), or on the contrary, vestimentary elements which are, so to speak, transpersonal, and which are related to a genre, not to a person (*linen for every coat*). In order to divide up the utterances of type B, it should be remembered that, in the Fashion magazine, descriptions of clothing duplicate information derived from a

---

[15] And besides, what is a sentence? (Cf. A. Martinet, "Réflexions sur la phrase," in *Language and Society*, essays presented to Arthur M. Jensen, Copenhagen, De Berlingske Bogtrykkeri, 1961, pp. 113–18.)

structure other than "speech," whether it be an image or a technique: description accompanies a photograph or a set of instructions, and it is, in fact, from this external reference that description gets its structural unity; and since, in order to shift from these structures to "speech," the magazine makes use of certain operators, which we have called *shifters,* any portion of vestimentary description introduced by a shifter will be considered as an utterance of signification in set B: *Here is the waist-length bolero,* etc. (shifter: here is); *a rose stuck in at the waist* (shifter: the anaphoric at degree zero); *Make yourself a halter top buttoned down the back,* etc. (shifter: make yourself).

VI. Second Division: Subsidiary Utterances

4.15. *Utterance of the signifier, utterance of the signified*

Once the endless garment has been divided up into utterances of signification, there is no difficulty in extracting subsidiary utterances on which we shall be working. For both sets A and B, the utterance of the signifier will be constituted by all the vestimentary features contained in a single utterance of signification. For set A (only), the utterance of the signified will be constituted by all worldly features contained in a single utterance of signification. In set B, since the signified is implicit, it is by definition deprived of an utterance.[16]

---

[16] The structuration of the written garment will thus involve the following steps: I. Inventory of the vestimentary code (mixed or pseudo-real): (1) structure of the signifier (sets A and B); (2) structure of the signified (set A); (3) structure of the sign (sets A and B). II. Inventory of the rhetorical system.

I

THE
VESTIMENTARY
CODE

1. *Structure of the Signifier*

5

The Signifying Unit

"A cardigan sporty or dressy, if the collar is open or closed."

I. THE SEARCH FOR THE SIGNIFYING UNIT

5.1. *Inventory and classification*

We have seen that we were justified in treating any utterance that the magazine devotes to clothing as a signifier of the vestimentary code, provided it was contained within a single unit of signification. From the simple *suit* to *pants cut off above the knees, with a silk scarf tied round the waist,* the harvest promises to be immense and outwardly anarchic; at times we glean only one word (*blue* is in Fashion), and at other times a highly complicated ensemble of notations (*pants cut off*, etc.). In these utterances of varying length and syntax, we must discover a constant form or we shall never know how vestimentary meaning is produced. And this order must satisfy two methodological requirements: first, we must be able to divide up the utterance of the signifier into spatial segments as reduced as possible, as if each utterance of Fashion were a chain whose links must be located; we must then compare these segments with one another (without further concerning ourselves with the utterance to which they belong), so as to determine according to which oppositions they produce different meanings. To speak in the vocabulary of linguistics, we must first determine which are the syntagmatic (or spatial) units of the written garment, and second, which are the systematic (or virtual) oppositions. The task, then, is twofold: inventory and classification.[1]

5.2. The compound character of the utterance of the signifier

The distinction between signifying units would be immediately apparent if each change of signified necessarily entailed an integral change of signifier: each signified would possess its own proper signifier, which would be attached to it in an immobile way, so to speak; the signifying unit would then have the same measurement as the utterance of the signifier, and there would be as many different units as there were different utterances; the definition of syntagmatic units would then be quite simple, but on the other hand, reconstituting the lists of virtual oppositions would be nearly impossible, for it would be necessary to include all the units of these utterances in a unique and unending paradigm, which would be tantamount to defying all attempts at structuration.[2] This is clearly not the case with written clothing: it suffices to compare a few utterances of the vestimentary signifier with one another in order to establish the fact that they often contain common elements, i.e., these elements are mobile and can participate in different meanings: *cut off* can be applied to several vestimentary objects (skirt, pants, sleeves), producing a different meaning in each case; which suggests that this meaning depends neither on the object nor on its qualification, but rather, at the very least, on their combination. Thus, it must be understood that the utterance of the signifier has a syntactical character: it can and must be broken down into smaller units.

II. THE SIGNIFYING MATRIX

5.3. Analysis of an utterance with a double concomitant variation

How are we to discover these units? We must start once again with the commutation test, since it alone can designate the small-

---

[1] This is at least the logical order of the research. But K. Togeby, *Structure immanente*, p. 8, has already pointed out that in practical terms it is often necessary to refer to the system in order to establish the syntagm. This is what we will in part be obliged to do.

[2] The structure comes apart whenever the paradigms are "open"; we shall see that this is the case for certain variants of written clothing, and that on this point the work of structuration has failed.

est signifying unit. We have several privileged utterances at our disposal, which we have already made use of in establishing the commutative classes of written clothing:[3] these are utterances with a double concomitant variation, in which the magazine itself expressly attaches a variation of signifieds to a variation of signifiers (*striped flannel or polka-dot twill, depending on whether for morning or evening*); these utterances themselves preempt the commutation test; we need only analyze them in order to determine the necessary and sufficient locus of the variation in meaning. Let us take an utterance of this type: *A cardigan sporty or dressy, if the collar is open or closed*. As we have seen,[4] there are in fact two utterances here, since there is a double signification:

$$cardigan \bullet collar \bullet open \equiv sporty$$
$$cardigan \bullet collar \bullet closed \equiv dressy$$

But as these utterances have fixed elements in common, it is easy to locate the part whose variation entails a change of signified: the opposition of *open* to *closed:* it is the opening or closing of an element which holds—doubtless for a certain number of cases —the power to signify. However, this power is not autonomous; without directly producing some meaning themselves, the other elements of the utterance participate in the signification: without them, such a signification would be impossible. It is true that there is what we might call a difference of responsibility between the *cardigan* and the *collar*, to the extent that these common elements do not have the same stability: the *cardigan* does not change, whatever its signified might be: it is the element furthest removed from variation (*open/closed*), but it is also the element which ultimately receives it: it is clearly the cardigan that is sporty or dressy, not the collar, which merely occupies an intermediary position between the variant and the recipient; as for the second element, its integrity is real insofar as the *collar* subsists, whether *open* or *closed*, but it is also precarious, being directly confronted with a signifying alteration. Therefore, in an utterance of this type, signification seems to follow an itinerary

---

[3] Cf., above, 2.2.
[4] Cf., above, 4.13.

of sorts: issuing from an alternative (*open/closed*), it next passes through a partial element (*the collar*) and, in the end, reaches and, so to speak, impregnates the garment (*the cardigan*).

5.4. *The signifying matrix: object, support, variant*

We begin to get a sense of a possible economy of the signifier: one element (*the cardigan*) receives the signification; another (*the collar*) supports it; a third (closure[5]) constitutes it. This economy seems to be sufficient since it accounts entirely for all stages involved in the passage of meaning, and since we cannot imagine other forms of articulation for this passage, whose model is informative.[6] But is this economy necessary? This is open to discussion: it is quite possible to conceive of the meaning directly confronting the garment it should modify, without passing through the relay of an intermediate element: Fashion can speak of *open collars* without reference to any other part of the garment; moreover, the substantial distinction between cardigan and collar is much less important than that between the collar and its closure: between the garment and its part there is a unity of substance, whereas between the garment and its qualification the substance is broken off: confronting the third element, the first and second elements form an affinitive grouping (we shall find this hiatus throughout the analysis). Yet we can foresee that the distinction between the element that receives (*the cardigan*) and the element that transmits (*the collar*) possesses at least one constant operational advantage:[7] for when the variation is not qualitative (*open/closed*) but merely assertive (for example, in *pockets with flaps/pockets without flaps*), it is necessary to maintain a relay (*the flap*) between the significant variation (*presence/absence*) and the garment ultimately affected by it (*the pockets*); it will be in our interest to consider the delineation of three ele-

---

[5] Here we run into a lacuna in the French (and English) vocabulary which will hamper us considerably throughout this work: we do not possess a generic vocable to designate the act of opening and closing; in other words, in many cases, we shall be able to designate a paradigm with only one of these terms. Aristotle long ago decried the absence of generic terms (κοινόν ὄνομα) to designate entities having common characteristics (*Poetics*, 1447b).

[6] Every message is comprised of a point of emission, a path of transmission, and a point of reception.

[7] Its operational role does not prevent the term receptor from having an original function in the theoretical system of Fashion (cf., below, 5.6).

ments as normal and the utterance with two terms (*open collars*) as simply condensed.[8] If the association of the three terms is logically sufficient and operationally necessary, it is legitimate to see in it the signifying unit of the written garment; for even if the phraseology jumbles the order of its elements, even if the description at times demands that we condense or, on the contrary, multiply them,[9] it is still possible to find an intended *object* of the signification, a *support* of the signification, and a third element, a variant proper, in any utterance of the signifier. Since, on the one hand, these three elements are simultaneously and syntagmatically inseparable, and since, on the other, each can be filled by a variety of substances (*cardigan* or *pockets*, *collar* or *flap*, *closure* or *existence*), we shall call this signifying unit a *matrix*. We shall, of course, put this matrix to good use, since we shall find it condensed, developed, or multiplied in every utterance of the signifier; we shall use current abbreviations to designate the object aimed at by signification (O), its support (S), and the variant (V); the matrix itself will be designated by the graphic symbol O.V.S. This will give us, for example:

$$\begin{array}{c}
\underline{\text{a pullover with a closed collar}} \equiv \text{dressy} \\
\text{O} \qquad\qquad \text{V} \qquad \text{S} \\
\underline{\text{a sweater with a boatneck collar}} \equiv \text{[Fashion]} \\
\text{O} \qquad\qquad \text{V} \qquad \text{S} \\
\underline{\text{a hat with a high crown}} \equiv \text{[Fashion]} \\
\text{O} \qquad\quad \text{V} \qquad \text{S}
\end{array}$$

5.5. *"Proof" of the matrix*

We can see that the matrix is not a mechanically defined unit of the signifier, although it is demonstrable by means of the commutation test; it is instead a model, an ideal and optional unit, provided by the examination of privileged utterances; its "proof" does not proceed from an absolute rationality (we have seen that its "necessary" character is open to discussion), but rather from an empirical commodity (it allows for an "economic" analysis of

---

[8] On the confusion of elements, cf., chap. 6.

[9] Language is entitled to condense them because the terminological system is not the real code; and since it is a matter of units, it is normal to anticipate a combination of these units, i.e., a syntax.

utterances), and from an "aesthetic" satisfaction (it is a sufficiently "elegant" manner of conducting the analysis, in the sense this word can have when applied to a mathematical solution): more modestly, we shall say it is sound insofar as it allows us to account for *all* utterances, taking certain *regular* adjustments into consideration.

III. THE OBJECT, THE SUPPORT, AND THE VARIANT

5.6. *The object, or meaning at a distance*

There have been indications of a close relation of substance between the support and the object of signification: at times there is a terminological confusion between the two elements (*open collars*); and at times there is a (technical) relation of inclusion between the support and the object: the support is a part of the object (*collar* and *cardigan*). But it is not at the level of this solidarity between support and object that we shall grasp the original function of the object aimed at by signification; it is rather in those utterances where the separation of the object from the support is greatest. In *A full blouse will give your skirt a romantic look,*[10] blouse and skirt are absolutely distinct, barely contiguous pieces; yet the skirt alone receives the signification; the blouse is only a relay, it supports the meaning, it does not benefit from it; all the *material* of the skirt is insignificant, inert, and yet it is the skirt which emanates romanticism. Here we see that what characterizes the object aimed at by the signification is its extreme permeability to meaning, but also its distance in relation to the source of this meaning (the *fullness* of the blouse). This trajectory, this emanation of meaning contributes to making the written garment into an original structure; in language, for example, there is no such object aimed at, since each fragment of space (in the spoken chain) signifies: everything in language is a sign, nothing is inert; everything is meaning, nothing receives it. In the vestimentary code, inertia is the original state of those objects which signification will seize upon: a skirt exists without signifying, prior to signifying; the meaning it receives is at once

---

[10] \ Skirt with a full blouse / ≡ romantic.
O V S

dazzling and evanescent: the "speech" (of the magazine) seizes upon insignificant objects, and, *without modifying their substance*, strikes them with meaning, gives them the life of a sign; it can also take this life back from them, so that meaning is like a grace that has descended upon the object; if the fullness takes leave of the blouse, the skirt dies to romanticism and is once again nothing but a skirt, it returns to insignificance. Hence Fashion's fragility does not inhere solely in its seasonal variability, but in the gracelike character of its signs as well, in the emanation of a meaning which touches, as it were, these elected objects at a distance: the life of this skirt does not come from its romantic signified, but from the fact that it possesses, for the duration of a spoken word, a meaning which does not belong to it and which will be taken back from it. Naturally, the circulation of meaning at a distance is related to the aesthetic process, in which a partial detail can entirely modify a figure of generality; the object aimed at is in fact close to being a "form," even when it is not materially coextensive with the support; it is this object which gives the matrix a certain generality, and it is by it that the matrices are enlarged: when they combine with one another, it is always in order to designate a final object aimed at, which thereby receives the entire meaning of the written garment.[11]

5.7. *Semiological originality of the support*

Like the object aimed at, the support of signification is always constituted by a material object, a garment, some part of a garment, or an accessory; in the chain of the matrix, the support is the first material element to receive one meaning or another which it must then transmit to the object aimed at; in itself, it is an inert entity which neither produces nor receives meaning, but merely transmits it. Materiality, inertia, and conductivity make the support of signification into an original element of the Fashion system, at least in relation to language. Indeed, language possesses nothing which might resemble the support of signification;[12] of course, the syntagmatic units of language are not direct signi-

---

[11] Cf., below, chap. 6.

[12] Obviously, we might consider pure sound or noise as the support of signification in language; but oral sound exists outside of language only in the state of the "inarticulate" cry whose extremely limited function has no relation to the functional importance of the support in a system like that of Fashion.

fiers, signs must pass through the relay of a second articulation, that of phonemes: the significant units of language rely upon distinctive units; however, phonemes themselves are variants, phonic matter is immediately significant, and, therefore, the linguistic syntagm cannot be divided into active and inert parts, significant and insignificant elements: in language, everything signifies. The support of signification draws its necessity and its originality precisely from the fact that the garment is not *in itself* a system of signification, as is language; in terms of substance, the support represents the materiality of the garment, in such a way that it exists outside any process of signification (or at least prior to this process): in the matrix, the support testifies to the garment's technical existence as opposed to the variant which testifies to its signifying existence. This suggests that all systems of communication based on objects that exist technically or functionally prior to signifying will inevitably include supports distinct from their variants; in food, for example, bread is meant to be eaten; however, it can also be made to signify certain circumstances (bread without crust for receptions, black bread to signify a certain rusticity, etc.): bread then becomes the support for variations in meaning (*no crust/black* ≡ a reception/the country).[13] In short, the support would be a decisive operational concept in the analysis of differential systems. It is likely that for all cultural objects originally intended to serve a functional end, the sufficient unit will always be composed, at the very least, of a support and a variant.

5.8. *The vesteme or variant*

The variant (for example: *open/closed*) is the point of the matrix from which signification emerges and, as it were, emanates all along the utterance, i.e., the written garment. We could call it the *vesteme,* for its role is not unlike those of the phonemes and morphemes of language,[14] or even that of the "gustemes"

---

[13] Cf. "Pour une psychosociologie de l'alimentation contemporaine," *Annales,* no. 5, Sept.–Oct. 1961, pp. 977–86.

[14] This is not the place to decide whether the variant or vesteme is closer to the phoneme or the morpheme, since we do not know if the Fashion system is doubly articulated, as is language. (The double articulation, which has been discussed by A. Martinet, designates the phenomenon by which language articulates itself into significant units—"words"—and into distinctive units—"sounds.")

analyzed by Claude Lévi-Strauss in relation to food:[15] like them, it is made up of oppositions of pertinent features. If after reflection we stick to the more neutral term *variant*, it is because the significant variations of clothing consist of modifications in being or in quality (for instance, measure, weight, division, addition) which are not peculiar to clothing and could be found in other systems of signifying objects. The original character of the variant is its non-materiality:[16] it modifies a material element (the support), but is not itself material; it cannot yet be said that it is constituted by an alternative, for we do not know whether all variants are binary (of the type: *presence/absence*),[17] but we can say that all variants proceed from a corpus of differences (for instance: *open/closed/half-open*); strictly speaking, this generic corpus (for which the French language, as has been indicated, rarely has a neutral vocable) should be called the *class of variants*, and each point of the differential system or paradigm should be called a *variant*; for the sake of terminological economy, and without any great risk of ambiguity, we shall henceforth call the ensemble of terms in the variation the *variant*: the variant of *length*, for example, will thus include the terms *long* and *short*.

IV. RELATIONS BETWEEN ELEMENTS OF THE MATRIX

5.9. *Syntagm and system*

We have already pointed out that both the object and the support are always material objects (*dress, outfit, collar, flap*, etc.), while the variant is a non-material value. This disparity corresponds to a structural difference: the object and the support are fragments of vestimentary space, they are *natural* (so to speak) portions of the syntagm; the variant, on the other hand, is a reservoir of virtualities from which only one term is actualized at the level of the support to which it is assigned. Hence, the variant constitutes that point of the system which coincides with the level of the syntagm. Here again we encounter an original characteristic of

---

[15] *Structural Anthropology.*

[16] There is an apparent infraction of the non-materiality of the variant in the case of variations in species (*linen/velvet*); but it is, in fact, the assertion that varies; cf. chap. 7.

[17] On the structure of variants, cf. chap. 11.

the Fashion system, at least in relation to language. In language the system breaks through, so to speak, at each point of the syntagm, for there is not one sign in language, phoneme or moneme, which is not part of a series of significant oppositions or paradigms.[18] In (written) clothing, the system marks an originally non-signifying mass in a sporadic manner, but this mark, by means of the matrix, has a sort of emanating action over the entire garment. We could say that, in language, the system has a value of being, while in clothing its value is merely attributive; or further still, that, in language, syntagm and system fill to capacity the two dimensions of symbolic space which they represent, while in (written) clothing this space is, in a manner of speaking, obstructed, since the systematic dimension is interrupted by inert elements.

5.10. *Solidarity between elements of the matrix*

The metaphor best able to account for the functioning of the matrix O.V.S. is perhaps that of a door under lock and key. The door is the object aimed at by signification; the lock is the support, and the key is the variant. In order to produce meaning, we must "introduce" the variant "into" the support, and run through the terms of the paradigm until meaning is produced, then the door is opened and the object takes on meaning; sometimes the key does not "fit": the variant of length cannot be applied to the support *buttons;*[19] and when it does fit, the meaning is different depending on whether the key turns to the left or to the right, and whether the variant says *long* or *short.* In this apparatus, no single element possesses the meaning; in a certain respect, they are all parasites on one another, even though it is the choice of variant which, in the end, actualizes the meaning, just as it is a gesture of the hand which carries out the act of opening or closing the door. This is to say that among the three elements of the matrix there is a relation of *solidarity,* or, as certain linguists would say, of *double implication:* object and sup-

---

[18] We know that even if the paradigms for phonemes are perfectly familiar (phonology), the paradigms for monemes (or signifying units) are still the object of preliminary studies.

[19] Here we have a rough sketch of one of the "constraints" whose ensemble will form a certain logic of Fashion (12.1).

port, support and variant are all presupposed by one another,[20] the one necessitates the other: no element will be found in isolation (with the exception of a certain instance of terminological license[21]). Structurally, this solidarity is absolute, but its force changes according to where it is placed at the level of the vestimentary substance or at the level of language; the object and the support are linked by a very strong vestimentary solidarity since both of them are equally material, as opposed to the variant, which is not: it is most often a matter of the same piece of clothing (in which case the object and the support are terminologically indistinguishable), or of a piece of clothing and one of its parts (*a cardigan and its collar*); on the contrary, from the point of view of language, it is between the support and the variant that the connection is closest, most often expressing itself through what A. Martinet calls an *autonomous syntagm;*[22] it is in fact easier, terminologically, to amputate the matrix from its object than from its variant: in *a hat with its brim turned up*, the fragment *brim turned up* has a sufficient (linguistic) meaning, while in the fragment *a hat with its brim . . .* , the meaning remains suspended,[23] and, moreover, since the operational manipulation of both the support and the variant occurs quite frequently, we shall call this part of the matrix, consisting of the support and the variant, the *feature.*

V. Substances and Forms

5.11. *Distribution of vestimentary substances within the matrix*

How is the vestimentary substance (entire pieces, parts of garments, fabrics, etc.) going to be distributed among these three

---

[20] This is why it is better to write the matrix as O)(V)(S, since)(is the sign of double implication; but as there is only one possible relation (of solidarity), we shall dispense with this symbol.

[21] On the confusions and extensions of elements, cf. the following chapter.

[22] A. Martinet, *Elements*. Although the feature may most often be comprised of the union of a substantive and an adjective, structural terminology is better because it is more pliant.

[23] To suppress the points of suspension is to close off the meaning, but it is also to change it (and to change the matrix):

a hat with its brim /	a hat with its brim turned up /
O VS	O S V

elements?[24] Can specific substances be attributed to each of them? Are cardigans always the intended objects of signification, collars the supports, and closure a variant? Can we draw up fixed lists of objects, supports, and variants? We must look into the nature of each element. Since the variants are not material, they can never be *substantially* confused with the supports and the objects (but terminologically[25] they can be confused quite easily): a skirt, a blouse, a collar, or a flap can never constitute a variant; inversely, a variant can never be converted into an object or a support. On the other hand, since all objects and all supports are material, they can exchange their substance quite readily: in one instance a collar may be a support, and in another the intended object; this depends on the utterance; if the magazine speaks of *collars with their edges turned up,* the collar becomes the intended object of signification, whereas before it was only the support: it is enough to raise the matrix a notch, if you will, in order to convert an intended object into a simple support.[26] We thus have only two lists of substances to establish: one for variants, and another for objects and supports alike.[27] We can see from this that the signifying matrix of the written garment is in fact half formal, and half substantive, since its substance is mobile or interchangeable in the first two elements (object and support) and stable in the third (variant). This rule differs notably from that of language, which requires that each "form" (phoneme) always have the same phonic substance (with all but insignificant variations).

---

[24] *Substance* is used here in a sense very close to Hjelmslev's: an ensemble of aspects of linguistic phonemes which can be described exhaustively without recourse to extra-linguistic premises (cf. L. Hjelmslev, *Essays*).

[25] For example, in *a hat with its brim,* since the word *brim* supports its own variation of existence.

[26] On the play of "notches," cf., below, 6.3 and 6.10.

[27] The mutual inventory of objects and supports will be conducted in chapters 7 and 8; the inventory of variants in chapters 9 and 10.

6

Confusions and Extensions

"A cotton dress with red and white checks."

I. Transformations of the Matrix

6.1. *Freedom of transformation in the matrix*

Since the matrix is merely a signifying unit, it stands to reason that it cannot account, in the canonical form in which it has been presented up to now, for all utterances of the signifier: most of the time, in their terminological state, these utterances are either too long (*a halter top buttoned down the back,* etc.) or too short (*This year blue is in Fashion,* i.e., *Fashion = blue*). We must therefore expect a double transformation of the matrix: one of reduction, when certain of these elements will be conflated in a single vocable, and one of extension, when there will be either a multiplication of an element within a single matrix or the linking of several matrices with one another. This freedom of transformation adheres to two principles: on the one hand, the terminological system does not necessarily coincide with the vestimentary code: one may be "larger" or "smaller" than the other: they do not obey the same logic, nor are they under the same constraints, which explains the confusion of elements; on the other hand, the matrix is a pliant form, half formal, half material,[1] defined by the relation of three elements: an intended object, a support, and a variant; the sole constraint is that these three elements be *at least* present in the utterance so that the economy of distribution of meaning is respected; but nothing keeps them

---

[1] Cf., above, 5.13.

from being multiplied,[2] which explains the extensions of the matrices. As for their linkage, it is nothing other than syntax which ordinarily unites the signifying units of a system. In other words, the analysis of every utterance of the signifier is subject to two conditions: a chosen matrix must be filled by at least these three elements; each term of the utterance must find its place in a matrix: the matrices must exhaust the utterance, and the elements must saturate the matrices: the signifier is then replete with signification.[3]

II. INVERSION OF ELEMENTS

6.2. *Freedom of inversion and its limits*

The order that has been assigned to the three elements of the matrix up to this point (O.V.S.) is a conventional one; it corresponds to a logic of reading, which reconstitutes the process of meaning in reverse, as it were, and gives the effect (the intended object) first, before going back to the cause (the variant). However, this order is not obligatory, and the magazine may very well invert certain elements of the matrix. The freedom to invert is considerable; it is not absolute, being subject to a perfectly rational constraint. Indeed, we saw that between the support and the variant there was a strong linguistic solidarity; it is therefore to be expected that we would be unable to dissociate that part of the matrix which is the *feature*. Of the six inversions of the elements O.V.S. which are theoretically possible, two are by rights excluded: those in which the support and the variant would be separated by the intended object:[4]

S. O. V.

V. O. S.

---

[2] Except the intended object, which is always singular, at least at the level of the matrix (cf., below, 6.8).

[3] Even if, as we have said (5.11), the meaning is distributed throughout the matrix with an unequal density.

[4] Exception being made, of course, for those matrices where there is a terminological confusion of the object and the support and where we can have V • (OS), as in:

$$\overset{\displaystyle \diagdown\ \text{a large collar made of organza}\ \diagup}{\overset{\diagdown\ \ \text{O} \qquad\qquad \text{SV}\ \ \diagup}{\text{V} \qquad\quad \text{OS}}}$$

The other formulas are all possible: whether within the feature itself there is an inversion of the variant and the support; or whether the feature itself exchanges its place with the intended object; or, finally, whether both these permutations occur simultaneously:

O • (V.S.): ＼ a blouse with a large collar ／
                O   V   S

O • (S.V.): ＼ a cardigan with its collar open ／
                O   S   V

(V.S.) • O: ＼ high waists for (evening) gowns ／
                V   S   O

(S.V.) • O: ＼ collars that are small for (sports) shirts ／
                S   V   O

As can be expected, the permutation of the two elements of the feature (V.S. or S.V.) is of little consequence, for its origin is purely linguistic: the order of the feature changes because the French (and less frequently the English) language requires, for instance, that certain adjectives precede the noun and others follow it. The displacement of the intended object has a more expressive value: the primacy of the feature entails a certain semantic accentuation of the support (*high waists for evening gowns*). Finally, it must be noted that from this point on, in a case where several matrices combine with one another, the intended object of the final matrix may, in a manner of speaking, subtend several elements of the intermediary matrices; the representation of the utterance then ceases to be linear and becomes architectonic; we can no longer say that the intended object precedes or follows its correlative elements: it is simply extensive with them.[5] All these permutations are obviously direct tributaries

---

[5] Example:

＼ a matched ensemble, straw hat and cache-peigne ／
            S_1 S_2 S_3
    V   O

In certain cases, the architectonic representation is necessary to account for a single matrix:

＼ this suit and its toque ／
        S_1 V S_2
              O

of the structure of the French (or English) language itself; Fashion would have to express itself in an inflected language like Latin if the order O.S.V. were to be consistently adhered to.

III. CONFUSION OF ELEMENTS

6.3. *Confusion of O and S*

It has already been indicated that two forms could receive the same substance and, therefore, the same name: consequently, there is a terminological confusion of two elements of the matrix in a single vocable. This is the case of condensations of object and support: *This year, collars will be open.*[6] In no way does this terminological condensation obscure the distinction of the respective structural functions of the object and the support; in *open collar,* we can say that the collar which materially receives the act of being opened (this year's collar) is not the same as the collar which is aimed at by the meaning of Fashion (collars in general): in fact, the genus-collar (the intended object) is actualized this year by the open collar (the collar thus becomes a support). How do these condensations of object and support usually come about? We could compare condensation to a knot that suddenly interrupts the sequence of links in a chain; in describing a garment, all that the magazine must do in order for the support, through an actual collision, to merge with the intended object and become identified with it is to *arrest* the meaning at the collar and thereby terminate the utterance at a certain moment; on the other hand, if the magazine extends its "speech" and takes the meaning beyond the collar, the outcome is a normal matrix having three explicit elements: in all condensed matrices, there is thus a kind of implicit amputation of a more remote object and a return of meaning to the old support: in *The open collar is in Fashion,* the collar receives the designation of meaning that elsewhere had fallen to an explicit object (*a blouse with an open collar*). This phenomenon undoubtedly has a general applicability, for it allows us to understand how a description draws a particular organization for its meaning from its own limitation

---

6 \ Fashion this year ≡ open collars /
V   SO

(and not only from its extension): *to say* is not only to note and to omit, but also to bring to a stop and to effect, by the very placement of this stop, a new structuration of discourse; there is a reversion of meaning, from the limits of the utterance toward its center.

6.4. *Confusion of S and V*

We have seen that the feature (the support and the variant combined) was most often constituted by an autonomous syntagm,[7] ordinarily formed by a substantive and a determinant (*open collar, rounded crown, two cross straps, slit side,* etc.). But it is not useful for language to confuse the support and the variant precisely because, on the one hand, the feature's linguistic cohesion is quite strong and, on the other, there is a disparity of material between these two elements: it is common to name both terms, insofar as they are linguistically stereotyped and yet substantially distinct. For the variant and support to be confused, the variant must lose its attributive value (the kind, for instance, that an adjective coupled with a noun can express) and reach the very being of the support. This explains why the elements of the feature are confused in only two sorts of variants: the variant of existence and the variant of species (here it is necessary to anticipate the inventory of variants[8]). If indeed the signification of the utterance depends upon the presence or absence of a piece, it is inevitable that the naming of this piece as support completely absorb the expression of the variant, since the support has nothing to uphold but its own existence or its own lack of existence: *a belt with tassels,* which means *a belt with existing tassels;* in the first utterance, the word *tassels,* as vestimentary material, is a support, and at the same time, as an affirmation that this material exists, it is a variant. Whereas in the case of the variant of species, we can say that it is the variant which absorbs the support: for instance, when the entire utterance is occupied by it: *a linen dress,* it is tempting to define the dress as a confusion of the object and the support and the linen as the variant (as opposed to velvet or silk, for example); however, since the variant

---

[7] Cf., above, 5.12.
[8] Cf., below, chap. 9.

is non-material, linen cannot directly constitute a variant; in fact, it is the fabric's materiality which supports the nominal variation of the species (*linen/velvet/silk*, etc.); in other words, between the intended object (the dress) and the *difference*, the relay of a material support must be reestablished. In generic terms, this is *the fabric*, whose terminological expression is identified with the naming of the species: as undifferentiated material (fabric), linen is a support, and as affirmation (i.e., as choice) of a species, it is a variant:[9] this would explain, if language permitted, an expression such as *a dress of "linened" fabric;* since the assertion of species is quite a rich[10] variant, the support and the variant are quite frequently identified; we find this to be the case with all utterances which include mention of a species of fabric, color, or pattern: *a linen (fabric) dress, a white (color) blouse of checked (pattern) poplin.* Thus the feature finds its precise measure in the unit of the word each time the primary source of meaning is the assertion, pure and simple, of existence or of species, for language cannot name without at the same time positing existence or particularizing.[11]

6.5. *Confusion of O, S, and V*

Finally, the intended object can quite easily be confused with the feature, even if the latter is normally developed or condensed. In the first case, we will have a support that is clearly separate from the variant, but the intended object will, in a sense, be subjacent to the feature-ensemble; if the magazine writes, *For spring, this suit and its toque*, it is easy to see that the object aimed at by signification is the ensemble of the suit and the toque, and that the meaning issues not from one or the other but from the association of the two; thus the object aimed at is the entire outfit, whose terminological expression in this instance is confused with each of the pieces it consists of and with the variant which makes it signify.[12] In the second case, the utterance of the signified

---

[9] Cf., below, chap. 7 on the assertion of species.

[10] A variant is *rich*, not necessarily because its paradigm includes a lot of terms, but because it can be applied to a large number of supports: this is "syntagmatic yield" (cf., below, 12.2).

[11] On particularization, cf., below, 7.4.

[12] $\diagdown$ Spring $\equiv$ this suit and its toque $\diagup$

$\qquad$ S1 $\quad$ V $\qquad$ S2

is reduced to a word; in *This year blue is in Fashion, blue* is simultaneously object, support, and variant: it is color in general which supports and receives the signification, it is the affirmation of the species *blue* which constitutes it.[13] This last ellipsis, the most powerful imaginable, is quite suitable to the major headings of the Fashion magazine, to the titles of its pages: beneath the foreshortened form of a single word ("shirtdresses," "linen"), we can read a signified (this year's Fashion) and a signifier, which is itself composed of an intended object, a support (the genre shirtdress, the fabric), and an assertion of species.[14]

IV. MULTIPLICATION OF ELEMENTS

6.6. *Multiplication of S*

Since each element of the matrix is a "form," it can in principle be "filled" by several different substances at once;[15] the matrix can be extended by the multiplication of certain of its elements. It is not uncommon, for instance, to encounter two supports in the same matrix; this is notably the case in all matrices containing a variant of connection, since it is precisely the nature of this variant to rely on (at least) two fragments of clothing; here is a classic case: *a (long-sleeved) blouse with a scarf under the collar*[16] (since there is no ellipsis). The most frequent case, though, is that of matrices in which there is a partial identification between the intended object and one of the two supports; for example, *the blouse tucked into the skirt:* the blouse is clearly the object aimed at, but at the same time it serves as partial support to the variant of emergence.[17] Of course, in such utterances the object

---

[13] This year's Fashion $\equiv$ \\(color) blue/ $\overline{\text{OS} \quad \text{V}}$

[14] The only confusion that may be ruled out is that between O and V, S remaining explicit, for the same reason that we cannot interpose the object between the support and the variant (cf., above, 6.2).

[15] Except the object aimed at by signification, which is always singular, as we shall see in section 6.8.

[16] \\a (long-sleeved) blouse with a scarf under the collar/ $\overline{\text{O} \quad \text{S}_1 \quad \text{V} \quad \text{S}_2}$

[17] \\a blouse tucked into the skirt/ $\overline{\text{OS}_1 \quad \text{V} \quad \text{S}_2}$

is most likely to be confused with the first support because language itself (we are dealing with a written garment) accords a stylistic privilege to the term placed at the beginning of the period; hence we can see how a simple "detail" can quite easily constitute the object aimed at, even if it is connected to a support materially more important than itself; in *a bracelet to go with the dress*, we are speaking principally of the bracelet—it is surely the bracelet to which we want to call attention, which is the object aimed at, even if a dress is more important than a bracelet.[18] In fact, this is one of the reasons for the existence of the Fashion system, that is, to give at least equal semantic power to materially disproportionate elements, and to combat the primitive law of quantity by a compensating function.

6.7. *Multiplication of V*

Since the matrix becomes more subtle from object to variant, it is to be expected that variants can be multiplied more easily than supports; the closer we get *to* the object aimed at, the denser the matrix becomes, and the more difficult the accumulation; on the contrary, the further we get *from* the object, the more use the elements of the matrix make of the liberties afforded by abstraction. Thus, it is common to have several different variants in a single support. In *a blouse slit on one side* (i.e., *a blouse, one side of which is slit open*), the support lends itself equally to two variants: fissure (*slit*) and number (*one*).[19] Here is an utterance with no fewer than four variants: *an authentic Chinese tunic, cut straight and slit up the sides*.[20] Moreover, it is quite possible for one variant to modify another linguistically, rather than to modify the support they both share: in *suspenders crossed in back*, the variant of position (*in back*) modifies the variant of closure (*crossed*).[21] There is nothing surprising about such an accumula-

---

[18] \ a bracelet to go with the dress /
    OS1   V   S2
[19] \ a blouse slit on one side /
    O V1 V2 S
[20] \ an authentic Chinese tunic, (cut straight) and (slit up the sides) /
    V1   V2   O   V3   V4
[21] \ suspenders crossed (in back) /
    OS V1 V2

tion of variant terms at a single point or even about the fact that a support may be in contact with a variant only through the intermediary of another variant: *mutatis mutandis,* in the French verb *chanterons* the marks of the plural number and of the future tense are grounded in the same root, which has the role of a prop (*chant-*).[22] At this point, it is enough to distinguish between ordinary variants, those which can modify both supports and other variants, and special variants—those which can only modify other variants; such special variants are intensives or variants of degree (*casually* in *casually knotted,* for example); these must be set aside, for if we want to draw up the inventory of features (SV), the intensives cannot take a direct part in it, since they are never directly attached to a support; we must examine their union with variants, not with supports.[23]

6.8. *Singularity of O*

There is only one element which cannot be multiplied within a given matrix, and that element is the object aimed at by signification.[24] It is to be expected that Fashion would refuse to multiply the object of a matrix: the entire structure of the written garment is, so to speak, an ascending one; through a maze of often disparate elements, it attempts to make its meaning converge toward a unique object; the very aim of the Fashion system is this difficult reduction from the many to the one; for, on the one hand, it must preserve the garment's diversity, its discontinuity, and the profusion of its components; and, on the other hand, it must discipline this profusion and impose a unified meaning under the various species of a unique aim. Thus, it is ultimately the singularity of the object aimed at by signification which guarantees the unity of the matrix; firmly based upon its unique object,

---

[22] The analogy stops at this point, because the difference of the vestimentary support *chant-* is a semanteme: it possesses meaning of itself, it is not an inert support.

[23] Cf., below, 10.10.

[24] We can now make the assertion that the singularity of the object aimed at by signification defines a matrix (the matrix would be that which contains one and only one intended object), and, by extension, the utterance of the signifier within its ensemble, as comprised of matrices: this utterance, as we shall see below, contains only a single intended object coextensive with the matrices whose linkage makes it possible to be designated.

it can freely multiply its supports and variants without risk of undoing itself. And in those cases where matrices are combined, they are combined according to a convergent organization,[25] in the end each utterance is filled by a single matrix, coextensive with all the others: since the intended object in this final matrix is unique, it takes on all the meaning gradually elaborated at the level of the preceding matrices: the singularity of the object aimed at by signification is, in a sense, the basis for the entire economy of the Fashion system.

V. ARCHITECTURE OF THE MATRICES

6.9. *Delegation of matrix to an element or a group of elements*

The combination of several matrices within a single utterance is based upon the freedom afforded every matrix to be represented by an element or a group of elements from another matrix clearly coextensive with it; thus, the matrices are linked together not by simple linear juxtaposition, like the words of a sentence, but rather by a kind of contrapuntal development and according to what might be called an ascending architecture since, ultimately, it is most common for the utterance to be occupied by a single matrix which has "assembled" all the others. Take, for example, a matrix already saturated: *white braid* ([SV].O); insofar as this white braid is a material element (even if this element is invested with a variant quality), it can easily assume a partial function in a larger matrix, where, for example, it will be either the object or the support; if the white braid must match the buttons (*white braid and white buttons*), the (white) braid and the (white) buttons can only be supports for a new variant of association, whose intended object is implicitly the entire outfit:

$$
\begin{array}{ccccc}
\diagdown & \text{white braid and white buttons} & \diagup \\
\diagdown\ \text{SV} & \text{O} \diagup & \diagdown\ \text{SV} & \text{O} \diagup \\
\diagdown\ \text{S}_1 & \text{V} & \text{S}_2 \diagup \\
& \text{O} \\
\end{array}
$$

---

[25] Cf. following paragraphs.

Three matrices are thus included within the same utterance, the last of which (S1.S2.V.O.) is coextensive with the first two, since each of its supports "represents" a complete matrix by itself. We could say that, in these syntactic developments, one matrix empowers an element of another to represent it and to transmit on its behalf some of the meaning it possesses to the final matrix. Matrices can be delegated to an element or to a group of elements when elements are conflated. However, not all formulas for such delegation are possible: since it is non-material, the variant cannot represent a matrix, and on the other hand, by virtue of its object and its support, the matrix is inevitably comprised of vestimentary substance;[26] it follows that the "point" of meaning (the variant) is always solitary (as opposed to elements which "represent") and seems to pull the meaning forward like the lead horse of a team; this is plainly seen in terminal matrices where the thinness of the variant contrasts with the density of its support and its object. On the other hand, the group OV can no longer represent any matrix because the variant cannot be identified with its object without the relay of a support. We therefore have the following forms of delegations:

I. Elements

VSO = V: impossible

VSO = S: \ white braid and white buttons /
       \ VS   O /
         S1 . . .

---

[26] When terminologically developing an utterance like *poplin with yellow dots*, it seems at first glance that the primary matrix (*yellow dots*) becomes the simple variant of the second matrix:

\ poplin (with a pattern of) yellow dots /
       \ O   V   S /
   OS   V

Actually, the second variant is one of existence, so we must reestablish the matrix:

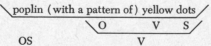

\ poplin with (a pattern of) yellow dots (that exist) /
       \ O   V   S /
   O   S   V

The *yellow dots* are nothing more than the support of their own existence.

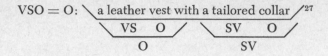

VSO = O: a leather vest with a tailored collar [27]

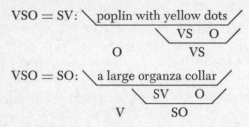

II. Groups of elements

VSO = SV: poplin with yellow dots

VSO = SO: a large organza collar

VSO = OV: impossible

6.10. *The pyramid of meaning*

By rights, the relation that governs the union of signifying units (matrices) is a relation of simple combination (and not of solidarity or implication as in other forms of syntax); formally, no matrix presupposes the existence of another, each can be sufficient to itself. Yet this particular combinative relation is a special one, for the matrices are linked together by development, not by addition. It is never possible to have a sequence of the type OSV + OSV + OSV, etc.; if two matrices appear in an order of simple succession, they are in fact subsumed within another, coextensive and underlying matrix. We could say that the written garment is constructed, like a canon, by augmentation, or rather, like an inverted pyramid: the base (at the top) of the pyramid would be occupied simultaneously by the primary matrices,[28] the fragmentary meanings within the described ensemble, and its literal utterance; the tip (at the bottom) of the pyramid would be the final secondary matrix, the one which assembles and sums up all the preceding matrices which allowed it to be built, thereby

---

[27] All primary matrices introduced by *with* or *of* (*à* in French) become a feature (SV) in the following matrix, whose variant is one of existence: *with a tailored collar/without a tailored collar*.

[28] What is here called a *primary matrix* is one in which no element represents another matrix, and a *secondary matrix* is one in which at least one element is "representative."

proposing to intellection, if not to reading, a final unified meaning. Such an architecture carries very precise implications. On the one hand, while it allows for a veritable profusion of vestimentary meaning through the utterance, this architecture preserves the final unity of meaning: the precious secret of the meaning of Fashion is enclosed, we might say, within the final matrix (and in a more singular way, within its variant), whatever the number of preparatory matrices which preceded it: it is association which gives a real Fashion-meaning to buttons and braids, not their whiteness. On the other hand, it makes the utterance of the signifier a sort of notched mechanism: it is the final notch which holds the meaning; to move up to the next highest notch or to skip a notch is to change the entire distribution of substances along the matrices;[29] the last meaning to be arrived at is always the most noteworthy meaning, but it is not necessarily situated at the end of the sentence: the utterance is an object of considerable depth; granted, it is perceived (linguistically) on its surface (the spoken chain), but it is read (in a vestimentary sense) in depth (the architecture of the matrices), as the following example clearly shows:

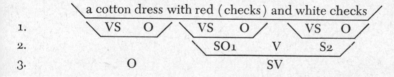

In this utterance there are, in a manner of speaking, three layers of meaning: the first is constituted by the species of materials and colors enlisted in the described garment (cotton, red, white); the second, by the association of red and white checks; the third, by the existence of a complex unit consisting of red and white checks on the cotton dress; this final meaning would be impossible without mention of the preparatory ones; and yet it is this final meaning that is the very point of the Fashion message.

---

[29] In *dotted poplin*, the meaning places the species of pattern (dots) in opposition to other unnamed species; while, in *poplin with yellow dots*, the species of pattern no longer has a direct responsibility in the building of meaning, which depends both on the color yellow (as opposed to other colors) and on the existence (as opposed to the lack) of a unit: *yellow dots*.

6.11. *Homographic syntax*

In order to comprehend the originality of this architectural syntax, we must return once again to language. Language is characterized by a double articulation: in it a system of "sounds" (phonemes) duplicates a system of "words" (monemes); there is a double system in written clothing as well: the forms of the matrix (O.S.V.) and the matrices in relation to one another. But the comparison stops there, for in language the units of each system are joined by a pure combinatorial function, whereas in written clothing the elements of the matrix are solidary: only the matrices are combinatorial. And in no respect does this combinatorial function resemble the syntax of language: the syntax of written clothing is neither a parataxis nor a government; the matrices are neither juxtaposed nor (linearly) subordinate; they engender one another by substantial extension (red and white checks form an ensemble that is coextensive with each of its parts) and formal reduction (an entire matrix becomes a simple element of the following matrix). We could say that the syntax of written clothing is a *homographic* syntax, to the extent that it is a syntax of correspondence and not of successive linkage.

VI. ROUTINES

6.12. *Routines V(SO) and (VS)O*

The elements of the matrix (O,S,V) are forms whose availability is limited only by the rule of distribution of substances (O and S are material, V is non-material). We could compare the matrix itself to a *pattern* and its elements to *pattern-points* as defined by certain linguists;[30] each pattern-point possesses a certain potential for substance, but there are obviously substances that fill certain forms more frequently than others. The most frequent, and hence the strongest, *patterns* are: the matrices (VS)O whose object consists of a piece or a part of a piece of clothing and whose feature (SV) consists of the material, the color, or the pat-

---

[30] Kenneth L. Pike, "A Problem in Morphology-Syntax," *Acta Linguistica*, V:3, p. 125. Pattern: *John came;* pattern-points: *John* and *came;* pattern-point replacement potential: *Bill, Jim, the dog, boys,* etc., can replace John.

tern, provided with a variation of species[31] (*flannel dress, white vest, checked poplin*); the matrices V(SO), whose object-support consists of a piece or a part of a piece of clothing, and whose variant consists of a qualification (*slit jacket, crossed suspenders, full blouse,* etc.); and, lastly, at the level of the secondary matrices, we were able to ascertain from some of the previously cited examples that the strongest *pattern* consists of the adjunction of a primary matrix to a secondary matrix, where it takes the place of the feature (SV) and functions as a variant of existence (*poplin with yellow dots*). As these *patterns* take the place of a single bloc within the utterance, we can consider them routines, analogous to the "elementary configurations" or "building blocks" of a translating machine;[32] so that if we wanted to construct a Fashion-making machine, we could often economize on detail in the primary matrices, whether these be V(SO) or (VS)O. A routine is, if you like, an intermediary state between form and substance: it is a generalized substance, since the routine is only fully valid at the level of certain particular variants.

6.13. *Routines and final meaning*

These routines have more than just an operational importance; they contribute to the ordering of the production of meaning: according to a well-known law, their frequency alone tends to banalize the message they transmit; thus, when they enter into a composition and occupy the rank of the primary matrices, they constitute a foundation whose very banality reinforces the originality of the final meaning; at the level of routines, the internal meaning thickens and fossilizes; thereby, however, all its vigor, all its freshness is left to the final variant which preempts them; in *a cotton dress with red and white checks,* the meaning of the cotton dress, the red checks and the white is a weak one according to that law which states that a cliché tends toward insignificance; the variant of association which unites the red and white of the checks produces a meaning that is already more vigorous;

---

[31] On the distinction between the species and its assertion, cf., below, chap. 7.

[32] On elementary configurations, cf. A J. Greimas, "Les problèmes de la déscription mécanographique" in *Cahiers de Lexicologie,* I, p. 58. The "building blocks" or "sub-routines" are "bits of calculation coded in advance and used like blocks in the construction of all codes" (B. Mandelbrot, *Logique, langage et théorie de l'information,* Paris, P.U.F., 1957, p. 44).

but ultimately it is the existence of red and white checks *in rela-tion to* the cotton dress which carries the strongest information, the newest meaning, the one which immediately makes itself evident upon first reading and which is the very goal of the utterance. From this we can guess what the profound finality of all this syntax will be: to concentrate the meaning little by little, to shift it from the banal to the original, to elevate it to the singularity of the never-before-seen or the never-before-read. The utterance of the signifier is thus something completely other than a compilation of noteworthy traits: it is the actual birth, patient and delicate, of a signification.

7

The Assertion of Species

"The twin set makes a noted appearance."

I. THE SPECIES

7.1. *The species of the garment*

We have seen that the object aimed at by signification and the support of signification could exchange their substance and that this substance was always material: a skirt, a blouse, a collar, a pair of gloves, or a pleat can sometimes be the object, sometimes the support, and at still other times both at once. Unlike the variant, which has a specific inventory of its own, objects and supports have an inventory that consists of a single substance common to both. This substance is nothing other than the garment in its materiality: the substantial inventory of objects and supports inevitably coincides with the inventory of the garment. But as we are dealing here with an article of clothing that is relayed through "speech," what we shall have to inventory are the vocables themselves which language uses to designate the garment (but not to qualify it, for that is the concern of the inventory of variants). In other words, what must be inventoried are names for clothing (ensembles, individual garments, parts of garments, details, and accessories); i.e., species. The species (e.g., *blouse, jumper, smock, bonnet, toque, capeline, necklace, flats, skirt*, etc.) forms the necessary and sufficient terminological unit required to constitute an object or a support. Another way of saying this is that in language the species belongs to the level of denotation; therefore, it is not at this level that we risk finding rhetorical elaborations, even if the origin of its designation is often meta-phorical (*Byron collar*, *shawl-warmer*, *moss-green*, etc.).

7.2. Real species, named species

Vestimentary species are so numerous that we naturally hope to be able to submit them to a reductive principle which dispenses with the making of an exhaustive inventory. Of course, if we had to establish the structure of real clothing. we would be justified in passing beyond the confines of the word; we would be free to define within the species the technical elements which constitute it—for example, to consider the toque as a hat having a high crown and no brim, i.e., to find both the primary species (the crown, the brim) and the implicit variants (the height, the lack)[1] within the species aimed at; this work of real analysis would no doubt permit us to reduce the profusion and anarchy of vestimentary species to a few simple species, of which the mere combinatorial function probably produces the entire garment. But since we must not infer a real structure from a terminological one, we cannot at this point proceed beyond the name of the species: it is with this name that we must deal, not with what it designates: we do not have to know how a blouse is made to know it differs from a polo shirt; in fact, we do not even have to know what a blouse or a polo shirt is: it is enough that the variation of their names be sanctioned by the variation of a vestimentary meaning. In short, the principle of species, strictly speaking, derives neither from the real in and of itself, nor from a vocabulary in and of itself, but only from that mixture of the two which is the vestimentary code.

7.3. Classification of species

It follows that in written clothing the classification of species cannot be submitted to either real (technological) or lexicological criteria:[2] species of written clothing must have their own order, one that is proper to the system itself, i.e., subject to criteria of signification and not criteria of manufacture or lexical affinity. In

---

[1] On the question of implicit (or "invested") variants, cf., below, 11.10.

[2] Lexicological criteria: cf. the notional classification of W. von Wartburg, J. Trier, and G. Matoré.

order to find out what this order is, we must obviously leave the syntagmatic level for a moment: the syntagm gives the chains of units but provides nothing that permits their immediate classification. This "resistance" on the part of the syntagm is so much stronger in the case of the species that the species become confused with the supports and the objects, i.e., with the inert elements of the matrix: it is the variant which both introduces meaning into the syntagm and represents the paradigmatic dimension;[3] and since, as opposed to the profusion of syntagmatic facts, the system is a principle of classification (since it allows us to constitute lists of oppositions), we must therefore try to find particular variants attached to species if we hope to classify these species. Such variants do exist: we find one each time that the meaning of a matrix emerges from the pure and simple affirmation of a particular species of garment:[4] we shall call this variant the *assertion of species,* and even though the inventory of object-supports should in principle precede the inventory of variants, we shall study this variant first, before returning to the classification of species.

II. The Variation of Species

7.4. *Principle of assertion of species*

The species can signify in and of itself. If it is stated that *the twin set makes a noted appearance,* this would mean at first glance that it is the twin set's existence itself which makes it signify Fashion, not its length, softness, or form; it is because the species *twin set* is distinct from other garments that it is immediately found to be endowed with the meaning Fashion: in order for the twin set to signify, it is enough that it assert its species.[5]

---

[3] Cf., above, 5.10.

[4] That is, in those matrices in which S and V are confused.

[5] Inversely, by virtue of the law of final meaning, the species is not significant if it is augmented by any other variant: the word that affirms it must be *matte,* for if one says that it is *close-fitting twin sets* which are making their appearance, it is clear that the twin set, while participating in the meaning as both intended object and support, no longer takes its final meaning from its nature as a twin set, but rather from its close fit. It will be recalled that matrices differ according to the particular case:

\ twin set /	\ close-fitting twin set /	
VSO	V	SO

This is not to say that the twin set itself literally constitutes the variant, for the variant cannot be material. In fact, if we take a closer look, we find that what undergoes the significant variation at the most fundamental level is not the material of the twin set at all; the opposition is not *initially* between the twin set and its sister species, but, more formally and more immediately, between the assertion of a choice (whatever it may be) and the silence of this choice. In short, when the nomination of the species is matte, two values, or, if one prefers, two forms, must always be distinguished in it: a material form which corresponds to the objective part of the matrix (object or support), and an assertive form, the affirmation that this material exists in a chosen form; and what signifies (as variant) is never the materiality of the species, but rather its affirmation. This distinction may appear Byzantine if we stick to the level of language, at least our Western languages, which in the utterance of a thing readily confuse its existence, the class to which it belongs, and the affirmation of its particularity all at the same time; on the one hand, it is after all an astounding phenomenon that language does not allow for the distinction between the simple utterance of a thing and the affirmation that it exists: to name is always to make something exist, and in order to take existence away from the thing the special tool of negation must be added to its nomination: there is a nominative privilege in being (what new Borges among us will imagine a language in which to say things would be by rights to negate them, and in which an affirmative particle would have to be added in order to make them exist?); and, on the other hand, there do exist languages (Bantu, Japanese, and Malay, for instance) which expressly mention both class and species in the utterance of the thing: so that one says, *3 animals-horses, 3 flowers-tulips, 2 round objects-rings*, etc.;[6] the example of these languages makes it clear that in *twin set* or in *white* it is legitimate to distinguish the material class of the garment (genus— twin set[7] or color) from the choice which affects a determination of species; for, in short, while implicitly developing *a linen dress*

<hr>

[6] Cited by L. Hjelmslev, "Animé et inanimé, personnel et nonpersonnel," in *Travaux de l'Institut Linguistique*, I, p. 157.

[7] The denomination "genus—twin set" is obviously provisional, since we do not yet know the class to which the twin set belongs.

or *a dress made of a linen fabric,* we merely separate the materiality of the support from the abstract affirmation of the choice
that makes it signify: semiologically, linen is nothing; it is not
the species in its materiality, but the assertion that one species is
chosen over and against all those that are relegated outside the
present meaning.

7.5. *The opposition x/the remainder*

Affirmation is nothing other than a suspended choice: if language,
which cannot speak without giving rise to substances, did not
require it, it would be useless to fill this choice with something
in order to render it significant. From the point of view of the
system (and consequently), as paradoxical as it might seem, from
the point of view of Fashion, of what importance is linen? Tomorrow it will be raw silk or alpaca, but the opposition between
a chosen species (whichever it might be[8]) and the mass of unnamed species will always be the same. Provided we are willing
to suspend substance, the significant opposition is a rigorously
binary one: it refers an entity not to its opposite (linen is not the
opposite of anything), but to the anonymous reservoir from which
this entity is drawn: this reservoir is, if you will, all *the remainder*
(a pole well known to linguistics). Hence, the formula for the
assertion of species would be:

$$x \quad / \quad \text{the remainder}$$
$$(linen) \quad (all\ other\ fabrics)$$

What is the nature of this opposition? Without recourse to very
complicated analytical techniques, and from the point of view
of the vestimentary code alone, the relation between *x* and *"the
remainder"* is the same as that which distinguishes a particular
element from a more general one. Also, to analyze the mechanism of the assertion of species further is to explore the nature
of "the remainder," whose opposition to the affirmed species constitutes the entire meaning of Fashion.

---

[8] The indifference of the choice is not absolute; reality itself is its limit, in
practice distinguishing heavy fabrics from light ones; linen, therefore, can only
be opposed semantically to another light fabric (cf., below, 11.11).

III. THE CLASS OF SPECIES: THE GENUS

7.6. Multiple "remainders": the path of opposition

It is obvious that "the remainder" is not all clothing minus the species named. In order to signify, it is not necessary for linen to be extracted from a "remainder" which would indiscriminately include necklaces, colors, packets, folds, etc.; there is no chance of a magazine stating: *In summer, wear linen, and in winter, wear flats;* such a proposition (the opposition of species it proposes: *linen/flats*) is properly *absurd*, i.e., it is located outside the system of meaning:[9] for there to be meaning, there must on the one hand be freedom of choice (*x/the remainder*) and on the other hand, this freedom must be limited to a certain grouping of oppositions (*the remainder* is only a *certain* part of the entirety of clothing[10]). We can thus expect the entirety of clothing to be made up of a certain number of groupings (or "rests"); properly speaking, each group is not the paradigm of the named species, for the significant opposition is only produced between the formulation (of a species) and the non-formulation (of the other species); at the least, it is the horizon which limits this opposition, the substantial reference which allows it to produce meaning.

7.7. The test of incompatibility

The operation which should allow for the reconstitution of the different "remainders" or groupings of the assertion of species can only be a formal one, for we cannot call directly upon the technical content or lexicological affinities of species. Since each inventory is constituted by all the species whose variation is prisoner of the same limits, it will suffice to find the principle of these limits in order to establish the inventories of species. It is clear that if linen, alpaca, and raw silk, for instance, enter into significant opposition,[11] it is in fact because these fabrics cannot be used

---

[9] Unless for rhetorical purposes one chose to parade absurdity itself: absurdity then becomes the signified of connotation of the entire sentence.

[10] Cf. the groupings of signification of modern logic, R. Blanché, *Introduction*, p. 138.

[11] Here we are speaking of significant opposition between species in order to simplify: in fact, the opposition is not between material species, but between assertion and non-assertion.

at the same time on the same part of the garment;[12] inversely,
linen and flats cannot enter into significant opposition, because
they can coexist perfectly well as parts of the same outfit; they
therefore belong to different inventories. In other words, what is
syntagmatically incompatible (linen, raw silk, alpaca) is *systematically* associated; what is syntagmatically compatible (linen,
flats) necessarily belongs to different systems of species. In order
to define the inventories, we must once again determine, at the
level of species, all syntagmatic incompatibilities (that is what
we could call the test of incompatibility); by collecting all incompatible species mentally, we produce a kind of generic species, which economically sums up an entire inventory of significant
exclusions: for example, linen, raw silk, alpaca, etc., form a generic
species (i.e., material); bonnet, toque, beret, etc., form another
generic species (i.e., headwear), etc. We thus obtain series of
exclusions summed up by a generic term:

$$a^1/a^2/a^3/a^4 \ldots\ldots\ldots A$$
$$b^1/b^2/b^3/b^4 \ldots\ldots\ldots B, \text{etc.}$$

It is quite useful to be able to handle the composite generic (A, B,
etc.) of each series with a degree of ease, for we shall thereby
be able to restore the profusion and anarchy of species to a certain
order which, if not finite, is at least accessible to method; we shall
call this composite a *genus*.

7.8. *The genus*

The genus is not a totality, it is rather a class of species; it logically unites all species semantically exclusive of one another;
hence, it is a class of exclusions; this should be emphasized, for it
may be tempting to fill a genus with all the species that seem intui-
tively affinitive; but, if the affinity and dissimilarity are actually
substantial characteristics of the species of a genus, they are not
operative criteria; the constitution of genera does not rest on a
judgment concerning substance,[13] it rests on a formal test of in-

---

[12] If they seem to be used at the same time, it is because they do not share
the same part of the clothes and because their coexistence is then preempted by
a special variant of association: species are nothing more than supports.
[13] Cf. the thematic classification of R. Hallig and W. von Wartburg, *Be-
griffssystem als Grundlage für die Lexicologie. Versuch eines Ordnungsschemas,*
Berlin, Akademie Verlag, 1952.

compatibility; we might, for example, be tempted to put hats and *cache-peignes* in the same genus, inasmuch as they seem to share an affinity; but the incompatibility test bars this, for a hat and a *cache-peigne* can be worn at the same time (one under the other); whereas, although a dress and a skiing outfit are formally quite different, they are both part of the same genus, since a "choice" must be made between the two, depending on the signified one wants to transmit. Sometimes language itself gives a genus a specific name which does not belong to any of the species comprising it: white, blue, and pink are species of the genus *color.* Most often, however, there is no generic term to designate a class of species linked by exclusion: what is the genus that "heads" pieces of clothing like blouse, caraco, camisole, and jumper, whose variation is nonetheless pertinent? We shall give these anonymous genera the name of the species most commonly found in it: the genus-blouse, the genus-coat, the genus-jacket, etc.: it will be sufficient, each time it is necessary, to distinguish between the blouse-species and the blouse-genus. This terminological ambiguity duplicates the confusion between the variant-class and the variant-term;[14] this is to be expected, since the genus is the class in which the variant of species isolates its point of assertion. Once the genus is defined, we can specify the formula for the assertion of species; it is no longer exactly x/"the remainder," but, if we call *a* the species and *A* the genus, it is:

$$a/(A\text{-}a).$$

IV. RELATION BETWEEN SPECIES AND GENERA

7.9. *Genera and species from the point of view of substance*

Once the genera are formally determined, can we assign them a specific content? What we can be sure of it that among species of the same genus there is a certain similarity and a certain dissimilarity simultaneously. In fact, if two species are absolutely identical, there cannot be significant opposition between them, for, as we have seen, the variant is essentially a difference; and if, on the contrary, two species are totally dissimilar (e.g., linen,

---

[14] Cf., above, 5.8.

flats), they cannot be opposed to one another semantically, their confrontation being literally absurd. Thus, for each species, the elements to which its "remainder" (or inventory, or genus) is limited are at once affinitive and dissimilar: *canezou* cannot be opposed to either *canezou* (total identity), or to *capeline* (total dissimilarity); but it will enter into opposition with a bolero, a halter, or a jumper because, from the point of view of substance, they present a relation of similarity-dissimilarity with regard to the *canezou*. We can say that, in general, similarity has to do with the way in which species of the same genus function (a *canezou*, a *jumper*, and a *halter* have nearly the same functional situation in the clothing ensemble), while dissimilarity has to do with the form of the species. The play of similarity and dissimilarity corresponds, of course, to the play of syntagm and system, since between any two given species the syntagmatic relation is exclusive of the systematic relation and vice versa; this is demonstrated in the following chart, each part of which we shall analyze below.

	Similarity	Dissimi-larity	Formula	Example	System	Syntagm
1	—	+	a • b	overcoat & toque	—	+
2	+	—	2a	two neck-laces	—	+
3	+	+<	a1/a2 a1 • a2	toque/ bonnet overcoat & rain-coat	+ outside the system	—

7.10. *Species of different genera:* a • b

We can see (example number 1) that two species, each belonging to a different genus, do not share a relation of similarity-dissimilarity, that their systematic relation is nonexistent and their syntagmatic relation possible: *an overcoat* and *a toque* can coexist, but there would be no sense in opposing them to one another, because there is no way of measuring between their similar (nonexistent) and dissimilar (fundamental) features. If it were a matter of actual clothing, it would be quite interesting to

compile the inventory of syntagmatic relations which genera can
enter into with one another (assuming that the genera of written
clothing could in fact be found in real clothing); for if, in written clothing, it is always a relation of solidarity (V)(S)(O)
which binds the elements of the matrix, there is nothing which
says that the associations of garments must be subject to the same
kind of relation in real clothing. Does a blouse require a skirt or a
skirt a blouse? Does the suit presuppose the blouse? Here, perhaps, is where we might find the three syntagmatic relations
established by linguistics (implication, solidarity, combination),
relations which would clearly constitute the syntax of real clothing.[15] As for the genera of written clothing, however, we cannot
treat their syntagmatic relations in terms of content, for there
is no syntagm other than that (double syntagm) of the elements
of the matrix and that between matrices themselves; when a
magazine wants to establish a relation of coexistence between
two species, it entrusts this relation either to the matrix itself
(*a belt with tassels*), or to an explicit variant of connection (*an
overcoat and its toque*):[16] the doubled species becomes, once
again, the simple support of this particular variant, and the assertion of species disappears.

7.11. *Identical species:* 2#

There cannot be systematic opposition between two identical
species (example number 2), but both species can obviously be
worn at the same time: two bracelets, for example; thus, a syntagmatic relation is possible in this case, but it is explicitly preempted by a particular variant (addition or multiplication), of
which the species itself is none other than the support.

7.12. *Species of the same genus:* a1/a2 *and* a1 • a2

Finally (example number 3), when both species belong to the
same genus (i.e., when they have a relation of similarity-dissimi-

---

[15] From the point of view of real clothing, going back to the criterion of covering the body, we might establish, for example, that for a man there is a simple
implication between covering the chest and covering the hips, but, for a woman,
the relation becomes one of double implication.

[16] \ a belt with tassels /		an overcoat and its toque /		
O	SV	S1	V	S2
			O	

larity), there is the possibility of assertion of species (*toque/ beret/bonnet*, etc.) between the two, and these two species cannot coexist. This incompatibility is obviously invalid by rights, for, in reality, nothing empirically prohibits the wearing of two species of the same genus: if a freezing rain is falling, one can throw a raincoat over one's overcoat in order to cross a garden; but such an "encounter" (or, if you will, syntagm) is always improvised and one only resorts to it with the awareness of (temporarily) violating an institution; it is a simple use of *dress*, which could best be compared, in linguistic terms, to an aberrant fact of speech (as opposed to facts of language).

V. FUNCTION OF THE ASSERTION OF SPECIES

7.13. *General function: from nature to culture*

The species occupies a strategic position in the Fashion system. On the one hand, as the pure and simple denomination of a garment, it exhausts the entire denotative plane of written clothing: to add a variant to a species (and particularly the variant of species itself) is already to depart from the literal, already to "interpret" the real, and to initiate a process of connotation which will naturally develop into rhetoric; as matter, the species is absolutely inert, closed in on itself, indifferent to all signification, as is evidenced by the tautology that spontaneously accounts for its denotative character: *An overcoat is an overcoat.* And, on the other hand, this matter is diversity itself; the diversity of techniques, forms, and uses, that is, everything there is in nature (even if already social) that cannot be reduced to any classification, is invested in the mobile list of species. Hence it is the *concrete diversity*, given by nature, which culture, by means of the assertion of species, seizes upon and transforms into the intelligible.[17] For this, it is sufficient to convert species-matter into species-function, the object into a systematic term,[18] an overcoat into a

---

[17] Cf. Claude Lévi-Strauss, *The Savage Mind.* "There exist only two true models of concrete diversity: the one on the level of nature is that of the diversity of species; the other on the level of culture is offered by the diversity of functions."

[18] We have seen, in a remark made by Saussure, that the word *term* implied the shift to a system.

choice. But, for this choice to be significant, it must be arbitrary; which is why Fashion, as a cultural institution, places what is essential in its assertions of species wherever the choice can in no way be dictated by any "natural" motivation; no free choice and, consequently, no signification can exist between a heavy overcoat and a light dress, for then it is the temperature that commands; there can only be significant choice where nature ends: nature does not impose any real distinctions between raw silk, alpaca, and linen, or between bonnet, toque, or beret; this is also why significant opposition does not occur between species of the same genus, but only between an assertion (no matter what its object) and its implicit negation, between a choice and a rejection; the systematic fact is not choosing linen, it is only *choosing something within certain limits;* we could say that the two terms of the paradigm are the choice and its limits (a/A-a). Thus, by transforming matter into function, concrete motivation into formal gesture, and, to use a well-known antinomy, nature into culture, the assertion of species truly inaugurates the Fashion system: it is the threshold of the intelligible.

7.14. *Methodic function*

This fundamental function of the assertion of species is to be found on the methodic level: it is the assertion of species which inaugurates the inventory of the system. By founding classes of incompatibilities, or genera, it allows for the handling of each of these genera in place of the species it "heads." As we have said, these species are the same substances which saturate the objects and supports of signification. Every species stands for an object or a support, by virtue of this principle: *the entire materiality of the garment is exhausted by the objects and the supports at the level of the matrix, and by the genera and the species at the terminological level.* The inventory of objects and supports ultimately leads back to the inventory of species and genera; we need only establish, by means of the incompatibility test, the list of genera, in order to have at our disposal an inventory of object-supports. The genus is the operative reality which is going to assume both object and support, as opposed to the variant which is irreducible, since it does not share the same substance as the strictly material (or vestimentarily syntagmatic) part of the matrix. The genera, the variants, and their modes of association (frequent, possible, or impossible, depending on the case) are thus the elements which make it possible to establish comprehensively the general system of the Fashion signifier.

8

Inventory of Genera

"Gauze, organza, voile, and cotton muslin, summer is here."

I. Mode of Composition of Genera

8.1. *Number of species by genus*

Formally, the assertion of species is simply a binary opposition of the type a/(A-a); strictly speaking, therefore, the genus is not a paradigm of various species, but only the grouping which limits the substantial possibilities of opposition. The number of species which are part of a genus is of no structural consequence; it matters little to the system whether a genus is assigned a species or not; as we shall see, the "richness"[1] of a genus depends on the number of variants which can be assigned to it, and, among these variants, the assertion of species never counts for more than one, whatever the range of its grouping might be.

8.2. *Subspecies*

Certain species can "head" other species: a *knot*, for instance, is a species of the genus "Fasteners," but it can have subspecies of its own: *hatter's-knot, cabbage-knot, butterfly-knot;* this means that a hatter's-knot is set in signifying opposition to all other knots before being more generally opposed to all other fasteners. We should consider the species-relay (the knot) as a sort of subgenus or, if one prefers, we should count each subspecies as an immedi-

---

[1] Cf., below, chap. 12.

ate species of the primary genus, thereby making the composite name which designates it a simple moneme equal to the others, which will be indicated by a hyphen (*hatter's-knot, cabbage-knot, butterfly-knot*). The existence of these subspecies does not alter the overall system of genera in the least, as long as the genus (primary or secondary) remains a class of exclusions.

8.3. *Varieties*

In certain cases, it is once again the rule of exclusion which requires us to make a careful distinction between *species* and *variety*. It might be helpful to regard certain species or even certain genera, taken together, as classes of inclusion; for example, necklaces, bracelets, collars, handbags, flowers, gloves, and coin purses all sustain a very important general category of Fashion: the *detail*. But the "detail," like the piece or the accessory, is a collection of objects, not a class of exclusions: there is neither signifying opposition nor syntagmatic incompatibility between two kinds of details, between a handbag and a coin purse. This is why we shall call the species or the genera which lexicologically comprise a grouping *varieties*,[2] without their having to comprise it semantically; in fact, the "detail," which is frequently mentioned in the Fashion utterance, can be its own genus: it can, for example, receive a variant directly: *a slight detail*, and coexist in the inventory of genera alongside certain of its *varieties*, which are not its species at all. This ambiguity between variety and species is the same as that found in written clothing itself: in Fashion, we are dealing with classes of exclusions, whereas language always tends to propose classes of inclusions.

8.4. *Genera with one species*

It may happen that a species does not enter into signifying oppositions with any other species mentioned, but that, from the moment it is named, even if only once, a place must be reserved for it in the inventory of genera, since it can serve as the intended object or the support of a variant. The *shirttail*, or *peplum*, for

---

[2] The variety and the grouping to which it is attached exist in the same intuitive relation as a rubric and its components in such thematic classifications as those of Hallig and Von Wartburg. We have seen that this type of classification has no structural value (cf., above, 7.3).

instance, mentioned in the corpus under study, belongs to no genus and includes no other species; we are thus obliged to consider it a species *and* a genus at the same time, or, one might say, as a genus with one species: formally, the shirttail is clearly a genus, since it is syntagmatically compatible with any of the other genera noted;[3] but substantially, despite its singularity, the shirttail is also a species, insofar as it was once or one day could be opposed to other species (*crinoline, buckram*): a grouping can be momentarily defective, while remaining theoretically and historically open; the linguistic consciousness of the species cannot in fact remain purely synchronic; the genus is thus based on a potential diachrony, from which synchrony releases only a single species.[4] But in all cases where genus consists of only one species (and is thus necessarily conflated with it), this species cannot, properly speaking, be the support of the opposition a/(A-a), and it is logical that we could not apply the variant of assertion of species to it: a *dress with floating panels* is not a dress that comes with a species of panel, but merely a dress with a panel added: it is thus the assertion of existence which encompasses all—temporary—cases in which, since the species is unique, its variation of assertion is impossible. Thus we see that if the assertion of species is the methodological key which opens the inventory of genera, we must acknowledge the fact that the inventory is to be completed by genera which do not derive directly from the assertion of species, but rather by genera somehow constituted by the residua rejected by this assertion.

8.5. *Species belonging to several genera*

Finally, it can also happen that a species appears to belong to several different genera at once; this is only an appearance, for in fact the (denotative) meaning of the word itself is not the same according to the genus to which the species is related: a

---

[3] It is understood, of course, that we are dealing with an incompatibility at the level of written clothing; for in real clothing, whose syntactic constraints are entirely different, we can easily find a singular species which may be incompatible with another species without our being able to list them within the same genus: *stockings* are generally incompatible with a bathing suit.

[4] It is not necessary to imagine a broad synchrony in order to found a genus, for Fashion easily invents new species, within its micro-diachrony (this is generally true when old vestimentary terms are revived).

knot in one instance can be a fastener, and in another an ornament (if it fastens nothing at all). Species can thus migrate quite
freely from one genus to another, depending on changes to which
context or, to put it more broadly, history subjects them. This is
because the genus, once again, is not a class of neighboring terminological meanings (as one might find in a dictionary of associated ideas), but rather of temporary semantic incompatibilities.
Hence, the task of distributing species among genera is a fragile
one, yet one which remains structurally possible nonetheless.

II. CLASSIFICATION OF GENERA

8.6. *Fluidity of the list of genera*

This list of genera and species is a precarious one, for in order to
identify new genera and new species all that is necessary is that
the corpus under study be enlarged historically. But, methodologically, this characteristic is of little consequence, for species
does not signify in and of itself, but only through its assertion:
this list of genera is not organic and we could not derive any
fundamental indication as to the structure of written clothing
from it.[5] Nonetheless, this list must be established, since it gathers
together the application points of the variants (the genera are
the object-supports of the matrix). For the corpus we are studying, the inventory of species gives rise to sixty-nine genera; but
certain of these are so particular, so visibly stated by the magazine from an eccentric point of view that, for economy of ex-
position, we shall henceforth consign them to a reservoir "for
memory."[6] So we shall draw up a list of only sixty genera.

8.7. *External criteria of classification*

Before enumerating the genera, we must decide upon their order
of presentation. Can we submit the sixty carefully identified genera to a methodical classification? In other words, is it possible to
derive all these genera from a gradual division of the totality of

---

[5] Contrary to the indications discernible in the number of terms of a variant
which concern the structure of written clothing (cf., below, chap. 11).
[6] Genera for memory: earrings—*cache-peigne*—arch (of a shoe)—tights—upper
(of a shoe)—background (color of printed fabric)—wig—overshoe—overskirt.

clothing under consideration? Such a classification is certainly possible, but only on condition that we leave written clothing and appeal to either anatomical, technical, or purely linguistic criteria. In the first case, we would divide the human body into more and more particular areas, and then group the genera concerning each area according to a dichotomous progression.[7] In the second case, we would essentially take into account the independence, the articulation, or the typical form of the genera, just as one does when classifying mechanical parts in an industrial shop.[8] But in these first two cases we would be appealing to judgments external to the written garment. As for linguistic classification, even though it is doubtless better suited to the written garment, it is, unfortunately, defective; lexicology has only proposed ideological groupings (notional fields), and semantics proper has not yet been able to establish structural lists of lexemes;[9] furthermore, linguistics has not been able to intervene in a lexicon as particular as that of clothing. Since the code being deciphered here is neither completely real nor completely terminological, it cannot easily borrow the principle for the classification of its genera from reality or from language.

8.8. *Alphabetical classification*

In the present instance, simple alphabetical order is preferable. No doubt, an alphabetical classification may appear as something of a last resort, the poor relation of richer classifications; but that is a prejudiced view, as well as an ideological one, to the extent that it grants by contrast a privilege and a dignity to "natural" or "rational" classifications. However, if an equally deep meaning is attributed to *all* modes of classification, we shall agree that an alphabetical classification is an emancipated form: the neutral is more difficult to institutionalize than the "loaded," the full. In

---

[7] For example: Trunk = bust + hips. —Bust = neck + bodice. —Bodice = front + back, etc.

[8] For example: clothing = pieces + parts of pieces. —Pieces = articulations + coverings. —Parts = planes + volumes, etc.

[9] We know that structural semantics is much less advanced than phonology, because the means of constructing lists of semantemes has not yet been found: "[Compared with phonology], *the oppositions seem to have a different character in the lexicon, one that is much looser, and whose organization seems to offer less advantage to systematic analysis*" (P. Guiraud, *La sémantique*, Paris P.U.F., *Que sais-je?*, p. 116).

the case of written clothing, alphabetical order has the precise advantage of being neutral, since it resorts to neither technical nor linguistic reality; it leaves the insubstantial nature of the genera (i.e., classes of exclusions) exposed, whose contiguity can exist only if it is taken up by a special variant of connection, whereas in every other system of classification we would be obliged to juxtapose the genera directly, without accounting for any explicit connection.

III. Inventory of Genera

8.9. *List of species and genera*

Here, then, listed by genus, is the inventory of species drawn from the corpus under study:[10]

1. ACCESSORY   We have seen that this genus contains varieties (handbag, gloves, coin purse, etc.), but that these varieties are not species. The accessory is a genus without species; its varieties are part of other genera; it is, of course, implicitly opposed to the *piece*.

2. APRON   *Apron (blouse-, dress-).* The genus *apron* is to be found at the limit of the sublime in Fashion: it is allowed when dignified by an adjoining subspecies which is fully vestimentary (*blouse-apron, dress-apron*); a skirt-apron seems excluded as too domestic.

3. ARMHOLE   The fact that the species of sleeve depends on the shape of the armhole does not warrant transgressing the terminological rule; it is the sleeve which is named, the sleeve which supports the species; the armhole remains semantically independent.

4. BACK   As with the side and the front, we shall distinguish the genus *back* from the variant *in the back, in back*.

5. BELT   *Belt (corselet-), chain, tie, martingale.* The martingale is not a belt, but in order for it to be a species of the genus *belt*, it need merely be syntagmatically incompatible with a belt.

---

[10] The genus is given here in the singular (except if it can exist only as part of a pair) to indicate that it is a question of type, of a class of exclusions, and not of a class of inclusions; it is named by an autonomous vocable if language allows, or by the name of one of its species (cf., above, 7.8).

6. BLOUSE *Blouse (smock-, sweater-, tunic-), blousette, bras-siere, caftan, canezou, caraco, casaque, chasuble, shirt, chemise, top, jumper, sailor, polo, tunic, middy.*

7. BRACELET *Bangles, bracelet, identification bracelet.*

8. CAPE *Cape (pelerine-).*

9. CLIP

10. COAT *Car coat, dustcoat, cloak, slicker, raincoat, coat (sweater-, mandarin-), overcoat, pelisse, riding coat, trenchcoat.*

11. COLLAR *Collar (bertha-, cape-, hoop-, shawl, shirt-, Peter Pan-, corolla-, wing-, Byron-, scarf-, funnel-, sailor-, military-, pil-grim-, dicky-, polo-, sailor's tie-, tailored-), ruff (Pierrot-).*

12. COLOR Species of colors are infinite and cannot be mas-tered without setting up a painstaking list; they range from sim-ple colors (*red, green, blue*, etc.) to metaphorical colors (*moss, lime, Pernod*), and even to purely qualitative colors (*gay, bright, neutral, shocking*); this infinity is compensated for by the sim-plicity of the implicit variant which makes these colors actually signify and which is the mark.[11]

13. DETAIL This genus calls for the same observation as that for *accessory*.

14. DRESS *Baby-doll, smock, jumpsuit, sheath, tank, dress (blazer-, blouse-, blouson-, shirtdress, chemise, sheath, coat-, sweater-, pinafore, tunic-), overalls.* This genus is not an inclu-sive class; it shouldn't be surprising to find garments of quite dif-ferent forms and functions, like the smock, the jumpsuit, and overalls, united here. (*Dress* is only the arbitrary name of a genus.) If there is affinity of substance among all these species, it occurs at the level of their extension (they cover the torso) and of their rank in the garment's thickness (they are *outerwear*).

15. EDGING *Band, bias, edging, scallop, fringe, galloon, gimp, binding, hem, piping, stitching, ruching, braiding, quill, ruffle.* Some of these species can be listed in other genera if they are not at the edge of the garment (*stitching* and *ruffle*, for example).

16. ENSEMBLE *Matching, bikini, suit, two-piece (blazer, blou-son, cardigan, casaque, jumper, sailor suit), jacket-, ensemble, separates, tailored suit (blazer-, bolero-, cardigan-, kimono, safari, tunic), three-piece, twin set.*

17. FASTENERS *Hooks, buckles, frogs, buttoning, buttons, studs,*

---

[11] Cf., below, 11.12.

zippers, laces, straps, knots (hatter's-, cabbage-, butterfly-), beads.
Buttoning is a collection or, better still, a line of buttons, but it
is all the same a semantic entity distinct from buttons; it supports
variants of position or balance in a more natural way.

18. FLAPS *Flap, lapel.*

19. FLOWER *Bouquet, camellia, flower, daisy, lily of the val-
ley, carnation, rose, violet.*

20. FOOTWEAR *Babouche, ballet slippers, boots, ankle boots,
shoes, pumps, loafers, mules, poulaines, oxfords, sandals, sport-.*
"Sport-" is an old signified fossilized into a species, i.e., into a
signifier.

21. FRONT *Bib, front, gorget, gorgerette, wimple, modesty,
dickey.* Like the side, but even more obviously, since this section
of the garment is materially distinct from its surroundings, as a
genus the *front* cannot be identified with its systematic synonym:
in front, on the front.

22. GLOVES *Gloves, mittens.*

23. HANDBAG

24. HANDKERCHIEF

25. HAT VEIL *Net, hat veil.*

26. HEADWEAR *Bandeau, bonnet (wig-), boater, capeline, hat
(Breton-, kerchief-, Peruvian-), chechia, cloche, coiffe, coiffure,
toque.*

27. HEELS *Heels (boot-, Louis XV-).*

28. HIPS As with the shoulders, we must distinguish between
the anatomical referant (*on the hip, down to the hips*) and the
vestimentary support (*narrow hips*).

29. HOOD *Capuchon, cowl.*

30. JACKET *Blazer, blouson, bolero, all-purpose-, cutaway, pea
coat, jacket (kimono-, Spencer-, sweater-).*

31. LINING *Inside* (in the singular),[12] *lining, reverse.*

32. MATERIAL Its species are infinite. But, as with color, it is
possible to submit this infinity to a regulating variant, obviously
implicit, which lists all materials under a single signifying opposition: weight.[13] The material may be leather as well as a fabric,
stones (for jewelry), or straw. Material is the most important of

---

[12] In an expression like: *better than a lining, the interplay of fabrics of equal
quality whose inside is constantly visible in some part of the outfit.*
[13] Cf., below, 11.11.

the genera; Fashion accords an increasing privilege to substances (as Mallarmé already noted).

33. NECKLACE   *Chain, necklace, locket.*

34. NECKLINE   *Decolleté (empire, sweetheart-, Florentine-, key-hole-), neckline (boatneck-, crewneck).* Although a collar necessarily implies a neckline, it is invariable that the neckline takes up, as it were, where the collar leaves off: it is when there is no collar that the neckline begins to signify.

35. NECKTIE   *Necktie, sailor.*

36. ORNAMENT (or trimming)   *Festoons, garlands, bows, ribbons, ruffles.*

37. PANEL

38. PANTS   *Pegged, jeans, pants (bell-bottomed, deck-), shorts.*

39. PATTERN   *Window-pane, mottled, ribbed, checked, floral, geometric, grained, printed, flecked, honeycomb, dotted, houndstooth (oversized-, large-, regular-, small-), satin stitch, polka dot, Prince of Wales, quadrilled, striped, cross-hatched, triangular.* This genus is constituted by the modes of aspect of the garment's surface material, in a word, by its designs, whatever their technical origin might be, woven or printed, and without regard to texture. This is one more proof of the autonomy of the semantic system in relation to the technological system: *the printed,* for example, cannot be set in opposition to *the woven,* which is not mentioned.

40. PETTICOAT (or slip)   Though invisible, the petticoat can contribute to meaning by altering the volume or the form of the skirt.[14]

41. PLEAT   *Drapes, gathers, godets, darts, pleats (fan-), fold, ruffles.*

42. POCKET   *Pockets (vest-, pouch-, breast-).*

43. SCARF   *Bandana, scarf (-ring, -end), foulard.*

44. SEAMS   *Seams, cuts, appliqué, trapunto, stitch, overstitch.* What is to be borne in mind regarding stitches is their semantic being, not their technological being; it does not matter that they serve to assemble; what is important is that a meaning be attributed to them, and for this they must be visible: thus, it is always a matter of apparent stitches.

---

[14] *The fullness of the skirt is often moderate and soft or else imposing and stiffened by petticoats.*

45. SHAWL   *Bertha, capette, shawl, warmer, stole, pelerine.*
This genus of pieces rests on the shoulders, while the neighboring
genus *scarf* rests on the neck; so there is no syntagmatic ambiguity between certain kinds of shawls (bertha shawl, for example) and certain species of collars (large, rounded, folded down),
because the distinction here arises implicitly only from technical
considerations: in principle, the collar is attached to the bodice,
while the bertha is an independent piece; this is why the bertha
is not set in opposition to the collar unless it is called a *bertha
collar.*

46. SHIRTTAIL (or peplum)   The shirttail (or peplum) is "the
part of a garment that falls below the waist." Naturally, we only
include those cases where the word itself is mentioned (*rounded
peplums*), without bothering with the thing itself, which exists
in most pieces of feminine clothing.

47. SHOULDER STRAPS

48. SHOULDERS   It is understood, of course, that by shoulders
we mean the shoulders of the garment, not those of the human
body. This distinction is necessary because, in certain utterances,
the shoulder is no longer the support of the variant, but a simple
anatomical reference (*on the shoulder*).

49. SIDES   There are no species mentioned. (We could, however, imagine one, e.g., gussets.) We must be very careful to distinguish between the genus *sides* and the variant *on the side* (or
on both sides). In the first case, it is clearly a material portion
of the garment, a syntagm, we are dealing with; in the second
case, the side is no longer an inert space, it is an orientation.

50. SILHOUETTE   *Line (A-, bubble, bell, hourglass, box-shaped,
princess, sack, mermaid, sweater, tunic, trapeze).*[15] No genus is
more prestigious than this one: it contains the very essence of
Fashion, it touches the ineffable, the "spirit," and lends itself to
the sublime, inasmuch as, by unifying diverse elements, it is the
very movement of abstraction; in short, it is the garment's aesthetic meaning, and although it belongs to the vestimentary code,
we can say that it is already permeated with rhetoric and poten-
tially contains a certain connotative meaning. Yet it is a genus

---

[15] Although there is, in principle, only one fundamental line by synchrony, the
magazine can be led to cite other lines; several species of line are given here in
order to account for the variety of this genus.

whose components can usually be discovered and enumerated: each one of these species is made up of the conjunction of a certain number of implicit variants (of form, stiffness, movement, etc.); these variants are combined with basic supports (skirt, bodice, collar) like the operations of a machine that result in an *idea:* ultimately, the silhouette is a long *calculation* whose terms vary each season.

51. SKIRT   *Skirt (wrap-around-, hoop-, short-).*

52. SKULLCAP

53. SLEEVE CUFFS   *Sleeve ends, French cuffs, paraments, sleeve-cuffs (musketeer-).*

54. SLEEVES   *Mancheron, sleeve (balloon, shirt, bell-, shawl-, bishop-, kimono-, leg-of-mutton-, pagoda-, penguin-, raglan-, fichu-).*

55. STOCKINGS

56. STRAP   *Barrette, bridal, sliding loop, braid, belt loop, tab.*

57. STYLE   *Style (California-, cardigan-, Chanel-, shirt-, sailor-, sport-, sweater-).* Style has a certain affinity with the silhouette (like it, it tends toward connotation); but the silhouette is a "tendency," it presupposes a certain finality: the "sack" is that toward which the garment tends; style, on the contrary, is a reminiscence, it derives its qualities of being from some origin. Hence, from the point of view of substance, pieces of a certain style can represent either signifiers (*cardigan-style*) or signifieds (*Watteau-style*); we have already come across this ambiguity in the case of sport shoes, an expression in which the signified is lodged in a signifying species. This very closeness between silhouette and style demonstrates that, in a signifying system, there is a kind of infinite circularity between the sign's formal origin and its tendency; the relation between signifier and signified is inert.

58. SWEATER   *Chandail, overblouse, pullover, sweater, jersey.*

59. VEST   *Cardigan, vest, waistcoat, surcoat.*

60. WAISTLINE   The word is ambiguous; it is often understood to mean a line of demarcation, higher or lower, separating the chest from the hips; but the mark is already a variant, and the genus could not act directly on a systematic element: hence we must reserve the word *waistline,* in as neutral a manner as possible, for the circular portion of a garment situated between the hips and the bottom of the chest.

9

Variants of Existence

"The true Chinese tunic, flat and slit."[1]

I. The Inventory of Variants

9.1. *Constitution and presentation of variants*

The genus designates the material substance which can fill either the object or the support of signification equally. There remains one form within the matrix that cannot be filled except by an independent and irreducible substance: the variant. Indeed, the substance of the variant can never be confused with the substance of the genera, for the one is material (*a coat, a clip*), while the other is always non-material (*long/short, slit/unslit*). This disparity of substances necessitates a separate inventory of variants, but we can be certain that the inventory of genera, combined with an inventory of variants, exhausts the substance of all matrices and thereby makes up a complete inventory of the features of Fashion.

Before undertaking the inventory of variants, however, it should be remembered that, like species, these variants do not present themselves as the simple objects of a nomenclature, even when sorted into classes of exclusions, but rather as *oppositions* having several terms, for they possess the specifically paradigmatic power of the matrix. The principle for constituting these oppositions is the following: wherever there is (spatial) syntagmatic incom-

---

[1] \ the true Chinese tunic, flat and slit /
    V1   V2   OS V3   V4

patibility, there is an opening for a system of signifying oppositions, i.e., of a paradigm, i.e., of a variant; for what defines the
variant is that its terms cannot be actualized on the same support *at the same time:* a collar cannot be *open* and *closed* at the
same time; and if *half-open* is the description, this means that
half-open is as valid a term of the differential system as *open* or
closed. In other words, all variant terms which cannot be actualized at the same time constitute a homogeneous class, i.e., a variant (in the generic sense of the word). In order to identify these
classes or variants, we need only arrange the terms resulting from
the commutation test into lists of syntagmatic incompatibilities:
a skirt, for instance, cannot be both *full* and *fitted* at once; these
terms are therefore part of the same class, they both partake of
the same variant (fit); but as this skirt can quite easily be at once
full, supple, and *flowing,* each of these terms belongs to a different variant. There will, of course, be times when it is necessary
to refer to the context in order to decide upon the distribution of
certain variants: if someone speaks of *a buttoned dress,* we understand that the meaning of the dress (e.g., Fashion at that
moment) derives from the fact that it has buttons, as opposed to
the same (unfashionable) dress which has none: the variant is
thus constituted by the existence *or* the absence of buttons; but
we can also understand that the dress derives its meaning from
the fact that it is closed by buttons and not by a zipper: the variant is thus concerned with the manner in which the dress is
fastened, not with the existence of buttons; the paradigm differs
with each case: in one instance there is opposition between
existence and absence, and in another between *buttoned, laced,
knotted,* etc.[2] Each variant consists of a variable number of terms;[3]
a binary opposition is obviously the simplest (*to the right/to the
left*); but on the one hand, according to a schema of Brøndal's,
a simple polar opposition can be enriched by a neutral term
(*neither to the right nor to the left = in the middle*) and by a
complex term (*both to the right and to the left = on both sides*);

---

[2] The matrix also changes:

$$\diagdown \text{a dress with buttons} \diagup \text{(existing)}$$
$$\text{O} \qquad \text{S} \qquad \text{V}$$
$$\diagdown \text{a buttoned dress} \diagup$$
$$\text{V} \qquad \text{SO}$$

[3] Cf. chap. 11.

and on the other hand, certain paradigms consist of a list of terms
which do not readily lend themselves to structuration (*fixed/set/
knotted/buttoned/laced*, etc.). Finally, certain terms of the paradigm can be terminologically defective, which does not, however,
prevent them from having a place: for example, *openwork* and
transparent, which though entering into significant opposition,
are logically nothing more than intermediate moments in a longer
list whose maximum degree (*opaque*) and zero degree (*invisible*) are never stated; it must be kept in mind that meaning is
not born of a simple qualification (*long blouses*), but from an
opposition between what is noted and what is not; even if the
synchrony being studied mentions only one term, the implicit
term upon which its own distinction depends must always be
reestablished (here it will be written between brackets); thus,
though blouses are never short, their length is sometimes noted
(*long* blouses), so it is necessary to reconstitute a significant opposition between *long* and [*normal*], even if this term is not
explicitly stated,[4] for here, as elsewhere, priority must be given
to the internal necessities of the system over those of language.
In the same manner, it will be granted that a single vocable
could sometimes belong to one variant and sometimes to another,
insofar as the play of opposition in the system does not necessarily
overlap the opposites of language: *large* can refer in one case to
a flat dimension (variant of size: a *large* knot) and in another
case to a dimension of volume (variant of volume: *large* skirt);
this depends, in fact, on the nature of the support. Lastly, since
it is always the vestimentary (and not the linguistic) meaning
which determines the signifying oppositions, we must grant that
each term of the variant could eventually consist of differing
terminological expressions: *in relief, puffed, fluted*, for example,
are non-signifying variants of the same signifying term [protrud-
ing]; strictly speaking, it is not a question of synonyms (a purely
linguistic notion), but of vocables indistinguishable by any variation of vestimentary meaning; if, however, they do vary terminologically, it is because of the support to which they are assigned:
granulated and *pasted* clearly do not have the same meaning, but
since, along with [protruding], they share the same relation of

---

[4] Throughout the inventory of variants, the *normal* will be noted by brackets:
[——].

opposition to *hollow*, they are part of the same paradigmatic term; their linguistic value changes according to whether they are applied to the fabric-support or the pocket-supports. The principal paradigm for each variant will therefore be given horizontally (insofar as possible, in the form of a structured opposition), and the non-signifying variants of each term of the paradigm will be given in columns.

narrow /	normal /	wide
slender thin		

Using the test of syntagmatic incompatibility, we arrive at thirty variants.[5] These variants might have been presented in alphabetical order, as were the genera. We have preferred—at least provisionally[6]—to group them in a rational (but not yet directly structural) order, so as to be able to formulate a few remarks common to a certain number of them. We shall therefore find the thirty variants divided into eight groups: *Identity, Configuration, Substance, Measurement, Continuity, Position, Distribution, Connection*. The variants of the first five groups (i.e., variants I to XX) pertain to their supports in an attributive manner as it were, determining a feature of existence (*long dress, light blouse, slit tunic*): these will be variants of existence (chap. 9). In the last three groups (variants XXI to XXX), each variant implies a certain placement of the support in relation to a field or to other supports (*two necklaces, a dress buttoned on the right, a blouse tucked into the skirt*): these will be variants of relation (chap. 10). Although the paradigms of variants that will now be presented have been established in a purely formal way, by recourse to the test of syntagmatic incompatibility, this will not prevent us from making a few brief comments from the point of view of substance, i.e., from justifying each variant beyond its systematic value by using morphological, historical, and psychological factors in such a way as to demonstrate the relations between a semiological system and the "world."

[5] There is a supplementary variant or a variant of variants, for it only modifies another variant (and not a genus): it is a variant of degree (intensity or integrity), which will be dealt with in 10.10.
[6] Cf., below, 12.12.

II. Variants of Identity

9.2. *Variant of assertion of species* (I)

A garment can signify because it is named: this is the *assertion of species;* because it is worn: this is the *assertion of existence;* because it is true (or false): this is *artifice;* and because it is accentuated: this is the *mark.* These four variants have this in common, that they turn the identity of a garment into its meaning. The first of these variants is the *assertion of species:* the principle behind this variant has already been discussed.[7] We saw that its paradigm can only be a formal one, and despite the multiplicity of species, this is a binary paradigm we are speaking of, since it always and only opposes an individual to its class, independently of the substance whose utterance fills this opposition; therefore, we shall simply recall that the formula for the variant of assertion of species is the following:

$$\boxed{a/(A\text{-}a)}$$

9.3. *Variant of assertion of existence* (II)

If the magazine states: *pockets with flaps,* there can be no doubt that it is *primarily* (i.e., *prior to* its quality as a species) the existence of the flap which gives the pockets their fashionable "look," their meaning; in other words, inversely, in the phrase *a dress without a belt,*[8] it is the lack of a belt which makes the dress signify. The paradigm then does not oppose one species to other species, but rather the presence of an element to its absence. Thus, species is determined in two ways: by setting itself, *in abstracto,* in opposition to other species, and by setting its appearance, *in vivo,* in opposition to its absence.[9] The variant of

---

[7] Cf., above, chap. 7.

[8] We can if we like (and have already done as much here) develop the terminological expression of presence by reestablishing the participle: *existing:*

$$\frac{\text{pockets with (existing) flaps)}}{\text{O} \qquad\quad \text{V} \qquad \text{S}}$$

[9] It is inevitable, as we have already hinted, that, from a terminological point of view, there is sometimes interference between the two assertions: in *a jacket with a belt,* the belt can be opposed to a half-belt or to its own absence.

existence is well known to linguistics, where its equivalent is the opposition of full degree to zero degree. We shall structure the opposition in this manner:[10]

with	/	without
with (or having) provided with		free of without . . .

9.4. *Variant of artifice* (III)

The variant of artifice opposes the natural to the artificial, as indicated by the following chart:

natural	/	artificial
genuine true		false fake imitation pseudo

A mythological history of this variant would be a rich one: it seems as if our garment had ignored the very existence of an alternative between the natural and the artificial for centuries; one historian[11] has assigned the birth of *similia* (false sleeves, dickey, etc.), to the beginnings of capitalism, perhaps under the pressure of a new social value, *appearance*. But it is difficult to know whether the promotion of nature as a vestimentary value (since the birth of artifice has inevitably produced a significant opposition, *real/artificial*, which did not hitherto exist) has been the direct result of a change in mentality or of technical progress: *to make real* implies a certain number of discoveries. Whatever the case may be, inasmuch as the real is general, it is assimilated into the *normal*, and it is then the artificial which is especially noted, except in those cases where it is precisely the technical which facilitates direct rivalry between the model and the imitation (real woolens, hand-sewn, etc.[12]). However, the preemi-

---

[10] This type of chart has already been explained (cf., above, 9.1).
[11] J. Quicherat, *Histoire du costume en France,* Paris, Hachette, 1875, p. 330.
[12] Machines exist which give the illusion of hand-sewing (*Entreprise,* no. 26, 15/4, pp. 28–51).

nence of the real tends to be weakening nowadays, thanks to the promotion of a new value: play.[13] Henceforth, play guarantees that to the majority of the notations of artifice we either attribute the power to vary personality and, thus, to manifest its potential richness, or that it constitute a modest alibi for the economic accommodations made by the garment. Thus, artifice tends to advertise itself as such; it usually applies either to function, which can be bogus (a fake knot is one that doesn't tie), or to the status of the piece, that is, to its degree of material independence: a piece of clothing is often declared false if it seems to be independent when in fact it is technically parasitic to a principal piece to which it is surreptitiously sewn; the *false ensemble* thus derives its artificiality from the fact that it consists of a single piece. Perhaps fabric alone is able to resist this promotion of artifice; we sometimes take note of it, which is to say we praise its authenticity.[14]

9.5. *Variant of mark* (IV)

It is proper for certain elements to give an accent and for others to receive it. However, vestimentary syntax does not establish a structural difference between *underlining* and *underlined;* this contrasts with language, which opposes the active and passive forms; what is important for the vestimentary code is the acknowledgment that between two elements (usually between the object and the support) *there is a mark*. This ambiguity can be seen clearly in cases where, since the object and the support arc identified, we would say that it is the substance which marks itself: to say that *the waist is (barely) indicated* is to say that the waist both produces and receives the mark by being more or less itself.[15] The *underlined* is thus in no way opposed to *underlining;* both of them are part of the same term constituted by the indeterminate presence of the phenomenon of marking; the opposing

---

[13] Cf., below, 18.9.

[14] There is almost no further semantic opposition between synthetic (or artificial) fabrics and natural fabrics, except perhaps right at the beginning, when the new synthetic begins to appear and imitates a new material (supersuede and plush). For the rest, "adult" synthetics no longer need to seek out the caution "real."

[15] \ waist barely indicated /

OS (intensive) V

term can be none other than *unmarked* (or the non-marking), which could be called the neutral: it is such an ordinary term that it remains unexpressed (except for color). What follows is the table for the variant of mark.

marked-marking	/	[unmarked–non-marking]
accentuated-accentuating indicated-indicating underlined-underlining		neutral (color)

By accentuating the existence of certain genera without adding anything to them except themselves (*the waist barely indicated*), the mark approaches the assertion of existence; we could say that it takes up where the other leaves off; for instance, if the lack of an element is physically impossible and if, consequently, the variant of existence cannot be brought into play, the mark will then allow the fact of existence to be significant; we cannot take the seam out of a garment (except for stockings), which should make it pointless to note that they exist; but they can exist emphatically, in the form of visible stitches, which is precisely what the variant of existence can account for. And because the mark is a superlative existence, its opposite itself is, we may say, raised a notch; it is no longer lack, it is simple existence deprived of accent—the neutral; we shall see how strong the signifying power of the variant *marked/neutral* can be (under occasionally remote names), when invested in the varieties of the genus *color:* for color cannot know non-existence: nothing fails to be furnished with a color:[16] in Fashion, what is colorless is simply neutral, i.e., *unmarked*, while *colored* is a synonym for lively, i.e., *marked*. Finally, it will be noted that the variant of mark has a strong rhetorical tendency: accentuation is an aesthetic notion which to a great extent belongs to connotation: it is, if you will, precisely because the garment is written that the emphasis placed on it is uniformly possible: it depends on the speech of the commentator; in real, extra-linguistic clothing, we can probably only grasp the encounter of two elements or, in the case of the marked waistline, the presence of another variant such as fit.

---

[16] Cf., below, 11.12.

III. Variants of Configuration

9.6. *Form and speech*

In image-clothing, the configuration[17] (*form, fit, movement*) absorbs nearly the entire being of the garment; in written clothing, its importance diminishes in favor of other values (existence, material, measurements, etc.): to combat the tyranny of visual perception and to tie meaning to other modes of perception or sensation is obviously one of the functions of language. In the order of forms, speech brings into existence values which images can account for only poorly: speech is much more adept than images at making ensembles and movements signify (we are not saying: at making them more perceptible): the word places its force of abstraction and synthesis at the disposal of the semantic system of clothing. Thus, as far as form is concerned, language can quite easily be made to retain only its constituent principles (the *straight* and the *round*), even if the transformation of these principles into real clothing is extremely complex: a *round skirt* consists of many lines other than the curve. The same thing applies to fit: the complex "feel" of a contour can be rendered by a single word (*clinging, bouffant*). And finally, the same holds true for the subtlest formal value, movement (*a cascading blouse*): it is the photograph of the real garment which is complex; its written version is immediately significant. In effect, language allows the source of meaning to be attached quite precisely to a small, finite element (represented by a single word), whose action is diffused through a complex structure.

9.7. *Variant of form* (V)

Terminologically, the variant of form is one of the richest: *straight, rounded, pointed, cubic, squared, spherical, tapered*, etc. All these terms can enter into significant opposition with one another, and we should not expect a simple paradigm for this variant. The confusion here stems from two circumstances which

---

[17] It is understood that we mean an *animated* configuration, close to the notion of *gestalt*.

are related to the elliptical power of language: on the one hand, voluminous pieces are sometimes qualified in terms of plane projection (*a straight vest, a squared coat*); on the other hand, even though the variant of form often deals with only one part of a piece (its edges, for example), it is the entire piece which receives the formal qualification: *flared gloves* are really gloves whose cuffs are flared. Nonetheless, although commutation does not permit the dozen or so terms which constitute the variant of form to be reduced to a simple opposition (since each term can be opposed to all the others), all the evidence seems to indicate that the paradigm does have a certain rational structure; it is composed of a mother-opposition, which suggests a very old Heraclitean couple: the *Straight* and the *Curved;* each one of these two poles is transformed in its turn into subsequent terms, depending on the fact that two accessory criteria are made to intervene: first, a criterion of parallelism—or divergence—of the lines engaged in the principle form: the *straight* thus gives birth to the *squared,* the *tapered* (or *pointed* or *darted*), and the *beveled;* the curve to the *round,* the *flared,* and the *oval;* next a geometric criterion, since form is sometimes considered as a plane and sometimes as having volume; the *straight* thus furnishes the *square* (plane) and the *cubic* (volume); the *curve* furnishes the *ball* and the *bell.*[18] We thus obtain the following paradigm with the understanding that each of its traits can be opposed to any other:

straight	/	curved
squared/tapered/angled square/cube		round/flared/oval spherical/bell-shaped

9.8. *Variant of fit* (VI)

The function of the variant of fit is to make the degree to which a garment adheres to the body significant; it refers to the feeling of a distance; it is very close to another variant, the variant of volume; but whereas in the case of volume, as we shall see, this distance is appreciated, so to speak, at the level of its external surface and in relation to the general space surrounding the gar-

---

[18] Examples of associations: *Box jacket, square collar. —Tapered shoes. —Beveled necktie, spike heels. —Round collar. —Bell skirt. —Flared skirt. —Pegged pants. —Oval neckline. —Cloche hat. —Circumflex (pocket) flap.*

ment (*a bulky overcoat* is one which takes up room), in the case
of fit, on the contrary, the same distance is evaluated in relation
to the body; here the body is the core and the variant expresses a
more or less constraining pressure on it (*a vague overcoat*); we
could say that in the variant of volume the distance of reference
is open (onto the surrounding space), and that in the variant of
fit it is closed (round the body); what counts in the first case is
the measure of a totality; in the second, it is a feeling of plas-
ticity. Moreover, fit can implicitly encounter other variants: mobility in the case of *floating:* a piece can be loosed from the body
to the point of appearing unattached to it (a panel, a scarf);
rigidity[19] in the case of *bouffant.*[20] The body is not the only center
of contraction for the piece; at times it is the element itself which
is its own referent: as in *a tight knot* or *a loose knot.* It is a matter of a general movement of constriction or dilation. The ultimate unity of the variant is, in short, to be found at the level of
sensation: though formal, fit is a coenesthetic variant: it makes
the transition between form and matter; its principle is the significant alternation between tight and loose, between choking and
relaxed: hence, from the point of view of a psychology (or a
psychoanalysis) of the garment, this variant would be one of the
richest.[21] Since this variant rests upon the feeling of a distance,
it is normal that the scale of these variations be intensive, even
if, according to the terminological rule, its expression remains
discontinuous; we therefore have two signifying states (but not
two beings): the *tight* and the *loose,* whose terminological variations can appear to be quite distant, depending on whether it is
a question of the relation of the piece to the body (fitted) or of
the relation of the piece to itself (tight). To each of these terms
a superlative must be added (at least as a reserve measure): the
skin-tight for the fitted and the *bouffant* for the loosened (in this
instance, under the influence of the variant of suppleness). Still,

---

[19] Variant of suppleness (IX).

[20] Clearly, it is impossible to have a real distance between the garment and the
body at every point: the garment must come in contact with the body somewhere;
but think of certain historical costumes that are bouffant nearly everywhere
(notably Elizabethan costumes, cf. N. Truman, *Historic Costuming,* London,
Pitman, 10th ed., 1956, p. 143).

[21] Fit lends itself quite readily to psychoanalytic commentary; Flügel attempted
this by sketching out a character typology based on the degree of the garment's
constriction considered as both protection and prison (*The Psychology of Clothes,*
London, The Hogarth Press, 3rd ed., 1950).

if by the very fact of its species the piece has a certain fit, language will obviously note only the eccentric term; the first term, corresponding to a normal state, will remain implicit: a blouse cannot be fitted without departing from its species; hence it can only be *normal* or *flowing*. Here, then, is the table for the variant of fit:

skin-tight	/	tight	/	loose	/	bouffant
clinging		fitted drawn in form fitting contoured strict[22]		full free flowing large soft casual boxy		

9.9. *Variant of movement* (VII)

It has already been pointed out that the variant of movement is responsible for animating the generality of the garment. The vestimentary line is vectorial, but its direction is most commonly inspired by the stature of the human body, which is vertical; these then become the terms of another variant (*high/low*) invested in the principal opposition of the variant of movement: *rising/falling;*[23] no doubt a *high-necked sweater* is a piece with a high neck; all the same, from the point of view of the ensemble, this term is clearly one of movement: technically, it is the piece that gives the collar its rise; linguistically (i.e., metaphorically), it is the entire piece which, as it were, aspires upward. The same is true for *full gloves:* they simply have long cuffs; but what defines them semantically (i.e., what opposes them to other types of gloves) is that they seem to rise along the arm. In all these cases, there is a carry-over from a real feature of a part of the piece to the overall look of the piece as a whole; this is why this variant is not far removed from a certain rhetorical state: it owes a good deal to the very nature of written clothing. The two poles

---

[22] *Strict* is a mixed term which straddles the terminological and rhetorical levels, like *small* (cf. 4.3 and 17.3).

[23] Cf., below, 10.1. *Hanging down* is quite close to *turned down* (variant of flection), but the two cannot be confused, for *turned down* implies the idea of a hem or a flap folded over.

of the opposition are thus constituted by *ascending* and *decending*, to which terms must be added their metaphorical variations (*upswept, plunging, hanging*), whose use depends on the support. The combination of *ascending* and *descending* in a single motion yields a mixed or complex term, *swaying; swaying* implies the existence of two correlative surfaces and, consequently, a new parasitic orientation: *forward/backward;*[24] this same nuance can sometimes be found in *protruding* and *receding;* but since there is no longer any trace of high or low, we can consider *protruding* and *receding* as a neutral category in relation to the principal poles, since they do not explicitly participate in either the action of *ascending* or *descending*. We can see that the differential armature of this variant is in fact constituted by the orientation, not the movement, which is present in all terms of the opposition; otherwise, the zero term (*motionless*) would be something like *slack*, which is obviously not warranted. One proof that movement is a de facto value is that its absence is not euphemistic, it cannot be noted; it is the various kinds of movement which are thrown into semantic relief: this is why we cannot avoid constituting it as an autonomous variant, independent of the variants of position or even of measurement (*long gloves*), which contribute so strongly to its structuration. Here is the table of paradigms for the variant of movement:

1	2	mixed	neutral
ascending /	descending /	swaying /	protruding
rising upswept	hanging plunging falling down falling		receding

IV. Variants of Substance

9.10. *Coenesthesia*

Here is a group of variants whose function is to make certain states of the material signify: its weight, its suppleness, the relief

---

[24] *Swaying* breaks down into *rising in front + falling in back*. We may remark that the inverse movement (*rising in back + falling in front*) is considered to be thoroughly unaesthetic (hence, never noted): this is the silhouette of Punch.

of its surface, and its transparency. We could say that, except for transparency, these are tactile variants; in any case, it is better not to subject the feeling of the garment to one particular sense; when it is heavy, opaque, stiff, or smooth (at least when these traits are noted), the garment participates in that order of sensations central to the human body, an order that we call *coenesthesia:* variants of substance (and therein lies their unity) are coenesthetic variants; and by this very fact, of all variants these are the ones which come closest to a "poetics" of clothing; furthermore, no variant is in fact literal: neither the weight nor the transparency of a fabric can be reduced to isolated properties: transparency is also lightness, heaviness is also stiffness;[25] in the end, coenesthesia leads back to the opposition between *comfortable* and *uncomfortable;*[26] these are in fact the two great values of clothing whether, as was the case in the past, we signify what is *heavy* in association with authority or whether, as is the case today, we give a general privilege to comfort and thereby to lightness; this privilege explains why today the *heavy,* having unpleasant connotations, is rarely noted; or further, why the *transparent,* being associated with the euphoric, is singled out as a desirable sensation far from its opposite the *opaque,* which is never written, since it is the norm: this play of oppositions is thus somewhat troubled by an implicit system of sensual (as well as historical) taboos. These variants of substance should in principle concern only the fabrics, fibers, woods, stones, and metals of which the garment and its accessories are made; in short, they should logically be applied only to the genus *material;* but that would be a technological viewpoint, not a semantic one; for by synecdoche, written clothing invariably transfers the nature of the substance onto the piece or (less often) onto the composition of pieces: *a light blouse* is one made of a light fabric, *an openwork coat* is one woven with a crochet stitch; but since the terminological rule requires that we stick as close as possible to the letter of what the magazine actually says (unless terminological substitutions are insignificant from the point of view of the vestimentary code), we must assume that the variants of substance apply to most genera, without bothering to reduce the piece to its material. We might be

---

[25] We could group these notions into thematic networks according to the method of analysis used in literary criticism.

[26] An opposition which has already been discerned in the variant of fit.

tempted to contradict our (assumed) capacity to reduce *a linen dress* to *a dress made of a linen fabric* by our (imposed) impossibility of reducing *a heavy coat* to *a coat made of a heavy fabric;* but linen is a species of the genus *material,* and heaviness, if it were a species, would always belong to the genus *weight:* linen exists by a relation of exclusion, heaviness by a relation of contrariety ($\neq$ light). Furthermore, other elements can contribute to the "lightness" of a blouse (its cut, its pleats, etc.), as soon as we recognize that, thanks to language, the weight = estimate of a garment is more a "poetic" than a molecular fact: weight in fact lends itself quite readily to this confusion between the substance and the article of clothing itself; with regard to relief, on the contrary, such confusion is unlikely: it is difficult to separate this variant from the material it modifies; language balks at transferring it to individual garments or accessories; the fabric of a coat can be rough without this characteristic being terminologically transferable to the piece: hence the rarity of this variant; hence it is not reality (there are many nubbly or non-smooth fabrics) which absolutely determines the yield of a variant,[27] it is, once again, the power language possesses to distribute this reality.

9.11. *Variant of weight* (VIII)

Fashion technicians are well aware that nothing defines a fabric better than its physical weight; we shall see later in the same manner that it is precisely the variant of weight which implicitly allows the countless species of materials to be divided into two large signifying groups;[28] semantically (and no longer physically), it is also weight which best defines the material. Here the garment seems to reencounter Parmenides's ancient couple, the light thing, which is on the side of the Memory, the Voice, the Vital, and the dense thing, which is on the side of the Dark, the Forgotten, the Cold; for weightiness is a total sensation;[29] the language which assimilates the *thin* (and sometimes even the *fine*)

---

[27] We shall call a variant's capacity to attach itself to an obviously variable number of genera its yield.

[28] Cf., below, 11.11.

[29] Weightiness can be reinforced or diffused by auxiliary variants: a garment with a broad base is heavier than a tapered garment; wide pleats weigh more, etc.

to the light, and the *thick* (the *bulky*) to the heavy;[30] here perhaps is where we grasp the garment's most poetic reality: as a substitute for the body, the garment, by virtue of its weight, participates in man's fundamental dreams, of the sky and the cave, of life's sublimity and its entombment, of flight and sleep: it is a garment's weight which makes it a wing or a shroud, seduction or authority; ceremonial garments (and above all charismatic garments) are heavy; authority is a theme of immobility, of death; garments celebrating marriage, birth, and life are light and airy. The variant's structure is polar (*heavy/light*). But we know that Fashion only notes (i.e., makes signify) euphoric traits; when joined to a given support, it suffices that a term have negative connotations (for example, *the heaviness of stockings*) for it to be disqualified and disappear from the opposition; the favored term remains (*light*, for example); but if it is notable (i.e., signifying), it is so in relation to an implicit term, which is the *normal:* a normal blouse is neither heavy nor light: heavy, it would be obtrusive; but its lightness can be noted against the neutrality of ordinary blouses. It is true that today lightness is most often euphoric, so that the constant opposition of this variant is [*normal*]/*light*;[31] *heavy*, however, is not pejorative whenever the protective or ceremonial function of a piece is sufficiently acknowledged to justify a thematics of the thick and compact (shawl, overcoat), or whenever (though this is quite rare) Fashion seeks to glorify an obscure style (necklace, bracelet, veil). Here is the table of this variant:

heavy	/	[normal]	/	light
thick bulky				fine thin

9.12. *Variant of suppleness* (IX)

Language has only one partial term (*suppleness*) at its disposal to cover two opposites (*supple/stiff*), but by *suppleness* we must

---

[30] *Bulky* and *thick* are commonly used as terms of measure; however, they refer to weight if the genus cannot be used by the variant of volume.

[31] This displacement from *heavy* to *light* is corroborated by the evolution of real clothing; sales of overcoats are falling in favor of lighter garments (raincoats, gabardines), perhaps due to the urbanization of the population and the development of the automobile (cf. *Consommation*, 1961, no. 2, p. 49).

obviously understand a general quality which allows the garment to hold its shape more or less well. Suppleness implies a certain consistency, neither too strong nor too weak: objects that are rigid by nature (clips, for instance) and elements that are either too limp or entirely parasitic on another piece cannot receive the variant. Like weight, suppleness is essentially a variant of matter, but as was the case with weight, there is a constant carry-over of the variation onto the entire piece. As is also true of weight, the opposition is, in principle, polar (*supple/stiff*); but although *stiffness* has been highly valued in the past (in armature and starching[32]), today it is suppleness which garners all the notations; *stiff* is only acknowledged by certain species of fabric (*stiff taffetas*), and *starched* is almost considered a defect (even in men's clothing); in the majority of cases where *supple* alone is noted, the opposition is found to be shifted a notch up and plays between the *supple* and the *less supple;* it must therefore be completed by an implicit term, which is the same as *normal,* as shown in the table of the variant which has many analogies to that of weight.

supple	/ normal	/ stiff
loose		starched rigid

9.13. *Variant of relief* (X)

The variant of relief has a very limited use, for it concerns only those accidents which can affect the surface of the support:[33] it is truly a variant of matter: terminologically it is difficult to isolate it; language does not readily transfer it to the piece, and only with difficulty does it do so in the case of parts of garments (trim, collars). Its terms can only be understood when placed in relation to an average surface (that of the fabric), from which we note surface variations (indentations or bosses).

---

[32] Flügel (*Psychology of Clothes,* p. 76) has proposed a psychoanalytic interpretation of the *starched,* by making a phallic symbol out of it.

[33] This is not to say that it isn't important psychologically. An investigation by Lazarsfeld has shown that people with small incomes prefer smooth fabrics (as well as chocolates and strong perfumes), and people with larger incomes, "irregular" fabrics (bitter substances and light perfumes as well) (P. F. Lazarsfeld, "The Psychological Aspect of Market Research," *Harvard Business Review,* 13, 1934, pp. 54–57).

1		2		Neutral		Mixed
(protruding)	/	hollow	/	smooth	/	bumpy
rippled [convex] crimped puffed nubbly appliqué in relief bossed raised fluted		[concave]				

This variant makes everything which renders the line of the fabric concave or convex signify (but not the line of the body, whose contours depend on the variant of fit); it is what authorizes us to consider *appliqué pockets,* for instance, as falling under the term *protruding:* these are pockets that are added to the garment and are separate from it. Though rare, this variant presents a complete structure: two polar terms (*protruding/hollow*); a mixed term (*protruding and hollow*), *dented* (*a small dented hat*), which is not pejorative since it is noted as an "amusing" detail.

9.14. *Variant of transparence* (XI)

The variant of transparence should, in principle, account for the degree of the garment's visibility; it consists of two poles: a full degree (the *opaque*) and a zero degree which corresponds to the total invisibility of the garment (this degree is obviously unreal, since nudity is taboo); like the "seamless," a garment's invisibility is a mythical and utopian theme (The Emperor's New Clothes); for from the moment we validate the transparent, the invisible becomes its perfect state. Be that as it may, of the two terms *opaque* and *invisible,* one represents a quality so constant it is never noted, and the other a quality which is impossible; notation can only apply to intermediate degrees of opacity: *openwork* and *transparent* (or *veiling*);[34] between these two terms there is no

---

[34] It is perhaps significant that, in Fashion, *veiling* indicates a transparency, hence an invisibility (albeit an attenuated one), while, psychically, *veiling* belongs above all to the mask (veiling-enveloping in veils). —On *veiling-veiled,* cf. *underlining-underlined,* 9.4.

difference in intensity, only in aspect: *openwork* is a discontinuous visibility (fabric or crochet), transparence is an attenuated invisibility (gauzes, mousselines). Everything that breaks down the garment's opacity, either in extent or in density, falls under the variant of transparence. Here is the table for this variant:

[opaque]	/	openwork	/	transparent	/	[invisible]
		with holes		veiling veiled		

V. Variants of Measurement

9.15. *From the definite to the indefinite*

In Fashion, the terminological expression of measurement is quite varied: *long, short, wide, narrow, full, vast, deep, high, important, to the knees,* ¾, ⅞, etc.: the usage of all these expressions often seems to be confused; in them we no doubt find, in approximative terms, the three fundamental dimensions of space (length, width, volume), but certain terms do not fit into these dimensions easily (*important, big*), and others can obviously be double entries (*narrow* can be a matter of either width or volume). The reasons for this confusion are threefold; first, it is a constant (as we have seen with regard to other variants) that the utterance terminologically refers the dimension of part of a piece to the piece as a whole: *a large hat* is in reality a hat with a large brim; second, in this complex object called a garment, Fashion notes real components less often than dominant impressions: although, in principle, *wide* cannot refer to the measure of volume, Fashion will use the phrase *wide sleeves* quite readily because it prefers to note how the piece appears in a plane; and finally, by entrusting itself to language, Fashion is obliged to make absolute measurements (the "long," the "wide") which are in fact completely relative,[35] and whose functional character could only be systematized by structural analysis;[36] the three-dimensional system can only have a degree of consistency, stability, and therefore clarity if it is established within a homogeneous and con-

---

[35] Littré says: "If one considers the three dimensions of a body, length is always the largest, width is usually in between, and thickness the smallest."

[36] Analysis analogous to that which has been made of the relational system of deictics (H. Frei, "Système des déictiques," *Acta Linguistica* IV, 3, 116).

stant field (an object or a landscape, for example); but without any indication that it is doing so, Fashion often mixes two fields together: that of the human body and that of the piece itself: so that headwear will be described as *high* (since it is a matter of its relation to the body) and a necklace as *long* (because it is a matter of the piece itself). The result of all this is that if traditional notions of measurement (length, width, volume) are clearly present in the Fashion system, they must have their own proper order, which cannot be that of simple geometry. Each variant of measurement seems in fact to deliver a double message: the measure of a physical dimension (length, width, thickness), and also the degree of precision of this dimension. The variant which is naturally the most precise is that of length (*long/ short*): on the one hand, since the human body is a longitudinal form, the length of pieces which cover it can vary quite easily and precisely; and, on the other hand, there is such disproportion between the body's length (or height) and its other dimensions, that the garment's length does not lend itself to much ambiguity; *length* thus separates itself from other variants of measurement by its precision and independence.[37] Variants of *width* and *volume* are much more imprecise; no doubt, when *width* (*wide/ narrow*) concerns pieces which are flat by nature (*a front*), its application is precise; but such cases are not very numerous; and when the piece is flat in projection (*a wide skirt*), its width tends to be confused with its volume; *volume* itself (*voluminous/thin*) is a precise notion when it concerns pieces that are distinctly spheroid (the crown of a hat); but very often, in fact, what Fashion requires is not so much the exact measurement of the width or thickness of a particular element as it is the notation of a certain totality, a certain "importance" of the piece, its fullness, both transversal and latitudinal, in relation to its length; of course it is necessary to distinguish a variant of width from a variant of volume, for there exist flat elements and spheroid elements; but in addition these two variants form something like the imprecise pole of an opposition whose precise pole would be length; an opposition itself headed by a generic term of measure, *size* (*large/ small*), which functions as the indefinite aspect of the first three

[37] Human verticality dominates our perception and what could be called our visual sensibility (G. Friedmann: "La civilisation technicienne et son nouveau milieu," in *Mélanges Alexandre Koyré*, Hermann, 1942, pp. 176–95).

variants, either by substituting for one of them, or by summarizing all three at once. The four variants of measurement are thus organized according to a hierarchy of functions:

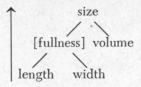

At each level, measurement becomes more imprecise, notation more arbitrary; *length* is certainly the most objective measurement; it alone receives a notation in inches (*a skirt five inches above the ground*); *width* and *volume*, on the other hand, readily exchange terms (*with wide sleeves*); and in the end, all three are to be found within a final generality, that of size. These four variants have the same structure. The opposition consists of two polar terms and a neutral [*normal*] term; but here the neutral term is less important than it is in variants of substance, for measurement runs into fewer taboos: *wide* is disqualified less frequently than *heavy*. Yet the neutral term is still necessary: *a long cardigan* is not opposed to *a short cardigan*. Although language cannot present an opposition in other than discontinuous terms, it is understood that the difference between terms is in fact progressive: ⅓, ½, ⅔, ¾, etc.: each one of the two poles (*long/short, wide/narrow, thick/thin, large/small*) represents less an absolute state than the imprecise term of a movement; what Fashion sets in opposition is a pole of reduction (which we clearly sense in a term like *shortened*[38]) and a pole of expansion; this intensive opposition of *more* and *less*, of major and minor, is the exact opposite of the absolute alternative we encountered in variants of identity (*yes or no*). But this progressive structure, when uttered by the magazine, quite easily becomes a fixed structure: everything happens, or at least is stated, as if it were an essence of the *long* and an essence of the *short:* the most mobile of definitions, measurement tends to be absorbed into the most passive of notations, i.e., assertion: which can clearly be seen when proportion (¾), the most relative of measurements, finally establishes an absolute species (*a three-quarter length*).

---

[38] *Shortened* implies a double relativity: in relation to a physical norm and in relation to the past.

9.16. *Variant of length* (XII)

Length is the most precise variant of measurement; it is also the most common; this is no doubt due to the fact that, taken vertically, the human body is not symmetrical (the legs differ from the head);[39] length is thus not an inert measurement, for it seems to participate in the body's longitudinal diversity; since the garment must come to rest on certain parts of the body (ankles, hips, shoulders, head) in order to hold its shape, its lines are vectorized, they are forces (there is no doubt that latitudinal costumes, those of the Spanish Renaissance for example, are much more inert, more "dead" than modern clothing); of these forces, some seem to move downward from the hips or shoulders: the garment *falls*, pieces are *long;* others on the contrary seem to rise from the ankles or head: such pieces are *high;* it is of course a matter of the same longitudinal measurement, but the difference in terminology clearly attests to the existence of true vestimentary forces; and depending on the manner in which these forces are distributed, the garment can undergo a fundamental change of type; thus, in our own feminine costume, there are two ascending vectors (*high* pieces being supported by the head and feet: high headwear, high socks) and two descending vectors (*long* pieces being supported by the shoulders and hips: coat, skirt); these four vectors are tied together like the inner and outer rhymes of a quatrain; but we can still imagine other "rhymes" and other "stanzas": couplet rhymes in the case of Oriental women's clothing (veil and dress *falling* in the same direction), alternate rhymes in traditional Oriental clothing for men (high headwear and falling robes):

	Modern women's clothing	Oriental women's clothing	Oriental men's clothing	13th-cent. English women's clothing, etc.
Head	a ↗	a ↘	a ↗	a ↘
Shoulders	b ↘	a ↘	b ↘	a ↘
Hips	b ↘			a ↘
Ankles	a ↗			

---

[39] "Symmetry . . . based upon the human figure, whereupon it appears that we seek such symmetry in width alone, not in height or length" (Pascal, *Pensées*, I.28).

Each system obeys a particular rhythm of taking flight and being weighed down; our system obviously tends toward neutrality, and it does not seem likely to change, for, in order for a notable revolution in type to take place, either headwear would have to start falling (veils) or ankles would have to be covered once again. All this clearly attests to the fact that longitudinal measurement, what we call length or height, depending on the point of support and the area of development, is of major structural importance; what is more, it is through variations in length that Fashion attempts to renew itself most spectacularly, and it is an "animated" length (a "slender" style) which defines the canonic body of the Fashion model. The variant of length includes four modes of expression. The first (and most frequent) consists of making the dimension absolute in the form of a pure adjective (*long/short*); we could call this absolute length (which is actually relative, since it implies a referent, which is the garment's point of support). In the second mode of expression, proportional length (¾, ⅞), the relativity is explicit, it passes into the language; in principle, we are dealing with a variant of connection, since the measurement unites two elements (a skirt and a jacket, for instance), noting by how much the one proportionately exceeds the other; but here again, the proportion is quickly made absolute; verbally, it defines only the piece whose variation is significant; from the point of view of the matrix V.S.O., the variant remains simple, the language retains no trace of its connotative character: *a ⅞ length coat* constitutes a complete matrix in which the relativity of the length is absorbed in the absolute of the term and even tends toward the species (a three-quarter length[40]). In the last two modes of expression, rarer than the first two, length is noted in relation to a specific referent; this referent can be a limit; the terminological element is thus *as far as the . . .* or its synonyms, *just over the . . . , (resting) on, up to the . . . ;* the referent itself is anatomical (knee, forehead, nape, ankles, hips, etc.), which is why it cannot be considered as a support: formally, it is included within the variant, of which it simply constitutes a terminological element. This referent can also be a base (*[starting] from the . . .*): as a constant, it is therefore the ground, and

---

[40] In the proportional variant there is a trace of a zero degree of proportion: this would be the coincidence of the two pieces.

the length is noted in inches (*a skirt eighteen inches from the ground*); this notation in inches proceeds from a dream of scientific precision; semantically, it is all the more illusory because the norm can vary from one couturier to another in the same season,[41] which means leaving the institution in order to enter into an order intermediary between the facts of clothing and the facts of dress, and which could be called the "style" of Couture, since each measurement refers to each couturier as to a signified; but from a systematic point of view, the function of variations in inches is quite simply to oppose *longer* to *shorter* from one year to the next. This complex variant of expression can be summarized in the following manner:

	long / [normal] / short		
Absolute length	high deep		low small
Proportional length	⅓, ½, ⅔, ¾, ⅞, etc.		
Limit (as far as the . . .)	hips/waist/chest/knee/calf/ankle/shoulders/nape		
Base ([starting] from . . .)	3 in./4 in./5 in., etc., from the ground		

9.17. *Variant of width* (XIII)

A garment's width is a much more inert dimension than its length; it is not experienced as a force: since the human body is symmetrical in width (two arms, two legs, etc.), the latitudinal development of the garment is balanced by status: a garment cannot bulge out on one side only; the genus which best lends itself to latitudinal imbalance is headwear. This is perhaps because, since symmetry is a factor of immobility, it is necessary to vivify the spiritual part of the body with its opposite, which is the face (*a hat tilted or raked to one side*, etc.). Moreover, width can only vary within very narrow limits: clothing cannot exceed the width of the body by much, at least not current types of clothing (there have been costumes in history with powerful lateral expansion, like those of the Spanish baroque). This variant is thus ill-suited to major pieces, which receive their aesthetic sense and their limits from the human body, and which, as we

---

[41] For example, in the summer of 1959, length from the hem to the floor: Cardin, 58 cm.; Patou, 40 cm.; Grès, 41 cm.; Dior, 53 cm.

have seen, can only be called *narrow* or *wide* by the projection
of a volume, and on condition that the piece have enough "body"
for it to stand out (*cape, overcoat*). The variant is thus stablest
in pieces that are flat and long. Finally, *wide* exists at the frontiers of aesthetic taboos, at least in modern costume, which usually takes thinness and *finesse* for elegance; therefore, we can only
note it by making it signify the values of ease or good protection.
So the table of the variant is a terminologically reduced one:

wide	/	[normal]	/	narrow
				fine thin

9.18. *Variant of volume* (XIV)

In principle, volume represents the transversal dimension of an
element if it has a thickness of its own (*buttons*), or of an entire
piece insofar as it envelops the body (*overcoat*). But we have
seen that in fact this variant readily served to account for a total
dimension, thereby one much more imprecise than length and
width. Its major term is particularly notable, at least for principal
pieces of clothing, particularly when such pieces have a confirmed protective function (*full, broad*); as for the reduced term,
it encounters the body directly and tends toward fit; in sum, in
the case of principal pieces, the garment can only make the body
bigger by making it vague; if it seeks to reduce the body, it can
only follow and mark it (and this is *fit*). Furthermore, according
to certain analyses, these two variants correspond to two vestimentary ethics: the importance of volume assumes the existence
of an ethic of personality and authority,[42] while the importance
of fit, on the other hand, assumes an ethic of eroticism. The table
of the variant of volume can be set up in the following way:

voluminous	/	[normal]	/	thin
full bulky important wide broad				(narrow) (small)

---

[42] Flügel, *Psychology of Clothes.*

9.19. *Variant of size* (XV)

As we have seen, the variant of *size* serves to express the indefinite quality of dimension; *big* and *little* are the key terms; they can be applied to any one dimension (*a big necklace* is in fact *a long necklace*) and to all dimensions at once (*a big handbag*) whenever the magazine wishes to adopt, so to speak, the most subjective point of reading, where it can account for an impression without having to analyze it. The fact that Fashion may make use of an indefinite (perhaps it would be better to say "indifferent") measurement when faced with the three classical measurements (some of which already tend toward totality), should not surprise us: in the same manner, many languages use an indifferent deixis to complete their system of specialized deixes: German opposes *der* to *dieser/jener*, and French *ce* to *ce . . . ci/ce . . . la*.[43] There is no doubt that, structurally, size holds a neutral position; semantically, it nearly always has a rhetorical value: *giant, immense, monumental, audacious*, these variations of the term *big* are intentionally emphatic (which is not the case with the other variants), and the reduced term (*little*) almost always has an ethical connotation (simple, sympathetic).[44]

Here, then, is the table for this variant:

big	/	[normal]	/	little
audacious giant immense monumental				

VI. VARIANTS OF CONTINUITY

9.20. *Breaks in continuity*

The plastic meaning of a garment depends a great deal on the continuity (or discontinuity) of its elements, even more than on its form. On the one hand, we could say that in its profane way

---

[43] Cf. H. Frei, "Système des déictiques."
[44] Cf., above, 4.3 and, below, 17.3.

the garment reflects the old mystical dream of the "seamless": since the garment envelops the body, is not the miracle precisely that the body can enter it without leaving behind any trace of this passage? And on the other hand, to the extent that the garment is erotic, it must be allowed to persist here and disintegrate there, to be partially absent, to play with the body's nudity. Continuity and discontinuity are thus preempted by an ensemble of institutional features: the garment's discontinuity is not content merely to exist: it either plays itself up or plays itself down. Whence the existence of a group of variants destined to make the garment's breaks or seams signify: these are the variants of continuity. The variants of division and closure have been reduced to the two contradictory and complementary functions of dividing (or not) and joining (or not).[45] The variant of mobility accounts for an element's independence, for the principle that makes it either adhere or not adhere to another element (this second element remaining unexpressed). Furthermore, whatever has been divided or mobilized can be attached in a number of different ways: it is the role of the variant of attachment to make these different modes of attachment signify. Finally, an element can be materially continuous and yet receive inflections which disrupt its line: a piece can be either folded back or flattened out, for example: this alternative is taken up by the variant of flection. The order just given to these variants is intentional; for if we put aside the final variant (flection), a rather poor variant at that, we can see that, structurally, they control one another: whether to lace or to button a piece (variant of attachment) is an alternative that can only have meaning if the piece is mobile or closed (variant of mobility or closure); and the alternative implied by this final variant (*open/closed*) is itself only possible if the element is divided from the outset. The first four variants of continuity thus form among themselves a sort of program, in the cybernetic sense of the term: each variant receives the legacy, so to speak, of the preceding variant, and assumes its validity only from the alternative which precedes it. The "dispatching" which governs the course of meaning is subtle: a piece *obliged* to be closed

---

[45] Language—however unfairly—requires us to call *continuity* the alternative between the continuous and the discontinuous; *division* the alternative between the divided and the undivided; *closure* the alternative between closing and opening, etc.

(consequently escaping the variant of closure) can still support an alternative of attachment (a divided piece which is always closed can be so either by buttons or by zipper); an element which is *always* divided can be open or closed (a coat, for instance). This means that, despite the network they form, these variants retain their individuality: what has no meaning in one place (being deprived of freedom) nonetheless makes sense further on. We can get an idea of the vitality of these variants if we examine the "dispatching" table which governs their various possibilities of appearance, remembering that in order for a variant to come into play and for meaning to be born, the opposition which comprises it must enjoy a kind of *guarded freedom:* the nature of certain genera thus excludes or, on the contrary, permits the application of certain variants to them, as indicated here by *Excluded* and *Possible*.[46]

Division	Mobility	Closure	Attachment
E ⎰ Divided by nature (*vest*)		P[47]	P
Undivided by nature (*stockings*)		E	E
Bipolar[48] (*suspenders*)		P	P
P ⎱		Closed by nature (*blouse*)	E
		Open by nature (*side of a jumper*)	E
	P (*shoulders*)		E
	P (*detachable hood*)		P

---

[46] Cf., below, 12.2.

[47] P: Possible. E: Excluded.

[48] A piece with two symmetrical ends or flaps (*scarf, belt*) is assimilated to a piece divided by nature because it can be closed, open, buttoned (bandeau), tied, etc. (cf. following paragraph).

9.21. *Variant of division* (XVI)

The massiveness of the garment can be altered in two principal ways: the surface of an element can be divided, separated partially or completely into two edges (a dress, the upper of a shoe); but also the element, without being split at all, can be divided into two sufficiently autonomous regions: this is the case with pieces made of two flaps or ends arranged according to a certain symmetry; functionally, the two ends of a shawl, a bandeau, or a belt replicate the two edges of an opening: they can be "closed" (crossed or tied) or "open" (left loose, hanging); this is why the facts of bipolarity must be included in the variant of division; not that there is any likelihood that pieces split by nature should have a meaning (as is the case with bipolar pieces), but because this separation involves signifying variations of closure and attachment (*a wrapped scarf, a knotted bandeau*[49]). The structure of this variant is an alternative of existence: the element is split or it is not; it cannot undergo any variation of intensity or of complexity: the mixed term (split and unsplit) is no more possible than the neutral term (neither split nor unsplit);[50] the normal term can cover only one of the two poles, generally the negative: what is split emerges as notable against a usual background of indivision. Here is the table:

split	/	[unsplit]
notched scalloped interrupted separated		

9.22. *Variant of mobility* (XVII)

An element's mobility can signify only if it can exist or not exist; pieces are usually mobile by status: a piece is what is indepen-

---

[49] Whereby we see that if the structural order can encounter the technological order, it is not enslaved by it: the division is here defined much more by its structural function (it is what controls the other variants of continuity) than by its substance.

[50] *Partially split* derives from the variant of integrity.

dent:[51] so it cannot receive this variant; for meaning to emerge, the element must sometimes be fastenable to a principal body, sometimes freed from it; in other words, the elements must be neither too independent nor too parasitical by nature: this is usually the case with attached parts, notably the martingale, linings, and collars; this can also be the case (though less frequently) with pieces that are ordinarily mobile but can be sewn onto or incorporated into a principal element (*bertha, cape, belt*): this brings us very near to the "fake" and, consequently, to the variant of artifice. Naturally, freedom of mobility is a material freedom, not a freedom of usage or bearing (assertion of existence). The table of the variant of mobility is a simple one, for the opposition is an alternative:

fixed	/	movable
immovable attached		interchangeable detachable

9.23. *Variant of closure* (XVIII)

The divided piece can be open or closed: this is the variant of closure. We are not at all concerned here with the manner in which a piece is closed (the manner of fastening belongs to the variant of attachment) but rather with the degrees through which this closure is accomplished: a double-breasted jacket "closes better" than a single-breasted one. Hence, we are dealing with an intensive variant whose levels are established by language on different qualities. It follows that we are speaking here only of the institutionalized degrees of closure: for the *open* to signify, it must be a (noted) norm for the magazine, and not a personal habit of the wearer. Closure is in fact a very rich aspect of dress; but, as such, it becomes an index of temperament, not a sign. In order to dissociate closure from attachment properly and to grasp the progressive nature of the variant of closure, we must go back to its generative variant, division; real or implicit, divi-

---

[51] Here we have a new example of a definition which is structural and no longer substantial, syntagmatic and no longer systematic: the piece would be what, with certain reservations, rejects the variant of mobility (because it is always mobile).

sion brings two elements into being, edges or sides, which are usually longilinear; it is the degree to which these two bands are brought together that will furnish the terms of the variant: if the two bands are not joined at all, the element is open (in the case of slits) or loose (in the case of flaps); if they come together without overlapping, this is edge-to-edge (for which straps or laces are the mode of attachment); *closed,* despite the generality of the term, always implies, in clothing, that one edge of a piece somewhat overlaps the other: *closed* is more closed than edge-to-edge; if the first band overlaps the second to a large degree, the garment becomes crossed; finally, if the full length of one of the flaps or ends is thrown over the other, the piece (coat or scarf) is *wrapped.* As it proceeds through these five principal modes, closure becomes increasingly stronger, because we are always concerned with a supple material which simple contiguity cannot join, since, in the case of clothing, the contiguous constantly risks coming apart as the body moves. To which we must add two terms which are more specialized: *straight* corresponds to *closed* but takes its meaning only within a partial opposition, limited to shoulder pieces, that of *straight/ crossed;* finally, applied to shoulder straps, [*simply closed*] becomes *around the neck,* as opposed to crossed straps, which are, so to speak, better "closed" than when simply tied behind the nape of the neck. These different degrees of closure form (in actuality) an opposition of five terms:

open	/	edge-to-edge	/	closed	/	crossed	/	wrapped
loose				straight around the neck				

9.24. *Variant of attachment* (XIX)

Since attachment is prepared for by the variants of division and mobility, and its intensity established by the variant of closure, the manner of attachment remains to be noted: this is the task of the variant of attachment. Attachment can be postulated and still left imprecise; it is what is *set, situated,* or *placed,* a neutral term opposed to an entire series of full and defined attachments:

full term	neutral term
. . . clasped/buttoned/drawstring = fastened/ zippered/hooked/tied/snapped . . .	/set
	placed situated

The number of full terms which enter into a signifying opposition is of necessity open, since we can always invent or revive a method of attachment which has not yet been noted. This variant is therefore one of the least structured (it cannot be reduced to an alternative, even a complex one), and we can readily see why: this variant actually touches on the variation of species: the *knotted* is very close to the *knot*. Language itself participates in this ambiguity, since it uses only one word to designate both the act of attaching and the object which serves as the agent of this action (the word *attachment*); nonetheless, we are clearly dealing with a true variant, precisely to the extent that we cannot confuse an action with an object: as we have seen, the assertion of species sets in opposition fragments of substance (*knot, button, laces*); the variant of attachment sets in opposition non-material modes, states of being disengaged from their supports: the difference between the two is the same as that between a *zipper* and *zippered;* moreover, as a genre-support, the attachment may very well have no fastening function: a knot or buttons can be "fake": *a dress with buttons* is not necessarily *a buttoned dress.* It remains nonetheless true that from the viewpoint of the general effort of structuration to which Fashion testifies for the entire society that elaborates it, it is obviously through the species, or more precisely, through the *open* collection of species (or *nomenclature*)[52] that structure comes undone; there is a conflict between the variant and the species: a relatively unstructured variant, like the variant of attachment, is in a sense invaded by the species.

9.25. *Variant of flection* (XX)

An element's form can subsist at the molecular level and still change its orientation; it is this change which the variant of

---

[52] *At the level of the relations between language and reality,* nomenclature represents a major structuration; but at the level of a far more specialized field, that of written clothing, the nomenclature of species is a factor of minor structuration.

flection must account for: it must make all the accidents which counter the original or "natural" meaning of an element signify by turning or bending it. It is understood that the terminological summary of this variant depends not on an absolute orientation, but rather on the quite relative movement which the pieces assume according to their origin or their function; apparent contradictions ensue between terms of pure flection (*folded*) and terms of oriented flection (*turned up, turned down*); the *turned-up* brim of a hat is folded, but a turned-up collar is not; this same brim when turned down is not folded; while a turned-back collar is. Naturally, this terminological maneuver does not alter the variant's real organization at all, since there is no systematic relation between the genera. We shall therefore organize the variant in the following manner: two polar terms, one corresponding to flection downward (*turned down*), and the other to flection upward (*turned up*); a mixed term standing for both superior and inferior flection, *folded;* and a neutral term (neither turned up nor turned down, i.e., *straight*), which is actually defective but historically attested to, as in the case of the ruff:

mixed		1		2		neutral
folded	/	turned up	/	turned down	/	straight
		raised rolled up		lowered		

10

Variants of Relation

"A sailor top open over a knit dickey."[1]

I. VARIANTS OF POSITION

10.1. *Variants of position—horizontal* (XXI), *vertical* (XXII), *transversal* (XXIII)—*and orientation* (XXIV)

The variants of position are responsible for the placement of a vestimentary element in a given field; for example, a flower can be placed on the right or the left of a bodice, a pleat at the top or the bottom of a skirt, and a bow on the front or the back of a dress; a row of buttons can be either vertical or oblique. In all these examples, it is clear that, taken as a group of variants, position implies the relation between a particular element and a space; this space must be that of the body itself as it is traditionally oriented,[2] for the piece referred to (bodice, skirt, dress) does nothing but reproduce the space of the body; we thus have a horizontal field if it is possible for the object to be moved to the right or left, a vertical field if it can be moved up or down, and a transversal plane if it can be moved forward or backward; these three planes, each provided with its own internal variations, correspond to the first three variants of position. As for the last

---

[1] \ a sailor top open over a knit dickey /
\ VS   O /
S(1)O V   S(2)

[2] This is obviously the same space which generates the first three variants of measurement (9.V).

variant, which we shall call the variant of orientation, its organization is somewhat different: on the one hand, unlike the other variants of position, it places the space of the piece and the body in relation to a row of elements (*buttoning*) or an element which is itself linear (*neckline*), rather than in relation to a punctuating element (*clip, flower, bow*); and on the other hand, since there exists no expressly transversal line in Fashion clothing, the variant of orientation calls only the frontal area of the body into play; its variation deals only with the opposition between the vertical and the horizontal (*buttons running vertically* or *horizontally*). These variants have the same structure, one that is both simple and thoroughly saturated (except for the variant of orientation, which has one defective term); each of them has two polar terms: *to the right/to the left, on the top/on the bottom, in front/in back, horizontal/vertical;* a neutral term: what is neither to the right nor to the left is median (*in the middle*): what is neither on the top nor on the bottom is median as well (*at the middle*); what is neither in front nor on the back of the body is on the side (*on the sides, on the side*); what is neither vertical nor horizontal is *oblique;* and finally, a complex term: what is simultaneously to the right and to the left is on both sides (*lateral*);[3] what is simultaneously at the top and at the bottom is *the whole length* of the piece; what is simultaneously in front and in back is *all around;* only the variant of orientation does not have a complex term. In language, these are all terms of pure denotation, without any notable terminological variation (except *perched* and *tilted,* for headwear, and *wreathed,* for flowers); it is important that they always retain their adverbial value: *at the side,* and *on the sides, in front* (and even *on the back*) are non-material localizations, not to be confused with their corresponding genres, which are fragments of vestimentary matter (*side, front, back*). We can group the four variants of position into the table on the following page.

The first three variants of position are quite mobile, they easily occupy what we could call the point of meaning; they modify other variants readily (most notably those of division, closure,

---

[3] We must not confuse *on both sides* (right and left) and *on the sides* (at the side).

	1	2	neutral	complex
XXI. *Horizontal position*	on the right	/ on the left left	/ (me-dian) in the middle	/ in width on both sides
XXII. *Vertical position*	at the top high (adv.) perched	/ at the bot-tom low (adv.) deep-set	/ median at the middle centered	/ in length the whole length in height
XXIII. *Transversal position*	forward in front at the front	/ back-ward in back at the back	/ at the side on the sides on the side	/ circular all around wreathed
XXIV. *Orientation*	horizon-tal	/ vertical	/ oblique	/ —

and attachment: *buttoned along the entire length, crossed behind, closed on the left,* etc.).

10.2. *Right and left, high and low*

We know that, when applied to clothing, the alternative of right and left corresponds to a considerable difference in signifieds—sexual, ethnic,[4] ritual,[5] or political.[6] Why does this opposition produce such strong meanings? Probably because, since the body is perfectly symmetrical in its horizontal plane,[7] the placement of an element on the right or left is necessarily an arbitrary act, and we know how much a lack of motivation strengthens a sign; perhaps the old religious distinction between right and left (*the*

---

[4] The ethnic distribution of ways of crossing garments can be found in Leroi-Gourham, *Milieu et techniques,* p. 228.

[5] On the right/left opposition in ethnology, see Claude Lévi-Strauss, *The Savage Mind.*

[6] In 1411, the Burgundians carried the standard on the right and the Armagnacs on the left.

[7] Cf. the quotation from Pascal, above, 9.15.

sinister) was only a way of exorcising the natural emptiness of these two signs, the (dizzying) freedom of meaning they liberate. For example, *right* and *left* cannot be used metaphorically; this can clearly be seen in politics, where a single circumstance (the disposition of places in a legislative arena) produces a simply denotative opposition (*right/left*), whereas, when it is a matter of *high* and *low,* the opposition can quite easily become metaphorical (*mountain/marsh*). The variant of vertical position (*high/low*) is in fact of less importance because on this plane the body's own divisions are no doubt sufficient to distinguish the different zones of orientation by nature and not by decision; there is very little symmetry between the upper and the lower parts of the body;[8] thus, to mark off a region of an element is not to create any new dissymmetry (which in the case of *right/ left* was all the more valuable since it was artificial); because of the very form of the human body itself, *high* and *low* are difficult regions to interchange, and, as we know, there is little meaning where there is almost no freedom;[9] *high* and *low* are thus positions which we always tend to make dynamic, i.e., to transform into *rising* or *falling,* terms which belong to the variant of movement.

II. Variants of Distribution

10.3. *Variant of addition* (XXV)

Apprehended within a semantic process, numbers themselves, in defiance of the progressive, regular, and infinite nature of the numerical scale, become functional entities whose opposition signifies;[10] thus, a number's semantic value depends not on its

---

[8] *Head/feet, trunk/hips, arms/legs* are useful oppositions, but they are situational (in relation to the middle of the body), not formal.

[9] At least the body is so perceived in our civilization; but elsewhere Claude Lévi-Strauss has noted the strength of the high/low opposition, which allows Hawaiian natives to tie the loincloth around the neck, and not around the waist, to mark the death of a chief (*The Savage Mind*); what we call *nature* here is obviously *our* nature.

[10] A semantics of numbers is yet to be established, for its connotation is one of incredible richness: all that is necessary to be convinced of this fact is to open a magazine and notice the considerable attention given to notations of numbers (cf. Jacques Durand, "L'attraction des nombres ronds" in *Revue Française de Sociologie,* July–Sept. 1961, pp. 131–51).

arithmetical value but on the paradigm of which it is a part: 1 is
not the same entity when it is opposed to 2 as when it is opposed
to *several*;[11] in the first case, the opposition is definite (variant
of addition); in the second case, it is repetitive and indefinite
(variant of multiplication). Therefore, the terms of the variant
of addition can only be the first few numbers; it is generally the
case that number is not specified beyond 4, at which point we
pass on to the variant of multiplication. Actually, the generating
opposition is obviously that between 1 and 2, between the unit
and the dual; other terms appear as combinations and neutralizations; 4, applied primarily to pockets and buttons, is understood
as 2 times 2, because of the symmetry to which this number spontaneously leads (in short, it is the intensive of 2); as for 3, it is
possible that semantically, rather than representing a complex
term (2 + 1), it represents the neutral degree of the opposition
1/2 (i.e., neither 1 nor 2), due to the archetypal force of the pair
(or symmetry); 3 is a sort of eccentric pole of the dual, its denial;
it is a failed dual; moreover, in the same way, 1 is a sort of privative of 2, as it is made to be understood in the expression *only one*.
What is more, we know that historically the dual has provided
clothing with numerous symbols: the Fools of the Middle Ages
and the clowns of the Elizabethan theater wore two-part and
two-toned costumes, whose duality symbolized division of the
mind. The table of this variant can be set up in the following
manner:

polar terms		neutral	intensive
1 / 2	/	3 /	4
	two-toned cameo	[tricolor][12]	

10.4. *Variant of multiplication* (XXVI)

The variant of multiplication is that of indefinite repetition: if
Fashion spoke Latin, the terminological expression of its opposi-

[11] This is why it would be necessary to write 1 in the first instance and *a* in
the second.
[12] *Tricolor* is not a good Fashion term because of the strong patriotic connotation attached to the word.

tion would be precisely the multiplicative paradigm: *semel/ multiplex:*

one	/	many
once		variegated a lot of some (implied)[13] multicolored several several times

The variant of multiplication is used sparingly, for it readily encounters a taboo of an aesthetic order: taste. We can say that the structural definition of bad taste is linked to this variant: vestimentary depreciation most often occurs through a profusion of elements, accessories, and jewels (*a woman covered with jewels*). Since it is euphemistic, Fashion can only note multiplication if it contributes to certain "effects": for example, to create an impression of "airiness" (*petticoats, laces*), a term which generally serves as a relay between the vestimentary signifier and the signified of femininity, or one of "richness" (*necklaces, bracelets*), provided this richness is not too heteroclite, involving a large variety of different species, and respects a unity of substance which is precisely what the variant of multiplication makes signify.

10.5. *Variant of balance* (XXVII)

In order for a variant of balance to exist, the genus it affects must have an axis of some sort in relation to which symmetry or dissymmetry can declare itself: this axis can be the median line of the body, either vertical or horizontal; the entire piece can be described as asymmetrical (it is dissymmetry which is usually noted) when, for example seams pass through the vertical axis of the body in an irregular manner (*asymmetrical blouse, dresses, coats*); or when two or more elements are placed in asymmetrical relation to this axis (*buttons, ornaments,* for instance); and also,

---

[13] *Some* (implied; French "*des*") is obviously not significant unless it is vestimentarily opposed to *one*.

when elements which are found in pairs due to the structure of the body (*sleeves, shoes*) are dissociated and rendered asymmetrical by a difference in material or color: this last case does not exist in actual clothing, but it must be held in reserve, since it accounts for a vestimentary fact such as bipartism. In a more limited way, the axis that serves as referent can also be found within the element itself: dissymmetry thus becomes a partial disorder affecting the form of this element, making it "unequal," or "irregular" (the design on a fabric, for example). As for the opposition itself, it is based upon the opposition *symmetrical/asymmetrical; in contrast with* can be considered a sort of intensive term of symmetry: contrast is a symmetry at once strengthened and complicated, since it presupposes two lines of reference, not just one (we have already come across oppositions partially built on a relation of intensity, such as *closed/crossed/wrapped*). The table of the variant of balance is thus the following:

1		2		intensive of 1
symmetrical	/	asymmetrical	/	in contrast
equal geometric regular		unequal irregular		contrasted

Up to now, Fashion has upset the body's constitutive symmetry only with extreme caution; perhaps because, as has been suggested, women are linked to symmetry more than men; perhaps also because the insertion of an irregular element into a symmetrical ensemble is a symbol of a critical spirit and Fashion resists all attempts at subversion.[14] Whatever the reason, when Fashion alters the symmetry of a garment, it most likely does so in a marginal way, as a light touch, through the irregular placement of certain discrete bits of adornment (*clasps, jewelry,* etc.); it must never give the appearance of disorder, but instead it should give the garment a certain movement: a slight imbalance simply provides the suggestion of a tendency (*overhanging, tilted*); we know that movement is a metaphor for life; what is

---

[14] Buytendik, quoted by F. Kiener, *Kleidung, Mode und Mensch,* Munich, 1956, p. 80. Military costume is the most symmetrical of all.

symmetrical is immobile, sterile;[15] it is normal, therefore, that, in conservative epochs, costume has been rigorously symmetrical and that to emancipate clothing is, to a certain degree, to unbalance it.

III. VARIANTS OF CONNECTION

10.6. *Connection*

All variants listed up to this point, even the relative ones, have been likely to be applied to only one support at a time (*a long skirt, an open collar,* etc.); to use the language of logic, each of these variants constituted a singular operator. Fashion, however, also has binary operators, responsible for making meaning emerge from the coordination of two (or more) vestimentary elements: *a blouse floating over the skirt; a toque matching the coat; a twin set brightened up with a silk scarf:* it is the way in which these pieces are associated, and it alone, which constitutes here that point of meaning which must animate the signifying unit. In these examples, we can in fact find no other terminal variant than the combination of the material elements of the matrix. This combination can, of course, vary: *to float over, to match, to brighten up*—each of these relations presupposes paradigms, and, consequently, different variants; but the structure is the same in all three cases[16] and can be reduced to the formula: $OS_1 \bullet V \bullet S_2$. Language places two vestimentary supports in relation to one another (*blouse and skirt, toque and coat, twin set and scarf*) and locates the ultimate meaning of these clothes in the coexistence of two supports: it is the nature of this coexistence alone which constitutes the variant of the matrix. For this reason, we shall call this

---

[15] Without seeking to transpose unduly from the biological to the aesthetic order, we must nonetheless recall that dissymmetry is a condition of existence: *"Certain elements of symmetry can coexist with certain phenomena, but they are not necessary. What is necessary is that certain elements of symmetry not exist. It is dissymmetry which creates the phenomenon"* (Pierre Curie, quoted by J. Nicole in *La symétrie,* P.U.F., *Que sais-je?,* p. 83).

[16] ╲ a blouse floating over the skirt ╱
    OS_1 V S_2
  ╲ a toque matching the coat ╱
    OS_1 V S_2
  ╲ a twin set brightened up with a silk scarf ╱
    OS_1 V S_2

variant a *connective*. Strictly speaking, variants of distribution
are connectives, since they also place two (or more) material
elements of clothing (e.g., two pockets, the two parts of a blouse)
in relation to each other; but in a way this relation is an inert
one, either purely quantitative (addition and multiplication) or
profoundly incorporated into the structure of the support (*an
asymmetrical blouse*): the connection is not explicit at the level
of the matrix; and most important, the connection proper has a
particular structural value: we saw that the relation which unites
the elements of the matrix $(O)(S)(V)$ was one of double implication or, as was also pointed out, one of solidarity: it is clearly
a syntagmatic relation; whereas the relation introduced by a
connective between two supports is a systematic relation, since
it varies according to a potential play of oppositions or paradigm.
Yet solidarity and connection are notions quite close to one
another, and it is certain that at the level of the variants of connection this proximity produces a particular confusion between
system and syntagm; we might even be tempted to define connectives as simple rhetorical variations of the solidarity of the matrix.
What prevents this, on the one hand, is that there is real diversity
among modes of association (*floating over, matching, brightened
up by*), and on the other hand, all matrices with two elements
(*a suit and its toque*)[17] would be incomplete and, consequently,
non-signifying if we were unable to locate the vestimentary
meaning in the association of these two elements itself (*and*).
Here we must recall the law of final meaning:[18] if the matrix
has only one variant (*cardigan • collar • open*), it is this variant
which holds the meaning, and in this case the association of the
cardigan and the collar can only be syntagmatic or else the utterance ceases to signify; but if this variant is lacking (*a cardigan
and its collar*[19]), the meaning must revert, as it were, to the
elements which remain: the syntagmatic relation which unites
them is thus doubled by a systematic relation, i.e., one that truly

---

[17] a suit and its toque
S_1 V S_2
O
[18] Cf., above, 6.10.
[19] a cardigan and its collar
S_1 V S_2
O

signifies, since it is part of a paradigm (*matching/dissonant*):
transferred here to the opening of the collar, meaning is shifted
onto the association of the collar and the cardigan: it is the abstract nature of this connection which produces meaning, not
the materiality of the elements associated. Ultimately, connectives are systematic facts of full status. Furthermore, it is because
the fusion of the syntagm and the system in them is so strong that
signification is so delicate; we see this quite clearly in language,
where systematic facts extended to the entire phrase (rhythm,
intonation) take on a wealth of meaning: there is a sort of semantic maturity proper to ensembles having suprasegmental signifiers,
to use linguistic terms. The canonic formula of connection begins
to be manifest in matrices having at least two explicit supports:
O • S1 • V • S2 (*a blouse floating over the skirt*). Obviously, we
can find matrices having three supports as well (*matching suit,
boater, and cache-peigne*[20]). In all these cases, the intended object of signification is constituted either by the first support, on
which language focuses attention (*gloves matching the coat*[21]),
or by the two supports together, implicitly subsumed within the
notion of *outfit* (*suit, boater, and cache-peigne*); but it can also
happen that the intended object ·is explicit and the supports
implicit: in *matching colors,* the object is obviously all colors concerned, and the supports are constituted by each of these colors
matched to the others;[22] this vigorous ellipsis is very close to
features of the variant of distribution (*two pockets*), whose
implicitly connective character we have already seen.

10.7. *Variant of emergence* (XXVIII)

The variant of emergence accounts for the way in which two
contiguous elements are situated in relation to one another. The
contiguity can be vertical (*a blouse and a skirt*) or transversal
(*a coat and its lining, a skirt and a petticoat*). The first term of

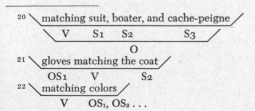

[20] matching suit, boater, and cache-peigne
    V   S1   S2   S3
[21] gloves matching the coat   O
    OS1   V   S2
[22] matching colors
    V   OS1, OS2 ...

the variant (*over/under*) corresponds to the movement which causes one of the two elements involved as supports within a feature to cover the other; since the two supports have an exactly complementary relation, the two terms of this movement are inevitably indifferent from a semantic point of view, yet they are opposed terminologically; if the blouse is *over* the skirt, the skirt is *under* the blouse: this statement of the obvious is not without its use, for it accounts for the fact that only the phenomenon of emergence is significant; the order in which it is expressed is not, since the terminology can be transformed without modifying the vestimentary meaning (we have come across the same ambiguity in *marked-marking* and *veiled-veiling*); what matters to the code is that between the two supports *there is* emergence; we shall thus catalogue all expressions of *exceeding* under one and the same term, no matter how the supports involved may actually be situated (*over, under, on, in, beneath, floating over, tucked in,* etc.); one piece can even cover another entirely: one is visible, the other is hidden, but the complementary relation between them does not change. This first term, one of abundant and varied terminology, can only be opposed to a negative degree: i.e., *flush with,* the expression for all cases where there is no emergence, where the two supports are exactly contiguous without one exceeding or covering the other. We thus obtain the following table of opposition:

over, under	flush with
visible, hidden, overlapping, in, floating over, inserted into, within, open over, sticking in, tucked into, on, emerging from	

The variant of emergence accounts for an important vestimentary fact relating to the history and psychology of costume: the appearance of "undergarments." It is perhaps a historical law that, over the course of time, pieces of clothing become animated by a kind of centrifugal force: the inside continually pushes its way toward the outside and tends to show itself either partially, at the collar, at the wrists, on the front of the chest, at the bottom of the skirt, or completely, when a piece that was an undergarment replaces an outer garment (sweaters, for example); the latter case is undoubtedly less interesting than the former; for what matters aesthetically or erotically is this suspended mixture of the seen and the unseen, which is precisely what the variant of emergence is responsible for making signify. The function of emergence would thus be to make the hidden visible, without, however, destroying its secret nature; in this way the garment's fundamental ambivalence is preserved, displaying nudity at the very moment it hides it; this at least is the psychoanalytic interpretation given by certain authors;[23] the garment would have the same basic ambiguity as a neurosis: it could be compared to the blush that comes across the face as a paradoxical sign of what is secret.

10.8. *Variant of association* (XXIX)

Two vestimentary elements can be described as *affinitive, dissonant*, or, in a neutral manner, simply *associated;* these are the three terms of the variant of association.

1		2		neutral
matching	/	dissonant	/	associated
blending with identical to paired with coupled with		cut off from clashing with		accompanying and on

The first term (*matching*) is by far the most frequent; it implies a real harmony (*alliance*) between the supports it unites; this harmony can go as far as identity if, for example, the two supports are made of the same fabric. When matching is presented as an absolute given, it is because either the second (implicit) support, or the outfit in general, or even the first support itself is doubled through a reflexive structure (*matching colors*). Matching provokes numerous metaphors, all those concerning affinity and particularly the couple (*Dots and light fabrics are made for each other*[24]). The second term (*dissonance, clashing*)

---

23 Cf. J. C. Flügel, *Psychology of Clothes.*
24 \ Dots and light fabrics are made for each other /
         V   SO /
\ S_1 S_2 /   V
     O

is obviously rare: Fashion, we know, is euphemistic; it does not admit contrariety except under the guise of the *piquant*. The neutral term occurs much more frequently; it corresponds to a pure correlation, signifying in itself, whatever its value may be; Fashion is so consistently euphemistic that the simple expression of a relation tends to turn this relation into an affinity: *a clip on the pocket* cannot be unharmonious; but this affinity remains unexpressed: the meaning is born of a simple coming-together of clip and pocket; this kind of nudity of relation shifts to the discretion of the terminology used; it is often a simple preposition (*on*) or a simple conjunction (*and*); and if the utterance of associative features is often complex, it is not because of the variant, but because of the chain of matrices, often quite long, when each of the two *relata* is at least one matrix all by itself.

10.9. *Variant of regulation* (XXX)

We have seen that the variant of balance controlled the distribution of identical and repeated elements (*pockets, buttons*). But it is the variant of regulation which gives a meaning to the balancing of disparate elements (*a blouse and a silk scarf*): it apprehends ensembles in order to explain how diversity, and often even contrast between elements, produces unity, and that this unity has a meaning; and as it generally concerns itself with nearly the entire vestimentary space, i.e., with the entire outfit, its action, remote yet imperious, rather resembles that of an intricate machine: Fashion regulates the way a woman dresses; here it increases, accentuates, develops; there it diminishes or offsets. This variant therefore includes two opposing terms: one of increasing what is already given, the other of restricting it; the two contrasting movements correspond to two types of balancing (accumulation and opposition); and as the balance of an ensemble, since it is no longer mechanical, can exist only at the level of a language (which in this case is the magazine's description), this variant, like that of mark, has a primarily rhetorical existence: the more a garment is *spoken*, the easier it is to regulate. The first term (*increase, enhancement*) is quite rare because emphasis is most often dealt with by the variant of mark; the two terms *marked* and *pronounced* are quite close; the difference is that the variation for *marked* is a negation (*unmarked*), while *pronounced* refers to an assertive opposite (*subdued*); it is also, and above all, that mark deals with simple supports and accent deals with double supports; in the first case, the support is marked absolutely, in the second there is a developed syntax, one support pronounces the other: *A stole will broaden your shoulders.*[25] The term of compensation, much more frequent, is comprised of numerous metaphors: *to subdue, to brighten, to warm, to enliven, to divert, to temper;*[26] it is always a matter of balancing one tendency with an allopathic dose of its opposite; also, it often suffices Fashion to combine two opposed signifieds in a single utterance in order to produce a regulation of signifiers: *These shirts are whimsical, cosmopolitan . . . wear them with classic slacks.*[27] In such cases, regulation is self-generated by the so-called endogenous interplay of opposites, as this example clearly shows: *The showiness of the jewels is due to the sobriety of the dresses.* All these facts of regulation, deliberate though they are, since Fashion is an intentional system, nonetheless suggest the mechanisms for transforming a natural object by a cultural correction; everything happens as if, initially, the model constructed itself, and then Fashion consciously intervenes in order to correct the excesses of this spontaneous rough sketch; the second support, from which the rectification generally derives, is moreover almost always of an inferior volume to the first support (confused with the intended object) which receives it: what is subtle and delicate acts forcefully: it is a "trifle" (*a rose, a scarf, an accessory, a little tie*) which regulates large ensembles (*a twin set, a fabric, a suit, a dress*), just as the brain commands the entire body: capital disproportion in the Fashion system, as

---

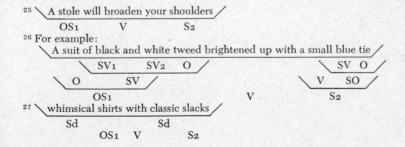

we saw in the case of the "detail." We can establish the table for the variant of regulation in the following manner:

increased by	/	offset by
emphasizing emphasized by enlarged		softened adding a note diverted by lightened up by enlivened by dressing up warmed up by tempered by

IV. THE VARIANT OF VARIANTS

10.10. *Variant of degree*

In order to complete the inventory of variants, it must be recalled that the Fashion system has one particular variant at its disposal which has been called an *intensive* or more generally a *variant of degree*, for it corresponds terminologically to adverbs of integrity (*halfway, completely*) or intensity (*little, very*), whose characteristic is that it can be applied only to another variant, and not sometimes to a genre and sometimes to a variant, like normal variants: it is, if you will, the variant of variants.[28] It possesses the fundamental characteristics of the variant (simple, memorable oppositions of immaterial substance), but its syntagmatic inventory could not follow the list of genera, only that of other variants. Its particular constitution sees to it that the intensive always occupies the extreme tip of meaning: nothing can be added to it; it crowns the utterance and is, nonetheless, substantially the emptiest element, though also the one which signifies most; in *slightly rounded skirt*,[29] there is an inarguable commutation of vestimentary meaning between (*fully*) *rounded skirt* and *slightly rounded skirt;* the former may be in fashion and the latter out of fashion: it is thus the variation of degree

---

[28] It is a pure auxiliary.
[29] \ slightly rounded skirt /
   V2   V1   OS

which carries the final meaning, and yet this variation is structurally tributary to the variant of form (*rounded*). The variation of degree can affect either the intensity of the supporting variant (*very soft, slightly transparent*) or the integrity of the support (i.e., of the species) to which it is applied (*a half-open collar*); rarely is a variant able to support both a variation of intensity and a variation of integrity simultaneously; this happens essentially in cases of form (*semi-rounded* and *slightly rounded*); we can thus envision two series of oppositions, two variants, if you will, which for economy of presentation we shall group in a single table:

	not at all	/	half-way	/	¾	/	nearly	/	entirely
Integrity			semi-demi-						com-pletely
	a little	/	not too	/	very	/	at the limits of the possible		
Intensity	discreet slightly moderately faintly								
	less	/	more						

Integrity establishes meaning on the proportion of space assigned to the variant it modifies; therefore, it can only be applied to variants linked by nature to the extensive quality of the support: formal spaces, lines of division, closure, attachment, flection, zones of position and emergence; in such instances the variant of degree indicates the amount of space deducted from the support by the supporting variant in order to make it signify; in the case of integrity, therefore, the variations are at closed, measured intervals: the thresholds are more clearly marked than they are for intensity. The variation of intensity is in fact less definite; although the terms of intensity, by the very nature of the language which takes each up in turn, are discontinuous, it implies that its support can vary continually; the progressive character of its oppositions is manifested in the use of the comparative: *a dress more or less long depending on the season, depending on the hour.* Here meaning is organized approximately around two poles, one reduced (*a little*), the other emphatic (*very*). The reduced pole includes numerous metaphors, whose use depends on the supporting variant (*a casually knotted scarf, a belt loosely attached, a discreet and moderate fullness,* etc.), because Fashion always seeks to make discretion "count." The variant of degree admits of only three cases of syntagmatic impossibility: the assertion of existence, addition, and multiplication: for these three supporting variants, progression is in fact excluded: their commutation is radically alternative: *to wear a jacket or not to wear it, one pocket or two.*

11

The System

"Here is linen, light or heavy."[1]

I. MEANING, SUPERVISED FREEDOM

11.1. *Systematic constraints and syntagmatic constraints*

The production of meaning is subject to certain constraints; this does not mean that constraints limit meaning, but, on the contrary, constitute it; meaning cannot appear where freedom is absolute or nonexistent: the system of meaning is that of a supervised freedom. Actually, the deeper we enter into a semantic structure, the more it appears that it is the sequence of constraints, and not that of freedoms, which best defines this structure. In written clothing, these constraints can be of two kinds; they can apply to the terms of the variant, independent of the support it concerns (the assertion of existence, for example, can only consist of the pure alternative between being and non-being): these are therefore systematic constraints; on the other hand, they can apply to the association of genera and variants: these are syntagmatic constraints. This is a useful distinction if we want to apprehend the structure of the signifier in its ensemble; hence, we must once again take up the problem of constraints, first at the level of the system, then at the level of the syntagm.

---

[1] \ linen light or heavy /
    OSV (species)

II. THE SYSTEMATIC YIELD

11.2. *Figured principle of oppositions: "spots"*

The principle underlying all systematic opposition[2] derives from the nature of the sign: the sign is a difference;[3] we could therefore compare a play of oppositions to a "spotted" fan run through by a needle; the fan is the paradigm itself or variant; each spot corresponds to a term of the variant; the needle is the utterance and, consequently, Fashion or the world, since by noting the feature, the world or Fashion actualizes one term of the variant to the detriment of the others. The spots untouched by the needle of the utterance, i.e., the terms of the variant which are not actualized, obviously form the reservoir of meaning; if information theory calls this reservoir a *memory* (granted, when applying this word to the ensemble of signs, and not to a simple paradigm), it actually does so because, in order to be active, an opposition has every interest in being memorable: the more organized the reservoir, the easier it is to call up the sign. Thus, the number of terms in a variant, and perhaps even more, as we shall see, the internal organization of these terms, has a direct effect on the process of meaning, independent of the associations to which this variant can or cannot be applied: we could call this the systematic yield of a variant. In turning back to the thirty variants which have been analyzed, it is possible to distinguish three groups of oppositions corresponding to three types of systematic yield.[4]

11.3. *Alternative oppositions*

Within the first group must be catalogued all strictly alternative oppositions of the type *yes/no* (*with/without, natural/artificial,*

---

[2] It is difficult to avoid a certain ambivalence in the word *system* (and *systematic*): system (in the restricted sense of the term) is the level of paradigms opposed to the level of syntagms, and in the broader sense it is an ensemble of units, functions, and constraints (the language system, the Fashion system).

[3] Saussure, *Cours de linguistique:* "*What distinguishes a sign is what constitutes it.*" The differential nature of the sign does pose some difficulties (cf. R. Godel, *Sources,* p. 196), but this does not alter the fecundity of the definition.

[4] The notion of systematic *yield,* as approximate as it still may be, has determined the classification which follows, even though it is much less refined than the classification of oppositions devised by J. Cantineau ("Les oppositions significatives," *Cahiers F. de Saussure,* no. 10, pp. 11–40).

marked/unmarked, etc.).⁵ These oppositions never consist of
more than two terms, not only de facto (we have seen elsewhere,
in certain oppositions, that there could be a defective term), but
also de jure: by the very nature of the difference which here
constitutes the sign, the opposition cannot receive any mediation
which language might sanction; a dress is worn *with or without
a belt,* and between the presence and the absence of a belt, no
intermediary state is possible. No doubt, such variations can lend
themselves to the variant of degree: a side can be *slit halfway,*
a waistline can be *lightly marked;* but, in this sense, the variation
of integrity or intensity affects only one term of the opposition
and does not introduce any qualitatively new term to it: what is
lightly marked, even at the limit of perception, falls entirely on
the side of what is marked. This is because in every alternative
opposition, conforming to the principle of phonological oppositions, the difference between the two terms is due to the presence
or absence of a character (precisely what we call the *pertinent
feature*): this character (existence, mark, slit) is or it is not:
the relation between the two terms is one of negation, not contrast, and negation cannot generate itself.⁶

11.4. *Polar oppositions*

The second group includes compound polar oppositions.⁷ Each
variant first includes two terms placed in equipollent opposition

---

⁵ Alternative opposition is found in the following variants:
    I. *Assertion of species* (a/[A-a]). (The assertion of species should be
      treated formally as a binary opposition and substantially as the re-
      pository of implicit variants. Cf., below, 19.10.)
    II. *Assertion of existence* (with/without)
    III. *Artifice* (natural/artificial)
    IV. *Mark* (marked/unmarked)
    XVI. *Division* (divided/undivided)
    XVII. *Mobility* (fixed/movable)
    XXVI. *Multiplication* (one/many)
  XXVIII. *Emergence* (exceeding/flush with)
    XXX. *Regulation* (increased by/offset by)
⁶ What we call an *alternative opposition* here would be a *privative opposition* in
linguistics, defined by the presence or absence of a mark.
⁷ Here the the variants of this group:
    VII. *Movement* (rising/falling/projecting/swaying)
    VIII. *Weight* (heavy/light/[normal]/——)
    IX. *Suppleness* (supple/stiff/[normal]/——)
    X. *Relief* (protruding/indented/smooth/crushed)
    XII. *Length* (absolute) (long/short/[normal]/——)

(*this/that*), then a neutral term which excludes both these terms (*neither this/nor that*) (we have seen that, as an ethical system, Fashion nearly always makes the neutral coincide with the normal, and that, as an aesthetic system, it refrains from noting it: the neutral term is thus often defective), and finally, a complex term (*both this and that*); this term is also inevitably defective whenever the polar terms imply a quality (weight, suppleness, length) extended to a space of the garment in such a way that the quality can only be applied to that place and nowhere else (a support cannot be partially supple); and whenever this complex term is mentioned, it can represent either a juxtaposition of opposing characters, the compromise being made at the level of the entire support (a crushed hat is formed by protrusions and indentations), or an indifference to noting one term rather than the other (*folded* corresponds to *turned up or turned down*). The opposition of polar terms usually appears to be of a contrasting nature, at least at the terminological level; in fact (but who knows precisely what a contrary is?[8]), the polar opposition is in no way defined by the presence or the absence of a mark, as in the case of alternative opposition, but by an implicit scale of accumulation, of which language notes the terms of arrival and departure, so to speak: from *light* to *heavy* there is a quantitative difference in weight, but weight is always present: it is not weight which constitutes the pertinent characteristic, it is its quantity, or its dosage, as it were. The mark's strong yield in oppositions discerned by linguistics (at least in oppositions of the second articulation) no doubt corresponds to a power of dissymmetry (or irreversibility), and it is precisely the extent to which equipollent oppositions are symmetrical or reversible

---

XIII. *Width* (wide/narrow/[normal]/——)
XIV. *Volume* (voluminous/thin/[normal]/——)
XV. *Size* (large/small/[normal]/——)
XX. *Flection* (turned up/turned down/[straight]/folded)
XXI. *Horizontal position* (right/left/in the middle/throughout)
XXII. *Vertical position* (high/low/at the middle/the entire length)
XXIII. *Transversal position* (in front/in back/at the side/all around)
XXIV. *Orientation* (horizontal/vertical/oblique/——)
XXIX. *Association* (matching/clashing with/associated with/——).,

[8] It is easy to determine the affinitive axis of two opposites, or further, their common semes, but this is only to sidestep the problem: how to define "contrastive" semes?

that they correspond to a more complex economy of signification; in order to remain effective, this structure needs language at this point more than ever: indeed, language manages to organize a cumulative variation into a polar variation and this variation into a signifying one because it is here concerned with qualities which humanity has essentialized into pairs of absolute opposites (*heavy/light*) for a very long time.

11.5. *Serial oppositions*

The third group of oppositions is quite close to the second; it includes all plainly serial oppositions, cumulative like the preceding ones, except that in this instance language does not organize them into immediately contrastive functions.[9] It is no doubt possible to distinguish two poles of attraction in a serial opposition, for example, *tight/loose* in the series of the variant of fit; but language does not isolate these contrastive terms absolutely and, furthermore, it does not normalize the degrees of the series; it follows that the series remains open-ended and that a new degree can always be inserted (this can be clearly seen in the case of proportional length); in this final group of oppositions, the series always escapes saturation one way or another.

11.6. *Combined and anomic oppositions*

Such are the three principal groups of oppositions. To these must be added a few variants of complex, or more precisely, combined structure.[10] In the variant of form, at least as far as we have been able to organize it, a generating opposition of polar type (*straight/rounded*) produces subsidiary oppositions, depending on whether spatial (plane, volume) or linear (convergence, divergence, complexity) criteria are made to intervene. In the

---

[9] Here are the variants with serial oppositions:
    VI. *Fit* (clinging/tight/loose/bouffant)
    XI. *Transparence* (opaque/openwork/transparent/invisible)
    XXII. *Length* (proportional) (⅓, ½, ⅔, etc.)
    XVIII. *Closure* (open/edge-to-edge/closed/crossed/etc.)
[10] The variants of this group are the following:
    V. *Form* (straight/rounded . . .)
    XXVII. *Balance* (symmetrical/asymmetrical/in contrast)
    XXV. *Addition* (1/2/3/4)
    XIX. *Attachment* (fixed/placed . . .)

variant of balance, one term of the alternative opposition (*symmetrical/asymmetrical*) includes an intensive of original expression (in contrast = doubly symmetrical). In the variant of addition, the numbers 1 and 2 have been assigned polar functions, the number 3 a neutral function, and the number 4 an intensive function in relation to 2. Finally, in the variant of attachment, a simple binary opposition (full term/neutral term) is profoundly destructured, as it were, by the development of a broad subsidiary opposition within the full term (*fixed/set/knotted/buttoned,* etc.); what we have here is not a serial (cumulative) opposition, since the terms serve to note modes and not degrees, but rather an anomic opposition: it can be given neither form nor order.

11.7. *Systematic yield: the problem of binarism*

What is immediately apparent in this inventory is that the Fashion system cannot be reduced to a process of binary oppositions. This may not be the place, as we proceed to a purely immanent description of a particular system, to discuss the general theory of binarism. We shall confine ourselves to an examination of the systematic yield of different types of vestimentary oppositions and of the possible meaning of their diversity. If we refer to the Fashion system, what matters, it would seem, so that an opposition may have an assured yield, is not so much that it be binary, but, more broadly, that it be *closed*, i.e., constituted by cardinal terms which delimit the variation's entire possible space, in such a manner that this space can be reasonably saturated by a small number of terms: this is the case of polar oppositions having four terms (group II); closed like alternative oppositions, they are, however, richer than such oppositions, built simultaneously out of a cell (polar terms) and a rough sketch of a combinatory (neutral term and complex term); as such, the three variants of position afford perhaps the best oppositions imaginable; the variant here (e.g., *right/left/in the middle/throughout*) is entirely saturated, i.e., its structure (in any given mental state) excludes the invention of a new term (which would not be the case with serial oppositions); here the vestimentary code is absolutely certain, barring a change in the language system itself, i.e., the segmentation of the real (for example, discarding the notions of *right* and *left*). We can now hazard that an opposition's excellence is due less to the number of its constituent terms (provided this number is reduced, i.e., ultimately memorable) than to the perfection of its structure. This is why serial oppositions have a less satisfying systematic yield than the others; a series is an unstructured object, it is perhaps even an anti-structure; and if the serial oppositions of the vestimentary code nevertheless have a semantic efficacy, it is because here, in fact, the series always coincides with a certain polarization of terms (*tight/loose*); if this polarization is impossible, the series becomes completely anomic (*fixed/sewn/knotted/buttoned*, etc.): it is obvious that what threatens—and sometimes spoils—the structural solidity of systems of oppositions is the proliferation of species—i.e., ultimately, language; an anomic series like that of the variant of attachment is very close to a simple list of species; it therefore could have no rigorous structuration other than that of the lexicon: structural analysis of the vestimentary code is thus defective to the extent that structural semantics is still feeling its way.[11] Here we arrive at the extreme ambiguity of translinguistic systems, i.e., systems whose signification passes through the relay of language; this ambiguity reproduces the duplicity of the linguistic system: language is clearly a digital system (with a strong binary predominance) at the level of distinctive units (phonemes), but this binarism is no longer constitutive at the level of significant units (monemes), which up to now has made structuration of the lexicon difficult; in the same manner, the vestimentary code seems divided between binary oppositions (even if they are compound) and serial paradigms; but while this conflict is resolved in language by doubling the articulation, which permits detaching, so to speak, the distinctive term of the combinator, it remains open in the vestimentary code, whose binary oppositions are here and there concurrent with (serial) nomenclatures derived from language. The present state of semiological inventories makes it difficult to say whether this (partial) defection of binarism fundamentally questions the universality (assumed by some) of digitalism, or whether it only refers to a certain moment in

---

[11] L. Hjelmslev, *Essays*.

the history of forms (our own): binarism is perhaps a historical property of archaic societies; in modern societies—where, moreover, meaning always tends to disappear beneath "reason" and form beneath content—binarism would tend on the contrary to mask itself and to let itself be overrun by language.

III. THE NEUTRALIZATION OF THE SIGNIFIER

11.8. *Conditions for neutralization*

Are systematic oppositions unalterable? Does the opposition between *heavy* and *light*, for instance, always signify? By no means. We know that, in phonology itself, certain oppositions can lose their pertinent character, depending on the placement of phonemes in the spoken chain;[12] in German, for example, the distinctive opposition d/t (*Daube/Taube*) ceases to be pertinent at the end of words (*Rad = Rat*): we say that it is *neutralized*. The same is true in Fashion; in an utterance like *Here is linen, light or heavy*, we clearly see that an ordinarily significant opposition (*light/heavy*) is explicitly rendered insignificant. How? By submitting the two terms of the opposition to a single signified; for it is quite obvious that in *a cardigan with its collar open or closed, depending on whether for sport or dress*, the opposition of *open* and *closed* escapes neutralization because there are two signifieds (*sport/dress*); in the first case, the disjunction (*or*) is inclusive, in the second it is exclusive.

11.9. *Role of the arch-vesteme*

To return once again to the phonological model, we know that the two terms of a pertinent but neutralizable opposition are conflated, in the event of neutralization, in what we call an archphoneme; thus, in the opposition o/ǫ (Fr.: *bótté/beauté*), usually neutralized at the end of a word to the advantage of ǫ (*pot/*

---

[12] A. Martinet describes neutralization thus: *"Phonology speaks of neutralization when, in a context defined in terms of phonemes, (supra-segmental) prosodic features and limits between signifying elements (junctures), the distinction appears to be unusable between two or several phonemes which alone possess certain phonic characteristics"* (*Travaux de l'Inst. de Linguistique*, Paris, Klincksieck, 1957, II, p. 78).

peau),[13] ọ becomes the arch-phoneme of the opposition. In a similar manner, a vestimentary opposition can only be neutralized to the benefit, one might say, of an arch-vesteme; for *light/heavy* the arch-vesteme is weight (*Here is linen, whatever the weight*); but here the vestimentary phenomenon departs from the phonological model; a phonological opposition is in effect defined by a difference in mark: one term is marked by a certain characteristic (pertinent feature) and the other is not; neutralization does not occur to the benefit of the free term, but rather to the benefit of a generic term; now not all these vestimentary oppositions conform to this structure; polar oppositions in particular have a cumulative structure: from *heavy* to *light*, there is always "some weight"; in other words, once the opposition is neutralized, weight still retains a certain conceptual existence. This explains why, whatever its provenance (alternative, polar, or serial oppositions), the arch-vesteme fulfills a certain function: neutralization is not indifferent: it constitutes a redundance (since linen of every sort has a certain weight), but this redundance is not without consequence for the intelligibility of the message: the final non-signifying character of the feature (*light or heavy*) shifts the effect of meaning back, as it were, onto the element which precedes it; in *Here is linen, light or heavy*, it is the linen which signifies, the effective variant is the assertion of species;[14] but this assertion is accentuated, so to speak, by the fact that it is followed by an utterance of indifferentiation: whatever its weight, it is the linen that signifies; in short, the function of the arch-vesteme is to tie the utterance together more strongly by the contrast of a full variant (the assertion of species) and an artificial variant, simultaneously uttered and avoided; this is doubtless a phenomenon of a rhetorical order, but we can see that within the vestimentary code itself it has a structural value: the expression of neutralization gives a particular emphasis to the rest of the utterance; in *This travel coat is worn with or without a belt*,[15] the neutralization of the variant of existence (*with*

---

[13] For 67 percent of the French people. Cf. A. Martinet, *La prononciation du français contemporain*, Paris, Droz, 1945.

[14] ＼ linen (light or heavy) ／

OSV　　　neutr.

[15] ＼ this coat with or without a belt ≡ travel ／

OSV　　　neutr.

or without) visibly reinforces the apodeicticism of the signifier (*this coat*); beyond the matrix itself (*coat*), the shifter (*this*) shifts an accrued meaning back onto the image to which it refers.

IV. THE SYSTEMATIC REDUCTION OF THE SPECIES: TOWARD REAL CLOTHING

11.10. *Beyond the terminological rule: invested variants*

We have seen on several occasions how language, by relaying the vestimentary code through open-ended nomenclatures of species, hindered the structuration of written clothing; this hindrance is certainly not without significance since it indicates a constituent tension of human societies torn between reality and language; in order to respect this very tension, we have attempted till now to inventory Fashion clothing without deviating from the terminological rule, i.e., without looking behind the word for the real features out of which the named object can be compounded. However, the inventory of variants permits us to undertake a new analysis of species, since henceforth we can hope systematically to reduce each species to a support provided with one or more implicit variants:[16] a short skirt (Fr.: *jupette*), for example, is nothing but a skirt constitutively provided with the variant of length (*skirt • short*).[17] This analysis can doubtless be only marginal to the system of written Fashion, since, by decomposing the named object into unnamed features, that system requires a transgression of the terminological rule; however, the inherent interest of this analysis is obvious, and it must be sketched out here as a guide, because if we try to proceed to a systematic reduction of species (by revealing the variants invested in each species), we open this very passage from written clothing to real clothing: it is thus the structural analysis of real clothing which is in question. For this sketch we shall choose two genres particularly rich in species (therefore seemingly refractory to struc-

---

[16] Implicit or invested variants.
[17] We have already seen that the species (*a three-quarter length jacket, a sport shirt*) is often constituted by the solidification of an old variant (length) or of an old signified (sport), fossilized, as it were, in the name of the species.

turation), material and color, and we shall attempt to order the mass of their species into signifying terms.

11.11. *Semantic classification of species of materials*

How are we to classify, *from the point of view of vestimentary meaning*, the various species of materials? We shall propose the following operational itinerary. The first step consists of reconstituting synonymic groups of species at the level of the corpus in its entirety, by putting all signifiers which refer to one and the same signified into a single group; we shall have, for example:

Group I: *Formal wear ≡ mousseline, silk, shantung.*
Group II: *Winter ≡ furs, woolens.*
Group III: *Spring ≡ crêpe de Chine, light woolens, jersey.*
Group IV: *Summer ≡ poplin, silk, raw silk, linen, cotton.*
  etc.

The second step is based upon the following fact: the semantics of Fashion is so fluid that quite often the signifier of one group also belongs to another group: *silk,* for example, is part of both groups I and IV; to follow the linguistic comparison, a signifier common to several groups may, of course, not have the same *value* in all places, just like two synonyms in language; formally, we are nonetheless justified in gathering into a single area all the groups which communicate with one another through at least one common signifier; they form a network of neighboring species, within which flow various meanings which, if not identical, are at least affinitive: there is reciprocal evidence of an affinity between the signifiers themselves and likewise between signifieds. Now not only are these areas quite vast, but in the case of material, all the species listed can be divided into two large affinitive areas linked by a relation of binary opposition, since the division of areas occurs when they no longer communicate, i.e., when meaning no longer passes from one to the other; hence, all the species of materials are catalogued under a unique opposition; on the side of the signifieds, pertinence (i.e., meaning) opposes a field dominated by the concepts of *formal wear* and *summer* to another field dominated by the concepts of *travel* and *winter;* on the side of the signifiers, the opposition passes between *linens, cottons, silks, organzas, mousselines,* etc., and *poplins, woolens, tweeds, velvets, leathers,* etc. Is this all? Can't the opposition we have just discovered be reduced or, at least, be made to conform to one already known (since for the moment we detect in it none of the variants already listed)? Here once again the commutation test should be our guide; it requires the identification of *the smallest element* whose variation entails the passage from one area to another, i.e., from one meaning to another. Now, the two areas clearly tend toward each other at the level of one species in particular, *woolens,* which is common to both areas *except for one difference;* and it is this difference, the smallest that can be discerned, which will make up the entire opposition of meanings: the woolens in area I are *fine,* in area II they are *coarse.* It follows that, from a signifying viewpoint, all species of materials end by being catalogued under an opposition of the type *fine/coarse,* or, to be more specific, since it is fabrics and not forms we are concerned with, *light/heavy:* this opposition is familiar, it is that of the variant of weight. We are thus led to acknowledge that in the species of materials, numerous as they may be, the system invests essentially only one variant: weight; so if we exceed the terminological rule, it is weight that signifies, not species. Once we consent to inventory the implicit, we must admit that species is not the ultimate signifying unit; a single species, for example, can be divided by the variant: meaning passes *inside* the species *woolens.*[18] Furthermore, since we are dealing with an alternation, there is nothing to prevent us from occasionally finding the neutral term mentioned (neither fine, nor coarse, nor light, nor heavy): here this is *jersey,* an amorphous and mobile signifier which can circulate from one area to the other; it naturally refers to a "pan-semic" (*all-purpose*) signifier.

11.12. *Semantic classification of the species of colors*

The same is true of color. Its species (in appearance quite numerous) are also catalogued into two opposed areas, which can be

---

[18] In the same way we have: *cotton (I)/brushed cotton (II). Brushed,* a rare term, seems to imply a variant of relief (smooth, without relief) and it would lead us to presume, in the last analysis, that weight itself refers to the degree to which the material is *closed* or *open,* ambivalent notions, since they are equally suited to the satisfaction of both coenesthetic needs (warmth) and erotic values (transparence).

reconstituted according to the same methodological itinerary used for material, by gathering synonymic species step by step. And here again, what meaning separates is not two color-types as we might imagine (for example, black and white), but rather two qualities; without taking the physical nature of colors into account, it puts *bright, light, pure, brilliant* colors on one side of the opposition and *dark, somber, dull, neutral, faded* colors on the other; in other words, color signifies not through its species but only insofar as it is marked or not; here again, therefore, it is a known variant which is invested in the species of colors in order to distinguish them semantically: the mark.[19] We already know that *colorful* or *colored* denotes not the presence of color but rather an emphatic manner of marking it; also, just as weight can divide a single species of fabric (woolens), so the mark can divide a single species of color: *gray* can be either light or dark, and it is this opposition which signifies, not the color gray itself. Hence, semantic opposition is fully capable of contradicting or ignoring the opposites of colors posited by common sense: in Fashion, *black* is a full color—one that is marked, in a word; it is a *colored* color (naturally associated with *formal wear*); thus, it cannot be semantically opposed to white, which is in the same area of *the marked*.[20]

11.13. *Implicit supports: reducible species and simple species*

This is not to say that it is possible to reduce every genus to the play of a single variant as easily as we did with material and color. We can at least be sure that a species can always be defined by the combination of a simple support and a few implicit variants. In other words, species is never anything but the nominal shortcut which economizes the utterance of a complete matrix. What is a simple support? It is a species which cannot be decomposed with the help of known variants; we could call these irreducible species *eponymous species*, for in general they are the ones which designate the genus to which they themselves belong:

19 These observations seem to coincide with those of ethnology (cf. Claude Lévi-Strauss, *The Savage Mind*).

20 We know that in the Middle Ages bright colors (and not this or that color) were highly valued and served as a medium of exchange or as gifts (G. Duby and R. Mandrou, *Histoire de la civilisation française*, A. Colin, 1959, Vol. 2, pp. 360–83).

blouses, jackets, vests, coats, etc.; these generic species lend themselves quite readily to explicit variants (*a light blouse, a waisted
jacket*), and in order to create new species it suffices that these
syntagms be given new names: a short skirt will be a *mini*, a hat
without a crown or brim, if it is supple, will be a *bandeau,* etc.;
thus, the more particular the species, the more reducible it is;
the more general it is, the less it can be decomposed, but also,
the more likely we are to find it as an implicit support in the
reducible species.

12

The Syntagm

"California-style shirts, with big collars, standing collars, small collars, military collars."

I. THE FASHION FEATURE

12.1. *Syntactical relation and syntagmatic association*

In Fashion, the syntax which unites the signifying units is a free form: it is the relation of simple combination which links a certain number of matrices into a single utterance; in *a cotton dress with red and white checks*,[1] six matrices are united by a relation which has no equivalent in verbal syntax, and whose homographic character has already been mentioned.[2] Within the matrix, on the contrary, the syntagmatic relation is constrained; it is a relation of solidarity or double implication which unites the object, the support, and the variant. Since it is free and infinitely combinative, the syntax of Fashion eludes any inventory; the matrix is a finite syntagm, stable and numerable; and since the distribution of the vestimentary substance among its elements is regular (supports and objects being filled by the genera, and the variant remaining non-material), it follows that the Fashion feature (union of genus and variant) has both a methodological and a

---

[1] a cotton dress with red (checks) and white checks

    VS   O   VS   O   VS   O

                  S_1O V S_2

      O   V   S

[2] Cf., above, 6.11.

practical importance, which is why we shall mean, when we say syntagmatic association, not the syntax of the matrices, but the union of genus and variant; indeed, the feature lends itself to inventory, it constitutes a unit of analysis whose handling makes possible both the control of the mass of magazine utterances and the postulation of a regular inventory of Fashion phenomena; and furthermore, since it is filled with substance, the feature encounters constraints which are no longer logical, but which derive from reality itself, whether physical, historical, ethical, or aesthetic: in short, at the level of the feature, the syntagmatic relation communicates with social and technical givens; this relation is the site in the general Fashion system where the world invests in meaning, because it is reality, by way of the feature, which dictates the chances for meaning to appear. Apparently, the systematic relation (even if the discussion of binarism still remains open) refers to a memory, in any case, to an anthropology; the syntagmatic relation, on the other hand, certainly refers to a "praxis": therein lies its importance.

12.2. *The impossibilities of association*

By virtue of certain determinations of fact, certain features are possible and others are not, for here it is substance alone (that of genera and variants), and not the law of Fashion, which governs the feature's possibilities to appear. In general, then, what are the *impossibilities* of association between genera and variants, at least as far as they can be determined in a civilization like our own?[3] First, there are impossibilities of a material order: an element which is too tenuous or filiform by nature (a strap, a seam) cannot receive the variant of form; a circular element cannot be long; and, in a more general way, for all elements which are entirely parasitic to another element (*linings, sides, waist, slips*) or to the body itself (*panty hose, stockings*), the association of genus and of certain variants is in a sense useless and rejects the variation of the *noted: a back* cannot have weight independent of the piece of which it is part, *stockings* cannot have a form of their own. Next, there are moral or aesthetic impossibilities: a certain number of pieces or parts of pieces

---

[3] On the historical relativity of the impossibilities, cf., below, 12.4.

(*blouses, pants, fronts*) cannot be submitted to the variant of existence, since denuding the chest or the trunk is not yet permitted; a back cannot be protruding, a garment cannot be "without a line," by reason of aesthetic interdictions coming from the civilization itself (and not only from Fashion), or even of certain "psychological" interdictions: stockings cannot be "falling," for they would be interpreted as an indication of slovenliness and negligence.[4] Finally, there are institutional impossibilities; it is the status of genus which prohibits certain associations (a jacket, protective by function, cannot be transparent; an accessory resists variations in mobility, since it is always mobile; a principal piece cannot be oriented, since it is a field of orientation), or better still, its definition: a cardigan is not free to be divided or undivided, since it is precisely its median division which defines it (in opposition to the sweater); we saw[5] that elements which were neither divided nor mobile did not have to be attached; in all these (many) cases, association is impossible because it would be pleonastic, so to speak; it is thus the very economy of information which excludes certain associations. And since the definition of the piece is after all implied in its name, it is ultimately language which often governs the feature's impossibilities to appear; the syntagmatic constraint could therefore yield only if language itself modified its nomenclatures.[6]

12.3. *The freedom of alternative*

As we have often seen, meaning can be born only from a variation. The impossibilities of association all tend to deprive the variant of its possibility of variation and thereby to destroy meaning. Ultimately, therefore, it is the syntagm which governs the power of the system, and the systematic yield of a variant[7] depends on the zone of freedom granted to it by the syntagmatic association, i.e., by the feature; this is why we can say that mean-

---

[4] However, a fad—i.e., literally, a "fashion"—can, of course, give a phenomenon of dress such as negligence the institutional value of a sign (in adolescent costume, for example).

[5] Cf., above, 9.20.

[6] Linguistics is naturally familiar with the problem of impossible associations; an analysis of syntagmatic incompatibility is to be found in H. Mitterand, "Observations sur les prédéterminants du nom," in *Études de linguistique appliquée*, no. 2, Didier, p. 128.

[7] Cf., above, 11.7.

ing is always the product of a supervised freedom. There is thus an optimal margin of freedom for each feature; for example, for a piece to lend itself to the variant of artifice (i.e., to be able to be "imitated"), its definition must not be too vague nor its function too constraining: an accessory is too imprecise and shoes too necessary for either to have the freedom to be "false." The optimum, therefore, is situated as far from a total freedom as from no freedom at all: a formless piece (total freedom) and a piece that is absolutely formed (no freedom) cannot lend themselves to the variant of form. In fact, the best chance that a genus can have of associating with a variant is to possess this variant implicitly, but only in an embryonic way, as it were: a skirt lends itself to variations of form quite readily because it already has a certain form in itself, though this form is not yet institutional. Meaning, in order to be born, thus exploits certain potentialities of substance; it can therefore be defined as the capture of a fragile situation, for if the potentiality of substance is prematurely fulfilled, it immediately forms a named species and the variant eludes us; if mobility is invested too soon, as it were, into the assemblage of two pieces, we obtain a species named *two-piece,* which is no longer free to lend itself to the variant of mobility because it is mobile by status.

12.4. *Reservoir of Fashion and reservoir of history*

Substance thus determines two great classes of associations of genus and variant: possible and impossible; these two classes correspond to two reservoirs of features. The reservoir of possible features constitutes the reservoir of Fashion proper, for it is from this reservoir that Fashion draws the associations from which it makes the very sign of Fashion; yet this is nothing other than a reservoir: since the variant consists of several terms, Fashion actualizes only one of them each year; the others, all participating in the *possible,* are *forbidden,* for they designate the *unfashion-able.* Whereby we see that the forbidden is possible by definition: what is impossible (we shall say excluded) cannot be forbidden. In order to change, Fashion thus makes the terms of a single variant alternate within the limits of possible associations; for example, it makes *long skirts* succeed *short skirts,* and a *flared line*

succeed a *straight line,* since the association of these genera and
variants is possible whatever the circumstances; a permanent
inventory of Fashion should therefore deal only with possible
features, since the rotation of the forms of Fashion is never concerned with anything but the terms of the variant and not with
the variants themselves. However, the features excluded from the
Fashion inventory, which corresponds to the impossible syntagms, are not thereby irrecoverable, for the impossibilities of
association, if they are imperative on the scale of a given civilization, are no longer so on a larger scale: none, doubtless, is universal or eternal; a civilization other than our own could accept
the fact of transparent blouses and protruding backs, and another
language could decide that cardigans are no longer divided pieces
by definition; in other words, time can make today's excluded
associations possible in the future, time can reopen meanings
which have long since, or even always, been closed; the class of
impossible features thus forms a reservoir, but this reservoir is
no longer that of Fashion, it is, one might say, the reservoir of
history. We assume that in order to draw upon this reservoir, i.e.,
in order to make an impossible association possible, there must
be another force besides that of Fashion, since it is no longer a
matter of effecting the passage from one term to another within
a single variant, but rather of subverting taboos and definitions
which civilization has made into a veritable nature. The observation of vestimentary features thus allows us to distinguish and
structurally define three tenses: actual Fashion, potential Fashion, and history. These three tenses outline a certain logic of
clothing; the feature actualized by the year's Fashion is always
noted, and we know that in Fashion the *noted* is *obligatory,* under
penalty of incurring the condemnation attached to the *unfashionable;* potential features which participate in the reservoir of
Fashion are not noted (Fashion virtually never speaks the *unfashionable*), they form the category of the *forbidden;* finally,
impossible features (which we saw were in fact historical) are
excluded, shifted outside of the Fashion system; here again we
find a structure known to linguistics: the mark (the noted), the
absence of mark (the forbidden), and what is situated outside
the pertinent (the excluded), but the structure of clothing—
wherein lies its originality—has a diachronic consistency; it sets

actuality (Fashion) in opposition to a relatively short diachrony (the Fashion reservoir) and leaves long duration outside the system:

Structure of the feature	Example	Diachrony	Duration	Logical category
1. Genus + one term of a possible variant	This year the flared line triumphs	Actual Fashion	One year	Obligatory
2. Genus + all terms of a possible variant	Line: straight/ round/ cube, etc.	Reservoir of Fashion	Short duration	Forbidden
3. Genus + an impossible variant	Slit sleeves	Reservoir of history[8]	Long duration	Excluded

II. THE SYNTAGMATIC YIELD

12.5. Syntagmatic definition of an element: "valences"

Genera and variants may—or may not—connect with one another according to rules issuing from the world (i.e., ultimately, history); consequently, we can consider each genus, on the one hand, and each variant, on the other, as endowed with a certain associative power, which will be measured by the number of adverse elements it can connect with in order to produce a significant feature; we shall call an element's associative relations *valences* (in the chemical sense of the term); if the association is possible, the valence will be positive, if the association is excluded, the valence will be negative. Each element (genus or variant) is structurally defined by a certain number of valences: thus, the genus *color* consists of ten positive valences and twenty negative valences, and the variant of suppleness thirty-four positive valences and twenty-six negative valences.[9] Every genus, like

---

[8] We know that slit sleeves were worn in the Middle Ages.
[9] It will be recalled that the corpus being studied has revealed sixty genera and thirty variants.

every variant, is therefore defined in a certain manner by the number of its valences, for this number measures as it were its degree of exposure to meaning; in reconstituting the chart of syntagmatic links for each genus and each variant, we establish a veritable semantic file with a definitional power as certain as a lexicographic rubric, even though this file includes no allusion to the element's "meaning." Parallel to an ordinary lexicon of Fashion (*raw silk* = *summer*), we can now imagine a veritable syntagmatic lexicon which would give the detail of possible and excluded associations for each element. Thus, we would obtain charts of combinative affinities which would have definitional value:

ACCESSORY: *Possible:* Existence, mark, weight, etc.
Excluded: Form, fit, movement, etc.

ARTIFICE: *Possible:* Accessory, fastener, shirttail, etc.
Excluded: Stockings, bracelet, etc.

Such a lexicon, which could be described as structural, would have at least as much importance as its lexicographic neighbor, for it is from this lexicon that Fashion derives its meaning, i.e., its being, far more so than from a table of arbitrary and contingent signifieds whose existence is often rhetorical. We must repeat that it is at the level of these syntagmatic paradigms that the world, reality, and history invest in the signifying system: before changing their meanings, signs change their surroundings, or rather, signs change their meanings by modifying their syntagmatic relations. History, reality, and praxis cannot act directly on a sign (inasmuch as this sign, while being unmotivated, is not arbitrary), but essentially on its links. Now, for written Fashion, such a syntagmatic lexicon is within reach (since the number of genera and variants is reasonably finite): it is obviously this lexicon which should serve as the basis for that perpetual inventory of Fashion without which the spread of the models of Fashion in real society (object of the sociology of Fashion) will escape any analysis.

12.6. *Principle of syntagmatic yield*

To confront all the syntagmatic charts furnished by the inventory is to compare the semantic power of genera and variants in relation to one another; for it is obvious that a genus provided with a high number of positive valences (the *edge*, for example) has more chances of signifying than a genus for which this number is low (the *clip*, for example). We shall call the degree of an element's exposure to meaning the *syntagmatic yield*, insofar as it is measured by the number of its valences; for instance, we shall say that the opposition *long/short* has a high yield, because it can be applied to a great number of genera. We must underline the fact that we are dealing here with a structural evaluation, so to speak, and not, strictly speaking, a statistical one, even though numbers are at issue (indeed, very simple numbers: at most, it is a bookkeeping matter); what is being counted is by no means the number of real occurrences of a syntagmatic relation in the corpus under study, but statutory encounters—encounters of principle; it matters little (at least for the moment) that we find a feature like *a light blouse* a hundred times in the Fashion magazines; if weight is a rich variant, it is not because of this entirely empirical repetition,[10] but because of the high number of genera that this variant can affect.

12.7. *Richness and poverty of elements*

The richness of an element, i.e., the high number of its positive valences, by definition translates the very state of the Fashion reservoir, since Fashion draws the change in its features from variants and genera that can be associated. In the case of variants, what is possible in Fashion is rich, principally at the level of the assertion of species, of mark, of artifice, of the assertion of existence, of association, of size, and of weight, and in the case of genera, at the level of edges, pleats, fasteners, headwear, collars, ornaments, and pockets. These then are the variants of identity which possess the greatest possibilities for meaning; since these variants, which are above all qualifiers, are the least technical of all (compared for example, to the variants of measurement or continuity), we might say that the "literary" development of Fashion is structurally well supported: Fashion tends to "recite"

---

[10] The number of real occurrences is not unimportant, but it should be interpreted from the rhetorical point of view: like any obsession, it refers to the user of the language, not to the system itself: it gives information about the magazine, for example, not about Fashion.

rather than fabricate the garment. As for the genera most widely susceptible of meaning, we see that they are essentially not principal pieces but rather parts of pieces (collars or pockets) or accessory elements (pleats, fasteners, ornaments); this explains the importance Fashion gives to the "detail" in the production of meaning.[11] On the contrary, the poverty of an element (or the high number of its negative valences), corresponds to the reservoir of history, since it refers to the least probable associations, which could not be actualized without a mental or linguistic upheaval. The poorest variants are the variants of position and distribution: there is a certain topological immobility of clothing, and it is in the orientation of elements that the revolution in clothing would be most perceptible. In the poorest genera, we find secondary elements, like the side, the back, or stockings, but also elements important in Fashion's eyes, such as material or color; this apparent paradox leads us to distinguish clearly between the strength of meaning and its extent.

12.8. *Extent or strength of meaning?*

Strength and "extent" of meaning are in fact in inverse relation since the extent of an element's combinative range, while banalizing it, weakens its power of information. We find the same inverse relation when passing from the systematic to the syntagmatic yield. When the association of genera and variants is limited in extension as a result of their poverty, the variation in meaning seems to shift intensively to the systematic level, i.e., where there exists a great freedom of choice; in the case of *style*, for example, the genus's syntagmatic poverty is balanced as it were by the systematic yield of the few variants with which this genre can be associated: notably, the assertion of species and form furnishes style with a wealth of variations which explains the genus's importance in Fashion. Which leads us to distinguish clearly between meaning's extension and its strength; meaning's strength depends on the perfection of the systematic structure,[12] i.e., on the structuration and the memorability of the associative terms; meaning's extent depends on its syntagmatic yield; and since this yield, as we have seen, is ultimately historical and cultural, mean-

---

[11] Cf., below, 17.8.
[12] Cf., above, 11.7.

ing's extension translates the power of history over meaning; to borrow an example from language, the associative paradigm of the word *industry* can be responsible for the term's "precision," for its semantic luster; but the syntagmatic association *Commerce and Industry,* participating in meaning's extension, refers to a history (the expression's fortune dates from the first half of the nineteenth century). To change Fashion thus implies overcoming quite different resistances, depending on whether we attack the systematic or the syntagmatic order; if we stick to the systematic level, there is no difficulty in shifting from one paradigmatic term to another, and this is Fashion's privileged operation, in the narrow sense of the word (*long/short skirt,* depending on the year); but to modify an element's syntagmatic yield by creating a new association (for example, *a protruding back*), is inevitably to appeal to cultural and historical instance.

III. THE PERMANENT INVENTORY OF FASHION

12.9. *Typical association*

We have seen that the analysis of the system could lead to a structuration of real clothing;[13] similarly, the analysis of the syntagm can furnish elements for a study of real (or "worn") Fashion; these elements are the features of Fashion which we shall call *typical associations*. The typical association is a feature (genus • variant) whose importance is designated by the high number of its real occurrences in the corpus, i.e., in short, by the banality of the information it transmits:[14] *with/without belt, marked or unmarked waistline, round or pointed collar, long or short skirt, wide or normal shoulders, collar open or closed,* etc. All these expressions, as we know, form stereotypes which endlessly recur in the inventory that Fashion itself makes of the clothing it chooses. The typical association expresses a double economy: on the one hand, it is the result of a representative selection: Fashion chooses, among an extremely large number of features, what we could call the sensitive points of meaning: the typical association is

---

[13] Cf., above, 11.IV.
[14] We might say that any insistent repetition of a feature constitutes a typical association: it is the impression of a stereotype which is determinant.

the stage of a conceptualization, it permits an essence of Fashion to be defined by a small number of features: it is a concentrated meaning; and on the other hand, since the typical feature always includes a variant whose paradigmatic interplay remains perfectly free, it forcefully designates the site where the opposition between *fashionable* and *unfashionable* is developed, i.e., the diachronic variation of Fashion: the *long skirt* is chosen on the one hand as a total feature against other, less important features (*a wide skirt* or *a long sweater*), and on the other hand against the adverse term of its variant (*short skirt*): in the typical association, the choice of Fashion is thus simultaneously reduced and full. It is therefore the typical associations which must be observed if we want to discern, on the one hand, a certain being of Fashion (what could be called its obsessional features) and, on the other, the freedom and hence the limits of its variations (since, in signification, all freedom is *supervised*). The typical association does not have a structural value, for its determination is statistical, but it does have a practical value, and here is where it prepares a passage from written to real Fashion.

12.10. *Basic Fashion*

The body of typical associations is accessible only through a certain analysis. Yet Fashion can proceed in an immediate manner to a summary of its features and give it to its consumers to read; this formula is a kind of *digest* of triumphant Fashion (which is generally advertised Fashion), the shortened definition of synchrony; we could call this basic Fashion. Basic Fashion includes, under the name *major lines* or *tendencies*, a very small number of features, for it is essential that the formula be memorable; thus, Fashion 19— is entirely defined by the following *digest: supple blouses, long jackets, oblique backs*. The passage from one basic Fashion to another (the following year) can be made in two ways: either by keeping the same formula but permutating the terms of the variants attached to them (*long jackets* becomes *short jackets*), or by making certain features disappear and noting new ones (*long jackets* might be replaced by *belts worn high*); furthermore, the change in formula might only be partial (*skirt lengths remain unchanged from last year*). The features involved in a basic Fashion are very often called Fashion *constants;* which is to say that the relation between the formula and the rest of the inventory is nearly the same as that between a theme and its variations; basic Fashion is given as an absolutely general constraint; it is, if you will, the *form* of Fashion; the variations, constituted by the ensemble of utterances in the magazine, correspond not to an individual speech (this would be the case of a "worn," i.e., "applied" Fashion) but rather to a speech which remains entirely institutional, a kind of very broad formulary from which the user can dream of selecting a ready-made "conversation." We recognize in this thematic organization the model of real clothing grasped in its broadest historical dimension (for example, "Occidental" clothing can also be summarized by a few features), as if Fashion reproduced in a diminishing mirror, *"en abîme,"* the relations of the basic inspiration or permanent type (*basic pattern*) postulated by Kroeber apropos of epochs of clothing.[15]

12.11. *Permanent inventory of Fashion*

Thus, Fashion itself makes a selection among its synchronic features, either in a mechanical manner at the level of typical associations or in a reflexive manner at the level of each basic fashion. This selection is empirical (although it is tributary to the system in its entirety), so, naturally, it introduces a real inventory of Fashion (and no longer one of principle). This inventory has to be double: dealing with the written corpus on the one hand and real (actually worn) clothing on the other. The inventory of written clothing would consist of recording and supervising each year's typical associations and the formulas of basic Fashion, in order to observe the variations they present from one year to the next; thus, after a few years, we could have a precise idea of Fashion's diachrony and the diachronic system would finally be within reach.[16] In another direction, each inventory of written Fashion should be confronted with an inventory of real clothing, attempting to determine if the features affirmed in the typical associations and the basic formula are discernible in the clothing women actually wear, according to what adaptations, omissions,

---

[15] A. L. Kroeber, quoted by J. Stoetzel (*Psychologie sociale*, p. 247). Cf. also Claude Lévi-Strauss, *The Savage Mind.*

[16] The basic formula obviously recalls the essential features of women's clothing dealt with by Kroeber in his diachronic study; the inventory suggested here deals with Fashions whose diachrony is weak.

and contraventions; the confrontation of these two inventories should permit us to grasp very precisely the speed of dissemination of the models for Fashion, provided the real inventory be taken in different regions and milieux.

IV. Conclusion

12.12. *Structural classification of genera and variants*

In order to complete this inventory of the vestimentary signifier, we must return to the methodological importance of the syntagm. We have seen that the classification of genera and variants hitherto adopted was not structurally founded, since it was an alphabetical classification in the case of the genera, and a notional classification in the case of the variants.[17] The syntagmatic charts established for each genus and each variant should allow us to approach a structural classification of elements which was hitherto premature. We can now envision three principles of classification, of differing usefulness. The first consists of classifying the ensemble of genera from the viewpoint of a single variant and vice versa; for example, we shall group all the genera which are associated positively with the variant of existence into a first class (positive), and those that cannot be associated with it into a second class (negative): in short, what we are concerned with is a classification internal to each syntagmatic chart and as it results from a simple reading of these charts; though much broken up, since it must be renewed with each chart, such a classification can be useful if we ever intend to make an exhaustive study (in the form of a monograph) of the diachronic field of a genus or of a variant, for instance: the transparence of clothing, or the historical structure of the blouse.[18] The second principle of classification, based upon the strictly functional yield, consists of considering all elements having the same number and the same kind of valences (positive or negative) as participating in a single class; isometric zones of syntagmatic yield would thus be re-

---

[17] Cf., above, 8.7 and 9.1.

[18] This assumes a translation from written clothing to real clothing which has been outlined in 11.IV, unless we limit ourselves to making the study concern the "poetics" of clothing (cf., below, chap. 17).

vealed, and these would be useful if we wanted to undertake a structural history of clothing, since we then could follow the stability or lability of each of these zones down through time. Finally, concerning the genera and assuming we keep the order of variants adopted here, by isolating sets of genera with the same valences from chart to chart, we would obtain extremely coherent groups of genera since such genera lend themselves to a certain group of variants in the same manner; for instance, the division-mobility-closure-attachment group (whose particularly structured character has been discussed[19]); with regard to this group, the genera *stockings, crown, clip, seam,* and *necktie* (among others) participate in a single class, since none of them can be associated with any of the four variants: for this group of genera, a community of rejections corresponds to the affinity between variants. Such a classification would have the advantage of presenting an ordered table of possibilities and impossibilities of association; and by subtly specifying the contingent reasons (deriving from physical, moral, or aesthetic constraints) for these possibilities and impossibilities, we could discern certain cultural affinities between genera of the same group.[20]

---

[19] Cf., above, 9.20.
[20] For example: "parasite" genera, "limit" genera, "filiform" genera, etc.

2. *Structure of the Signified*

13

The Semantic Units

"A sweater for chilly autumn evenings during a weekend in the country."

I. WORLDLY SIGNIFIED AND FASHION SIGNIFIED

13.1. *Difference between A ensembles and B ensembles: isology*

Before studying the signified of the vestimentary code, we must recall[1] that the utterances of signification are of two kinds: those in which the signifier refers to an explicit and worldly signified (*A* ensembles: *raw silk* ≡ *summer*), and those in which the signifier refers in a total manner to an implicit signified, which is the Fashion of studied synchrony (*B* ensembles: *a short bolero, fitted at the waist* ≡ [*Fashion*]). The difference between the two ensembles derives from the mode of the signified's appearance (we have seen that the structure of the signifier was the same in both cases: it is always the written garment); in *A* ensembles, contrary to what happens in language, the signified has its own proper expression (*summer, weekend, promenade*); this expression is most likely formed from the same substance as that of the signifier, since in both it is a matter of words; but these words are not the same; in the case of the signifier, they partake of the lexicon of clothing, and in the case of the signified, they partake of the lexicon of the "world"; here, therefore, we are free to deal with the signified apart from the signifier and submit it to a test of structuration, since it is relayed by language; on the contrary,

---

[1] Cf., above, 2.3 and 4.

in *B* ensembles, the signified (Fashion) is given at the same time as the signifier; it generally does not possess any expression of its own; in its *B* ensembles, written Fashion coincides with the linguistic model which gives its signifieds only "within" its signifiers; we could say that, in such systems, the signifier and the signified are isological, since they are "spoken" simultaneously; isology usually renders the structuration of signifieds very difficult, since they cannot be "unstuck" from their signifiers (unless we resort to a metalanguage), as the difficulties of structural semantics doubtless prove;[2] but even in the case of *B* ensembles, the Fashion system is not that of language; in language there is plurality of signifieds; in Fashion, each time there is isology, it is always a matter of the same signified: the year's Fashion, and all the signifiers of the *B* ensembles (vestimentary features), are, in short, merely metaphorical forms. It follows that the signified of the *B* ensembles escapes all structuration. It is only the signified of *A* ensembles (worldly and explicit signifieds) that we must try to structure.

II. THE SEMANTIC UNITS

13.2. *Semantic units and lexical units*

In order to structure the signifieds of *A* ensembles (henceforth, the only ones in question), it is obvious that we must segment them into irreducible units. On the one hand, these units will be *semantic*[3] since they will result from a segmentation of content; but on the other hand—as was the case with the signifier—they can be reached only through a system, language, which has its own form of expression and content: *a weekend in the country* is clearly the signified of a vestimentary sign whose signifier is given further on (*a thick wool sweater*), but it is also the signi-

---

[2] Difficulties underlined by all syntheses of the question (Hjelmslev, Guiraud, Mounin, Pottier, Prieto).

[3] According to the distinction made by A. J. Greimas which will henceforth be adopted ("Problèmes de la description," *Cahiers de Lexicologie*, 1, p. 48), *semantic* will be reserved for the level of content and *semiology* for the level of expression: the distinction here is not only valid but necessary, since there is an absence of isology in *A* ensembles.

fier (sentence) of a linguistic *proposition*. The semantic units will thus be verbal, but nothing requires that they always have the dimensions of the word (or moneme): technically speaking, they do not have to coincide with lexical units. And as it is their vestimentary value which interests the system of Fashion, and not their lexical value, we need not bother with their terminological meaning: *weekend* certainly does have a meaning (the final, leisure-time portion of the week), but we can abstract this meaning from the word in order to see in it only what is signified by *sweater*. This distinction is an important one, for it makes it possible to foresee that all ideological classifications of semantic units (by conceptual affinities[4]) must be challenged, unless this classification coincides with a structural classification stemming from the analysis of the vestimentary code itself.

13.3. *Significant units and semantic units*

In language, certain units of the signified coincide perfectly with certain units of the signifier, since there is isology: by segmenting an utterance of the signifier into minimal units (significant units), we thereby define units of concomitant signifieds.[5] But in Fashion the control of the signifier cannot be as determinant; in fact, combinations of matrices (and not one matrix alone) often include a single signified which cannot be terminologically decomposed (reduced to a single word): the unit of the signifier (the matrix V.S.O.) cannot designate the semantic unit with any certainty. In fact, in the Fashion system it is the unit of relation (i.e., of signification) which is constraining: a complete signified corresponds to a complete signifier;[6] in *a thick wool sweater = an autumn weekend in the country*, there is no coded correspondence between the components of the signifier and those of the signified: the sweater does not particularly refer to the weekend, the wool to autumn, and its thickness to the country, for even if there is a certain affinity between the coolness of autumn in the

---

4 For example, Von Wartburg and Hallig's classification, already cited.

5 These units of signifieds, however, are not necessarily minimal, since the majority of lexemes can be decomposed into semes.

6 This is something like what happens in language in the case of the sentence (cf. Martinet, "Réflexions sur la phrase," in *Language and Society*, pp. 113–18).

country and the warmth of wool, this affinity remains general and revocable besides, since the lexicon of Fashion changes each year: elsewhere, *wool* might signify *spring on the Riviera.*[7] Thus, we are unable to make the minimal units of the signifier and the minimal units of the signified correspond with one another in a stable manner; meaning can preside over the determination of meaning only at the level of total signification: the utterance of the signified has to be segmented under the control of the general signifier (the utterance of the signifier), not under that of its smaller units. This general control would be inoperative in Fashion whenever we encountered only integrally new or integrally repeated signifieds: how could what is unique or identical each time it is encountered be segmented? But this is not the case: the majority of utterances of the signified combine elements which are already known because we have come across them, variously combined, in other utterances; utterances such as *a weekend in the country, country vacations, society weekend, society vacations,* are all reducible because they are made up of common and, consequently, mobile elements: because *weekend, city, vacation,* and *country* are found in (partially) different utterances, we are justified in constituting these expressions into semantic units for the purpose of forming a true combinatory; for, by changing utterance, each of these units changes its total signifier, and it is clearly the sign's commutation which permits them to be repeated; all we must do, therefore, in order to establish an inventory of semantic units within the limits of the corpus under study, is to submit the utterances of the signified to this new commutation test.

13.4. *Usual units and original units*

Mobile (i.e., repeated) units do not, however, exhaust the totality of all utterances of the signified; certain utterances or certain fragments of utterances are constituted by unique notations, at least on the scale of the corpus; these are, one might say, *hapax legomena;* these *hapax* are themselves also semantic units, for they are attached to a total signifier and participate in meaning.

---

[7] Cf., below, on the sign (15.6).

Thus, we shall have two kinds of semantic units, one mobile and repeated (we shall call these *usual units*), the other constituted by utterances or residues of utterances which do not lend themselves to repetition (we shall call these *original units*). We can distinguish four ways in which usual and original units are encountered: (1) A usual unit can constitute an utterance all by itself (*for summer*). (2) An utterance can be formed exclusively of usual units (*summer evenings in the country*). (3) The utterance can combine usual units and an original unit (vacation—winter—in Tahiti). (4) The utterance can be constituted in its entirety by one original unit (it cannot be decomposed by definition), whatever its rhetorical amplitude (*for a spectacular entry at that little bistro you always go to*). We cannot assure this distinction of a stable content, since enlarging the corpus would perhaps be sufficient to transform an original unit into an ordinary unit, as soon as we find it in a combined form; moreover, it has no effect on the structure of the utterances: the modes of combination are the same for all units: this distinction is nonetheless necessary because the usual units do not come from the same "world" as the original units.

13.5. *Usual units*

Usual units (*afternoon, evening, spring, cocktails, shopping*, etc.) cover notions and uses which belong to the real social world: seasons, schedules, holidays, work: even if these realities are often present from a standpoint too luxurious not to be somewhat unreal, they are the basis for institutions, protocols, even laws (in the notion of a legal holiday), which depend on a genuine social praxis. Thus, we can assume that the usual semantic units of written clothing in essence designate the very functions of real (actually worn) clothing; by its usual units, Fashion communicates with reality, even if it stamps this reality with a constantly festive and euphoric mark; in short, the ensemble of written clothing's usual units would be the photogenic version of the real functions of the clothing actually worn. The quite practical origin of usual units explains why they correspond so readily, for the most part, to lexical units (*weekend, shopping, theater*), though structurally they are not required to do so: the word, in the ordinary sense of the term, is in fact a powerful condensation of a social use:[8] its stereotypic nature corresponds to the institutional character of the circumstances it sums up.

13.6. *Original units*

Original units (*to accompany the children to school*) usually belong to written clothing exclusively, and there is little chance of their having any warrant in social reality, at least in its institutional form; however, this is not a fixed rule, and nothing prevents an original unit from becoming a usual unit; in *vacation in Tahiti*, Tahiti is a *hapax*, but in order for this place-name to become a usual vestimentary signified, it would suffice that the current vogue, travel agencies, and, above all, a rise in the standard of living make Tahiti a resort as institutionalized as the Riviera. Until that point, the original unit is usually an indication of utopia; it refers to a dream world which has the entirely oneiric precision of complex, evocative, rare, and unforgettable contingencies (*just the two of you walking along the docks of Calais*); narrowly tributary to the Fashion magazine's discourse, original units participate quite readily in the rhetorical system of the utterance; rarely do they correspond to simple lexical units, but, on the contrary, demand to be developed phraseologically;[9] in reality, these units are rarely conceptual; they tend, like all dreams, to combine with the structure of a genuine narrative (*Living 20 km. from a large city, I have to take the train three times a week*, etc.). Since each original unit is "*hapax*" by definition, it carries a stronger message than usual units do;[10] despite their originality (i.e., in informational terms, their absolutely unforeseen nature), they are perfectly intelligible since they are transmitted through the relay of language and since the *hapax* exists at the level of the vestimentary code, not at the level of the linguistic code. Nevertheless, we can list them in order by

---

[8] We know that *the word* is a notion which has been questioned by many linguists, and this problematics is no doubt justified on the structural plane; but the word also has a sociological reality; it is an effect and a social power; furthermore, it is often at this very moment that it becomes connoted.

[9] *Tahiti*, for example, is developed rhetorically in the phrase *love and dreams in Tahiti*.

[10] A. Martinet, *Elements*, 6.10.

reason of their ordinarily phraseological nature (it would be easier to classify them by their rhetorical signifieds).

III. STRUCTURE OF THE SEMANTIC UNIT

13.7. *The problem of "primitives"*

In principle, nothing prevents us from examining whether it is possible to decompose the usual unit into smaller elements (provided they are vestimentarily significant); this would obviously amount to going beyond the word (for usual units easily assume the dimension of a word) and to distinguishing several interchangeable parts in the signified which this word represents; this attempt at decomposing the word-as-signified is well known to linguistics: it is the problem of "primitives" (the notion is found in Leibnitz), which has been raised most notably by Hjelmslev, Sorensen, Prieto,[11] Pottier, and Greimas; the word *mare*, though by itself constituting a minimal and indecomposable signifier (short of passing to the second articulation), covers two units of meaning: "horse" and "female," whose mobility is demonstrated by the commutation test (*"pig"* • *"female"* = /sow/). In the same manner, we could define /lunch/ as a semantic combination of action ("eating") and temporality ("at midday"); but this would be a purely linguistic analysis; vestimentary commutation does not permit us to go this far; certainly, it attests to a temporal primitive (*noon*), because there may be a garment for that hour; but the other primitive suggested by linguistic analysis (*eating*) has no vestimentary sanction: nowhere is there a garment for *eating*, and the decomposition of *lunch* cannot be fully justified: hence, *lunch* is the last unit we can attain, we cannot go any further: usual units are clearly the smallest semantic units afforded to the analysis of the worldly signified; this is to be expected: the Fashion system is inevitably less sophisticated than that of language, its combinatory is less refined, and it is one of the functions of semiological analysis as it was founded, "between words and things," at the level of the terminological or pseudo-real code, to

---

[11] Cf. G. Mounin, "Les analyses sémantiques," in *Cahiers de l'Institut de Science Economique Appliquée*, March 1962.

suggest that there exist systems of meaning within language, but possessing larger units and a less flexible combinatory.

13.8. *The AUT relation*

Given these units, we can still try to constitute them into lists of pertinent oppositions. We shall be helped here, once again, by the paradigms furnished by the magazine itself, each time it utters what we have already called, apropos of the signifier (for they are obviously the same examples), a double concomitant variation;[12] in *striped flannel or polka-dot twill, depending on whether for morning or evening*, it is asserted, by the variation of the signifier itself, that between "evening" and "morning" there is a pertinent opposition and that these two terms are part of the same semantic paradigm; they constitute, one might say, a fragment of system extended on the syntagmatic level; on this level, the relation which unites them is that of exclusive disjunction: we shall call this very particular relation (since it syntagmatically combines the terms of one and the same system) the AUT relation.[13] By its alternative nature (either . . . or else), AUT is, so to speak, the syntagmatic relation of the system or the specific relation of signification.[14]

13.9. *The problem of the semantic mark*

It remains to discover whether these pertinent oppositions of signifieds can be reduced to the pair *marked/unmarked*, as is the case with phonological oppositions (but not, as we have seen, with all vestimentary oppositions[15]), i.e., whether one of the terms of the opposition possesses a characteristic of which the other is deprived. In order for this reduction to be possible, there would have to be a rigorous correspondence between the structure of the vestimentary signifier and that of the worldly signified; for

---

12 Cf., above, 5.3.

13 As opposed to the VEL relation (cf. following chapter); we must resort to Latin vocables, since in French OU is both inclusive and exclusive.

14 Here are a few pairs of alternative terms furnished by the corpus under study: *sport/dressy; day/night; evening/morning; savage/civilized; classical/fantasy; practical/sophisticated; severe/light; reserved/gay; discreet/joyous; Islands/Ocean*: this opposition covers the climatic contrast between the warmth of the Mediterranean ("Island") and the coldness of the Atlantic ("Ocean").

15 Cf., above, 11.II.

example, in order for "dressy" to be marked in relation to "sport," the dressy garment would have to possess a mark, one specifically absent from the sport garment: this is obviously not the case: the "dressy" garment may sometimes be more "charged," sometimes less, than the sport garment. The oppositions of signifieds, whenever the magazine makes it possible to pick them out, thus remain equipollent oppositions; it is impossible to formalize their content, i.e., to transform the contradictory relation into a differential relation.[16] Therefore, distinctive analysis appears powerless to determine a classification *a minimo* of semantic units, solely under the sanction of the vestimentary code: usual units remain whole, and henceforth it is with respect to their grouping that we must pursue the analysis of the signified.

---

[16] In linguistics, the decomposition of the signified into marked and unmarked elements remains problematic. Cf., however, A. Martinet on the masculine and feminine, "Linguistique structurale et grammaire comparée," in *Travaux de l'Institut Linguistique,* Paris, Klincksieck, 1956, I, p. 10.

14

Combinations and Neutralizations

"Coquettish without coquetry."

I. THE COMBINATION OF SIGNIFIEDS

14.1. *Syntax of semantic units*

The usual semantic unit (henceforth the subject of our attention) is not only mobile (it can be found inserted into different utterances) but also sufficient: it can form an utterance of the signifier by itself (*raw silk* ≡ *summer*). This means that the syntax of semantic units is never anything but a combination:[1] a signified never requires another signified, it is always a matter of simple parataxis; the linguistic form of this parataxis must not create an illusion: the words can be combined with syntactic (and not paratactic) elements on the level of language (prepositions, conjunctions), but the semantic units they relay are purely combinatory (*evenings • autumn • weekend • country* ≡ *for autumn evenings during a weekend in the country*). The relation of combination can be filled, however, in two different ways: either we accumulate units whose meaning is complementary (*this raw silk dress for Paris in summer*), or we enumerate the possible signifieds of the same signifier (*a sweater for town or country*); all the

---

[1] Original units can also be submitted to combination (with usual units); but their singularity prevents us from pursuing the analysis as we are doing with the usual units: they can be recognized, not classified.

combinations of semantic units brought together in a single utterance result in one of these two cases; we shall call the first type of combination the ET relation, and the second the VEL relation.

14.2. *The ET relation*

The ET relation is cumulative; it establishes a relation of real complementarity (and not formal, as in the case of VEL) between a certain number of signifieds which it amalgamates in a unique, actual, contingent, and experienced situation (*in Paris, in summer*). The phraseology of this relation is varied, constituted by all the syntactic forms of determination: epithetical adjectives (*springtime vacation*), substantives as complements (*summer nights*), circumstantial determinants (*Paris summers; a promenade on the pier*[2]). How far can the power of the ET relation extend? Its field of extension is quite vast; at first sight, we might believe that it can unite only affinitive signifieds, or at least not contradictory ones, since they must refer to situations or states that can be actualized simultaneously: the weekend is normally compatible with spring, and it is true that affinity is the common rule in the ET relation;[3] the relation can also, however, juxtapose units of apparently contradictory meanings (*audacious and discreet*); here we must simply recall that the validity of such relations does not depend on rational criteria, but only on formal conditions: it suffices that these semantic units be governed by a single signifier; this is why it should not be surprising that the field of application of the ET relation is practically total, and that it ranges from pure redundance (*sober and discreet*) to unmistakable paradox (*audacious and discreet*). ET is the relation of actuality; it permits the notation of a particular contingency to be drawn from a general reservoir of usual functions; through simple combinatory interplay, Fashion can produce rare signifieds of rich and personal appearance, though starting from

---

[2] The variation is terminological when it cannot be linguistically further reduced (*Paris summers*); it is rhetorical when it presents the unit in a literary and metaphorical form (i.e., carrying a certain connotation): *springtime* is, one might say, more "spring" than *spring;* the pier is a metaphor for the ocean, a usual unit generally cited under the species of three places-as-climates: *beach* (≡ sun), *pier* (≡ wind), *harbor* (≡ rain).

[3] Other affinitive signifieds: *classic and easy to wear, young and pert, gay and practical, young and feminine, simple and practical, casual and easy, distinguished and Parisian, supple and free-and-easy.*

elements which are poor and common; this relation thus approaches a sort of *hic et nunc* of the person and the world, and seems to propose a garment for complex circumstances and original temperaments; furthermore, when the combinatory includes original units, ET permits the representation of a utopian world where everything is possible, *the weekend in Tahiti* as well as *a rigorous suppleness:* thanks to ET, the garment's meanings can appear from unimaginable horizons and designate unique, irreversible uses; the garment thus becomes a pure event: preserved from all generalization and all repetition (even though starting from repeated elements), the vestimentary signified then suggests the encounter with a moment so rich that it can be expressed only through the accumulation of units none of which destroys the other, contradictory though they may be. This is why we might say that ET is the relation of the experienced, even if imaginary.

14.3. *The VEL relation*

The VEL relation is simultaneously disjunctive and inclusive (as opposed to AUT, which is disjunctive and exclusive): disjunctive because the units it links cannot be actualized at the same time, inclusive because they belong to a single class, which is coextensive with them and which is implicitly the garment's real total signified: in *a sweater for town or country*, there is an alternative of actuality between the city and the country, for we cannot be in both places at the same time; the sweater, however, stands intemporally, or at least successively, for both, and consequently refers to a unique class, one which includes city and country at the same time (even if this class is not named by the language). Of course, the relation here is inclusive, not for reasons inherent in the meaning of its terms, but uniquely because it is established under the eyes, one might say, of a single vestimentary signifier: the relation between city and country is one of equivalence, or better still, of indifference, *from the point of view of the sweater;*[4] if, in fact, the two semantic units were no longer governed by one but rather by two signifiers, the relation would shift from

---

[4] This is why VEL can be nicely expressed through the conjunction *and: a sweater for the sea and the mountains.* On *and/or*, cf. R. Jakobson, *Essais*, p. 82.

inclusive to exclusive, it would pass from VEL to AUT (*sweater or blouse depending on whether for country or city*); here we would have *two* signs. What is the psychological function of VEL? As we have seen, the ET relation actualizes possibilities, however distant from one another they may appear to be (*audacious and discreet*); which is in fact to say that it puts an end to the possible and converts it into the real, and it is for this reason that it is clearly the relation of the experienced, even if utopian. The VEL relation, on the contrary, actualizes nothing and grants to the often contradictory terms it unites their character as possible; the garment to which it refers is a rather general one, not in order to satisfy a rare and intense function, but to saturate several functions successively, each one of which thus remains open to possibility; thereby, contrary to ET, which implies a garment of the moment, VEL supposes a duration, during which the garment will be able to pass through a certain number of meanings, without ever losing the singularity of the sign; we therefore witness a curious reversal: the garment to which the ET relation refers tends toward the utopian to the very extent that its signified has all the appearances of reality (it is truly rare): it is truly the Fashion garment, all the more imaginary because it seems to be detailed:[5] it is as natural to dream of a sweater *for autumn evenings, a weekend in the country, if you are carefree and serious,* as it is difficult really to possess it, i.e., economically; conversely, VEL implies a real garment to the very extent that its signified is only possible; each time the magazine uses the VEL relation, we can be sure that it is tempering its utopia and aiming at an actual reader: a garment *for the sea or the mountains* (VEL) is more probable than a garment for *a weekend at the seashore* (ET). And as it is impossible to equalize remote functions (*city and country, sea and mountains*) without rising to a general concept which abolishes the differences between them, VEL implies a certain intellectualization of the world: the same outfit cannot be worn ("indifferently") to the theater and to a nightclub, without implicitly referring to the more abstract idea of a nocturnal outing: as opposed to the ET relation, which is the

---

[5] The "detail" is a fundamental element of the imagination; how many theories of aesthetics there are which are fabulous because they are precise.

relation of the experienced imaginary, VEL is the relation of the intelligible real.[6]

II. THE NEUTRALIZATION OF THE SIGNIFIED

14.4. *Neutralization*

Since all semantic units can be combined either by ET or by VEL, without regard to the logical resistance of certain paradoxes (*coquettish without coquetry*) or certain pleonasms (*sober and discreet*), provided they are placed under the sanction of a single signifier, it would be futile to try to establish syntagmatic charts for the signified,[7] i.e., to enumerate for each unit the complementary units with which it can be combined: in principle, no association is excluded. But as the syntagmatic development of terms ordinarily placed in pertinent opposition (*"weekend"*/ *"week"*) inevitably entails the elimination of this pertinence (*a garment for the week as well as for the weekend*), combinations of semantic units under the control of a single signifier correspond to the phenomenon of neutralization already described apropos of the signifier,[8] and it is by neutralization that the analysis of semantic units must be pursued. We have seen that the AUT relation (*striped flannel or polka-dot twill, depending on whether for morning or evening*) was the relation of pertinent distinction or signification; in such utterances, *morning and evening* are the two alternative terms of a single system; in order for this opposition to be neutralized, it suffices that the two terms no longer be governed by two signifiers (*striped flannel/polka-dot twill*), but rather by a single one (for example: *striped flannel for morning or evening*); in other words, any transition from AUT to ET or to VEL constitutes the neutralization of a pertinent opposition whose terms, fossilized as it were, are found in the utterance of the signified as semantic units simply combined: we see here that what in linguistics is called the neutralizing context (or domi-

---

[6] Of course ET and VEL can be found in the same utterance:

\ this sweater ≡ a weekend for sports or high society /

1   ET   (2   VEL   3)

[7] Cf., above, 12.II.
[8] Cf., above, 11.III.

nance) is formed by the very singularity of the vestimentary signifier.[9]

14.5. *Arch-semantemes, functives and functions*

Thus units elsewhere opposed in a distinctive manner (*afternoon/ morning, casual/formal*) are sometimes subject, under the dominance of a single signifier, to a neutralization which dissolves them (ET) or equalizes them (VEL); but by being identified with or undifferentiated from each other, these units inevitably engender a second semantic class, which subsumes them: sometimes this is a circumstance of use general enough to cover the casual and the formal simultaneously, sometimes it is a temporal unit coextensive with afternoon and morning (day, for example); this new class, or this syncretic signified, is, *mutatis mutandis,* the equivalent of the arch-phoneme produced by phonological neutralization or of the arch-vesteme produced by vestimentary neutralization;[10] we could call it an arch-semanteme; we shall limit ourselves to the term *function,* which better accounts for the convergent movement of neutralization, since the terms a function "heads" are *functives;* often we possess a general name for this function or combination of functions; thus, *morning and afternoon* are the functives of the function *day;* but there are also times when the function is not sanctioned by any vocable of the language; there is no word in French to designate a concept coextensive with both casual and formal; the function is then defective on the terminological level, but this does not prevent it from being "full" on the level of the vestimentary code, since it derives its validity not from the language but from the singularity of the signifier;[11] hence, whether the function is named or not, a functional cell composed of a function and its functives can always be separated from a neutralized utterance:

(day)	(O)
(morning) (afternoon)	(casual) (formal)

---

[9] On the extension of neutralization to the lexicon and to morphology, cf. inquiry instigated by A. Martinet (*Travaux de l'Institut Linguistique, II*).

[10] Cf., above, 11.9.

[11] Terminologically defective functions primarily concern characterological, psychological, and aesthetic signifieds; in short, an ideological order subject to the notion of opposites.

14.6. *The pathway of meaning*

Once constituted by the neutralization of its terms or functives, each function obviously draws its meaning from its opposition to a new, virtual term, it too belonging to the system (even if it is not named by language), for all meaning is engendered out of an opposition; in order for *day* to possess a vestimentary meaning, it must itself be the simple functive of a potential function, it must be part of a new paradigm; for example, that of *day/night*. And as each function can become a functive,[12] a system of neutralization is thus constructed through the ensemble of Fashion signifieds, a system somewhat resembling a pyramid whose base would be formed by a great number of pertinent oppositions (*morning/afternoon; summer/winter/spring/autumn; city/country/mountains; casual/formal; audacious/discreet;*[13] etc.), while at the summit we would now find only a few oppositions (*day/night outdoors/indoors*); between the base and the summit, an entire scale of gradual neutralizations, or, one might say, intermediary cells, here functives, there functions, depending on whether there is the sanction of a double or a simple signifier. All transitions from AUT to VEL or ET are, in short, merely moments of a constant movement which drives the semantic units of Fashion to destroy their distinction in a superior state, to lose particular meanings in an increasingly general meaning. Naturally, at the level of the utterances themselves, this movement is perfectly reversible: on the one hand, pairs (or groups) of functives, drawn into the function, are merely devitalized fossil oppositions, endowed with only a sort of rhetorical existence, insofar as it is a matter of parading a certain literary intention through a play of antitheses (*the fabric for town and country*); and on the other hand, Fashion can always reconvert VEL or ET into AUT, can return from *day* to the opposition between *afternoon and morning,* by doubling the signifier. Hence, every

---

[12] Certain ensembles of the general lexicon of a language can be described in terms of functives and functions:

family

children   parents

son   daughter   father mother

[13] It is clear that the oppositions of signifieds are far from being entirely binary.

function is a confusion (ET) or an indifferentiation (VEL) which is unstable, reversible, strewn with "witness-terms"; any homogeneous series of neutralizations, from particular basic oppositions to the general function into which they are all absorbed, could be called the *pathway* of meaning. In Fashion, the movement of neutralization is so powerful that it allows only a few rare pathways to subsist, i.e., a few total meanings. These pathways generally correspond to known categories: temporality, place, climate; in the case of temporality, for example, the pathway includes intermediary functives like "morning," "evening," "afternoon," "night," absorbed into a final function: "any time";[14] the same is true for place ("wherever you go") or climate ("all-weather pants").

14.7. *The universal garment*

We might conceive of a moment when these different pathways come to a stop: when their terminal functions enter into a final opposition with each other: *"any time"/"wherever you go"/"all-weather"/"all-purpose."* However, even at the summit of the pyramid, it is possible for functions to be neutralized. We can already give one and the same vestimentary signifier to the semantic units of *day* and to those of *year: a little jersey dress worn all year long, from morning till night.* We can still combine the particular functives of one pathway with either the terminal function of another pathway (*gingham, for the weekend, for vacation, and for the whole family*) or the terminal functions of several pathways (*for all ages, for any occasion, and for all tastes*). What is more, the magazine can even neutralize these ultimate functions and produce a total pathway which then includes all the possible meanings of the garment: an *all-purpose* garment, a garment which *suits all occasions.* The unit of the signifier (*this garment*) then refers to a universal signified: the garment signifies *everything* at once. This ultimate neutralization does posit a double paradox. First, a paradox of content: it may appear surprising to see Fashion dealing with a universal garment, usually known only in the most disinherited societies, where, by force of poverty, people own no more than a single garment; but between the gar-

---

14 *"A cape for any time."*

ment of misery and the garment of Fashion there is (to speak here only in terms of structure) a fundamental difference: the former is merely an index, that of absolute misery; the latter is a sign, that of a sovereign domination over *all* uses; for Fashion, to gather the totality of its possible functions within a single garment is in no way to erase differences, but on the contrary to assert that the unique garment miraculously adapts itself to each of its uses in order to signify each of them at the faintest call; here the universal is not a suppression at all, but an addition of particularities; it is the field of an infinite freedom; functions prior to the final neutralization thus remain implicitly present like so many "roles" a unique garment can play: strictly speaking, an all-purpose outfit does not refer to a difference in uses, but to their equivalence, i.e., surreptitiously, to their distinctiveness. This leads to the second paradox (this one formal) of the universal garment. If meaning is possible only within a difference, then the universal, in order to signify, must be set in opposition to some other function, which is, it seems, a contradiction in terms, since the universal absorbs all the garment's possible uses. But in fact, from the point of view of Fashion, the universal remains one meaning among others (just as in reality an all-purpose garment hangs in the same closet with other garments with specific uses); having reached the uppermost line of the last oppositions, the universal is integrated with them—it does not dominate them; it is one of the terminal functions, along with time, place, and occupation; formally, it does not close the general system of semantic oppositions, it completes it, as a zero degree completes a polar paradigm.[15] In other words, there is distortion here between the content of the universal signified and its form: formally, the universal is merely a functive, for the same reason as and on the same line as the last functions of the main path-

---

[15] We can distribute the principal pathways in a table of regularly constituted oppositions:

1	2	mixed	neutral
at home work city sport day etc.	going out holiday nature classic year	all-purpose	a day without plans

ways; beyond this line, there are no more oppositions, hence no more meaning: signification stops (this, no doubt, is the case with the garment of misery): the pyramid of meaning is a truncated pyramid.[16]

14.8. *Why neutralization?*

This neutralization which incessantly torments its body of signifieds renders every Fashion lexicon illusory; no sure sign corresponds to the signifieds *morning* and *evening*, since they can sometimes have distinct signifiers, sometimes a single signifier; everything happens as if the Fashion lexicon were fake, composed finally of a single series of synonyms (or, we might say, of one immense metaphor). Yet this lexicon seems to exist, and this is the paradox of Fashion. At the level of each utterance, there is an appearance of full meaning, flannel seems to be forever attached to morning, twill to the evening; what is read, received, is an apparently complete sign, endowed with persistence and discretion; thus, on the level of its syntagm, which is that of reading, written Fashion seems to refer to an organized body of signifieds, in short, to a strongly institutionalized, if not even naturalized world. But as soon as we try to infer from the syntagm to the system of signifieds, this system eludes us: twill no longer signifies anything, and it is flannel which begins to signify evening (*in flannel for evening and morning*), i.e., to speak in terms of substance the opposite of what it just signified. From the syntagm to the system, the signifieds of Fashion thus seem the object of a magic trick, whose secret we must now discover. In all signifying structures, the system is an ordered reservoir of signs and thereby implies the mobilization of a certain tense: the system is a *memory;* to pass from the syntagm to the system is to restore fragments of substance to a permanence, to a duration; conversely, to pass from the system to the syntagm is, we might say, to actualize a memory. Now, as we have seen, the system of Fashion's signifieds, under the effect of neutralizations which endlessly displace its internal structure, is an unstable system. By shifting from a strong syntagm to a weak system, what Fashion

---

[16] Here are a few headings for pathways, as uttered by Fashion magazines: *the entire family; all day, even in the evening; city and sea, mountains and countryside; any beach, not just the Riviera; all ages; rain or shine,* etc.

loses is therefore the memory of its signs. Everything happens as if Fashion were preparing, on the level of its utterances, strong, clear, durable signs, but, by entrusting them to a fickle memory, forgetting them immediately. Herein lies the entire paradox of Fashion: strong on the level of the moment, signification tends to break down on the level of duration; nevertheless, it does not break down completely: it retreats. This means that Fashion actually possesses a double regime of signifieds: varied, particular signifieds, a rich world full of times, places, circumstances, and characteristics, distinct on the level of the syntagm; and a few rare signifieds, marked by a strong "generality," on the level of the system. The syncretism of Fashion's signifieds thus appears as a dialectical movement; this movement permits Fashion to represent (but not truly to signify) an apparently rich world through a simple system. But above all, if Fashion so easily admits the neutralization of its signifieds, at the risk of making its lexicon lose all rigor, it is doubtless because the final meaning of the utterance is not on the level of the vestimentary code (even in its terminological version) but rather on the level of the rhetorical system; now, even in the case of A ensembles (whose signifieds we have just analyzed), the first of the two rhetorical systems these ensembles consist of[17] has for its general signified: Fashion itself: it is ultimately of little importance that flannel signifies morning or evening equally, since the sign thus constituted has Fashion for its true signified.

---

[17] Cf., above, 3.7.

3. Structure of the Sign

15

The Vestimentary Sign

"The famous little suit that looks like a suit."

I. DEFINITION

15.1. *Syntactic character of the vestimentary sign*

The sign is the union of the signifier and the signified. This union, since it is classic in linguistics, should be examined from the point of view of its arbitrariness and its motivation, i.e., its double basis, social and natural. But first it must be recalled that the unit of the vestimentary sign (i.e., of the sign of the vestimentary code, divested of its rhetorical apparatus) is defined by the singularity of the signifying relation, not by the singularity of either the signifier or the signified;[1] in other words, though reduced to the unit, the vestimentary sign can include several fragments of signifiers (combinations of matrices and elements of the matrix itself) and several fragments of signifieds (combinations of semantic units). Therefore, we must not try to make any particular fragment of the signifier correspond to any other particular fragment of the signified; we can certainly assume that in *cardigan with an open collar* ≡ *casual*, it is the opening (of the collar) which has some affinity with casualness;[2] yet the object and the support participate closely in the meaning: it is not just any "opening" which produces the casual; the same is true for the

---

[1] Cf., above, 4.V.

[2] This is proved formally by the double concomitant variation: *cardigan with open collar or closed collar* ≡ *casual or dressy.*

chains of matrices (*a cotton dress with red and white checks*): even though the terminal matrix,[3] and consequently its variant (here the existence of checks), possesses the point of meaning, it nonetheless collects, like an absorbent filter, the signifying force of intermediary matrices; as for the signified, we have said that it owed its unit not to itself but to the signifier, under whose control it is read.[4] Hence, the relation between the signifier and the signified should be observed in its full range: the vestimentary sign is a complete syntagm, formed by a syntax of elements.

15.2. *Absence of value*

The syntactic nature of the sign gives Fashion a lexicon which is not simple: it cannot be reduced to a nomenclature that would provide bilateral (and permanent) equivalences between a signifier and a signified, both of them irreducible. Certainly, language is no longer a simple nomenclature; it derives this complex character from the fact that its sign cannot be reduced to a relation between a signifier and a signified, but is also, and perhaps still more importantly, a "value": the linguistic sign is completely defined, beyond its signification, only when we are able to compare it to signs which are similar: /*mutton*/ and /*sheep*/, to use Saussure's example, have the same signification, but not the same value.[5] Now, the Fashion sign appears defined outside any "value": for if the signified is explicit (worldly), it never allows a variation of value analogous to what sets "*mutton*" in opposition to "*sheep*"; the Fashion utterance never derives any meaning from its context; and if the signified is implicit, it is then unique (it is Fashion itself), which excludes any paradigms of the signified other than *in fashion/out of fashion*. The "value" is a factor of complexity; Fashion does not possess it, which does not prevent it from being a complex system; its complexity derives from its instability: first, this system is renewed each year and is valid

---

[3]
```
    \ a cotton dress with red (checks) and white checks /
     \  VS    O  /  \  VS    O  /  \  VS    O  /
                     \  S1O       V       S2  /
        O       V                  S
```

[4] Cf., above, 13.3.

[5] See Saussure, *Cours de linguistique*, pp. 154 ff., and R. Godel, *Sources*, pp. 69, 90, 230 ff.

only at the level of a brief synchrony; next, its oppositions are subject to a general movement of constant neutralization. Thus, it is in relation to this instability that the arbitrariness and the motivation of the vestimentary sign must be examined.

II. The Arbitrariness of the Sign

15.3. *Institution of the Fashion sign*

We know that in language the equivalence of the signifier and the signified is (relatively) unmotivated (we shall return to this point later), but it is not arbitrary; once this equivalence is established (/*cat*/ $\equiv$ "cat"), it cannot be overlooked if we are to make full use of the system of language, and it is because of this that we can say, correcting Saussure, that the linguistic sign is not arbitrary:[6] a general law narrowly limits the power of those who use the system: their freedom is combinative, not inventive. In the Fashion system, the sign, on the contrary, is (relatively) arbitrary: it is elaborated each year, not by the mass of its users (which would be the equivalent of the "speaking mass" which produces language), but by an exclusive authority, i.e., the *fashion-group*, or perhaps, in the case of written Fashion, even the editors of the magazine;[7] of course, the Fashion sign, like all signs produced within what is called mass culture, is situated, one might say, at the point where a singular (or oligarchical) conception and a collective image meet, it is simultaneously imposed and demanded. But, structurally, the Fashion sign is no less arbitrary: it is the result of neither a gradual evolution (for which no "generation" would in itself be responsible) nor a collective consensus; it is born suddenly and in its entirety, every year, by decree (*This year, prints are winning at the races*); what points up the arbitrariness of the Fashion sign is precisely the fact that it is exempt from time: Fashion does not evolve, it changes: its lexicon is new each year, like that of a language which always keeps the same system but suddenly and regularly changes the "currency" of its words. Besides, the language system and the

---

[6] Cf. E. Benveniste, "Nature du signe linguistique," *Acta Linguistica I*, 1939, pp. 23–29.
[7] Editing develops the fundamental themes of Fashion through signs which belong to it.

Fashion system do not have the same order of sanctions: to depart from the language system is to risk losing the power to communicate, it is to be exposed to an immanent, practical sanction; to infringe upon the (present) legality of Fashion is not, strictly speaking, to lose powers of communication, since the *unfashionable* is part of the system, it is to incur a moral condemnation; we could say that the institution of the linguistic sign is a contractual act (at the level of the entire community and of history), while the institution of the Fashion sign is a tyrannical act: there are *mistakes* in language and *faults* in Fashion. Moreover, it is in direct proportion to its very arbitrariness that Fashion develops an entire rhetoric of Law and Fact,[8] all the more imperative because the arbitrariness it must rationalize or naturalize is unchecked.

III. THE MOTIVATION OF THE SIGN

15.4. *Motivation*

The sign is motivated when its signifier is in a natural or rational relation to its signified and, consequently, when the "contract" (Saussure's word) which unites them is no longer necessary. The most common source of motivation is analogy, but there can be many degrees of analogy, from the figurative copy of the object signified (in certain ideograms) to the abstract schematism of certain signals (in the highway code, for example), from pure and simple onomatopoeia[9] to partial (relative) analogies known to language when it constructs a series of words according to the same model (summer—summertime; spring—springtime, etc.). But we know that, in essence, linguistic signs are unmotivated: there is no analogical relation between the signified "cat" and the signifier /cat/. In all systems of signification, motivation is an important phenomenon to observe; first, because a system's perfection, or at least its maturity, seems to depend largely on the lack of motivation of its signs, insofar as systems with digital functioning (i.e., non-analogic) seem more effective; next, be-

---

[8] Cf., below, chap. 19.
[9] See, however, the limits applied to the motivation of onomatopoeia by A. Martinet, *Economie des changements phonétiques*, Berne, A. Francke, 1955, p. 157.

cause in motivated systems the analogy of signifier and signified seems to found the system in nature and to free it from the responsibility of purely human creations: motivation clearly seems to be a factor of "reification," it develops alibis of an ideological order. For these reasons, the sign's motivation must each time be replaced within its limits: on the one hand, it is not motivation which makes the sign, it is its rational, differential nature; but, on the other hand, motivation leads to an ethics of signification systems, since it constitutes the articulation point of an abstract system of forms and of a nature. In Fashion, the stakes involved in this problem will appear fully when the rhetorical level is analyzed, and when it will be necessary to discuss the system's general economy.[10] Remaining within the vestimentary code, the problem of the sign's motivation is posed in different ways, depending on whether the signified is worldly (*A* ensembles) or belongs to Fashion (*B* ensembles).

15.5. *Case of* A *ensembles*

When the signified is worldly (*Prints are winning at the races. The accessory makes it spring. For summer, raw silk,* etc.), we can distinguish, under the relation of motivation, three modes of signs. According to the first mode, the sign is blatantly motivated, in the form of a function; in *ideal shoes for walking*, there is a functional conformity between the form or material of the shoes and the physical demands of walking; the motivation here is not, strictly speaking, analogical, it is functional: the garment's signaletic does not completely absorb its functional origin: the function establishes the sign, and it is the evidence of this origin which the sign transmits; we could say, pressing the point just a bit, that the more motivated the sign, the more present its function and the weaker the semiological nature of the relation: motivation is clearly a factor, one might say, of *de-signification;* by its motivated signs, Fashion plunges into the functional, practical world, which is nearly the same world as that of the real garment.[11]

---

[10] Cf., below, chap. 20.

[11] Still, we must point out that what appears to us as imperiously functional, i.e., natural, is at times merely cultural: how many other societies' garments there are whose "naturalness" is beyond our comprehension. If there were one general functional law, there would only have been one type of garment (cf. F. Kiener, *Kleidung, Mode und Mensche*).

According to the second mode, the sign's motivation is much looser; if the magazine asserts that *this fur coat works for you on the station platform, waiting for a train,* we can, of course, detect a functional trace in the conformity of a protective material (fur) and an open space exposed to the wind (the platform of a railway station); but here the sign is motivated only at a very general level, insofar as, in very vague terms, a cold place calls for a warm garment; beyond this level, there is no further motivation: nothing about the railway station requires fur (rather than tweed) and nothing about fur requires the station (rather than the street); everything happens as if in each utterance there were a certain kernel of substance (here the garment's warmth, there the world's coldness), and as if motivation were established from one kernel to another, without regard to the detail of the units involved in each utterance. Finally, according to the third mode, the sign appears at first glance to be quite unmotivated; it seems there is no "motive" to a *pleated skirt* entering into a relation of equivalence with the age of mature women (*a pleated skirt for the mature woman*), or a low-cut boat-neck collar being suited, naturally or logically, to *tea dance at Juan-les-Pins;* the meeting of signifier and signified here seems absolutely gratuitous; however, if we look closer, we can still recognize a certain substantial but diffuse correspondence between the area of the signifier and the area of the signified in this third mode: insofar as the *smooth* and the *curved,* suggesting contours, emphasize youth by antinomy, *pleats* can be thought of as "reserved" for maturity; as for the *low-cut boat-neck collar,* its harmony with a tea dance at Juan-les-Pins is established in relation to the usual signs of evening dances: the low-cut neckline by analogy and the boat form by contrariety (only a tea party); we see in these two examples that motivation does finally exist, but it is still more diffuse than in the case of *fur at the station,* and above all, it is established in relation to distinctly cultural norms; what serves as its basis here is neither a physical analogy nor a functional conformity, but rather a recourse to the uses of civilization, doubtless relative, but in any case much broader, much more durable than the Fashion which actualizes them (as, for example, the affinity between "casualness" and festivity): it is this *beyond* of Fashion, however historical it may be, which here serves as the basis for the signifying relation. We can see from this that the three regimes of signs we have just discussed do not, in fact, correspond to degrees of motivation: the Fashion sign (in A ensembles) is always motivated; but its motivation has two specific characteristics: on the one hand, it is blurred, diffuse, most often concerning only the substantial "kernel" of the two combinants of units (signifiers and signifieds); on the other hand, it is not analogical but simply "affinitive": this means that the motive for the relation of signification is either a utilitarian function or the imitation of an aesthetic or cultural model.

15.6. *The signified garment: play, effect*

At this point we must examine a particular case of motivation: when the signified is the garment itself; in *a jacket disguised as a coat*, the signifier *jacket* refers to a formal archetype, which is the coat and which, consequently, serves the ordinary function of the signified; it is true that this signified is vestimentary and, strictly speaking, no longer worldly; this is not to say it is a material object, rather it is a simple image of reference; the coherence of the A ensembles (those with worldly signifieds) is preserved here, insofar as the coat in this instance is nothing other than a certain cultural idea, issuing from a world of formal models; there is thus a complete relation of signification: the jacket-object signifies the coat-idea. Since the one imitates the other, there is obviously a fundamental analogical relation between the signifier-jacket and the signified-coat. This analogy usually contains a trace of temporality; the actual garment can signify an outmoded garment: this is *evocation (These coats evoke capes and togas)*; or again, the piece plays the role of its own origin, i.e., signals it (without following it exactly, of course); in *a coat cut from a mohair blanket* or *a skirt made from a plaid shawl, with the fringe showing*, the coat and the skirt act as signifiers for mohair and plaid; the plaid and the mohair are more than simply used, they are signified, i.e., it is more their concept than their substance which is manifested: the plaid shawl is present, not by its function, which is to provide warmth, but by its identity, which may very well be a feature external to its material: fringes.[12] The ana-

---

[12] It must be analyzed thus:

$$\diagdown \text{skirt} \bullet \text{fringes showing} \equiv \text{plaid} \diagup$$
$$\quad \text{OS}_1 \qquad \text{S}_2 \qquad \text{V} \qquad \text{Sd}$$

logical nature of these signifier-signifieds has a psychological implication which becomes quite apparent if we consider the rhetorical signified of these utterances; this signified is the idea of *play:*[13] by playing the game of clothing, the garment itself substitutes for the person, it displays a personality rich enough to change roles frequently;[14] by transforming our garment, we transform its soul; in this (analogical) doubling of the garment into signifier and signified, there is in effect both respect for a system of signification and the tendency to depart from it, for the sign here is imbued with a dream of action (of manufacture), as if the motivation it is based upon were both analogical and causal, the signified producing the signifier at the very moment when the signifier does nothing but manifest the signified; this clearly explains the ambiguous notion of *effect:* the effect is both a causal and a semiological term; in *A double row of buttons furrows the coat,* the buttons' *effect* is a furrow, but they also *signify* it: what such buttoning communicates is an idea of indentation, whatever its reality.[15] The ludic nature of these utterances becomes quite apparent when they take an extreme form, which through its excess indicates the very limits of the system, i.e., of signification; in *the famous little suit that looks like a suit* (or even *a very "suit" suit*), signification achieves its own paradox, it becomes reflexive: the signifier signifies itself.

15.7. *Case of* B *ensembles*

These remarks apply to *A* ensembles (with explicit and worldly signifieds). In *B* ensembles, it is obvious that the sign is unmotivated, since there is no Fashion substance to which the garment could conform by either analogy or affinity.[16] In all probability, the tendency which seems to impel any sign system (provided it is not purely artificial) to join a certain (relative) motivation,

---

[13] The signified *play* becomes apparent through the following kind of rhetorical signifiers: *Play with the blouse by playing with scarves and belts. A skirt does the trick,* etc.

[14] Cf., below, 18.9. A ludic theme *par excellence* is that of Janus; such a piece is *in back, a tight dress with a plunging martingale, and in front, a loose two-piece cut at the waist.*

[15] ╲ a coat with a double row of buttons ≡ furrow ╱

      O   V   S   Sd

[16] The Fashion sign is "tautological," since Fashion is never anything but the *fashionable* garment.

or at least to insert "motivation" into the semantic contract (this
is the case of language), as if a "good" system were the result
of a tension (or of an equilibrium) between an original non-
motivation and a derivative motivation, does exist in Fashion:
the fundamental model of the year[17] is decreed *ex nihilo*, its signs
are absolutely unmotivated; but the majority of Fashion utterances merely develop this annual countersign in the form of
"variations," and these variations are obviously in a relation of
motivation with the theme which inspires them (for example,
there will be an affinity between the form of pockets and the
basic "line"). This secondary motivation, derived from an original
lack of motivation, remains entirely immanent, it has no point of
application in the "world." This is why it can be said that in *B*
ensembles, the Fashion sign is at least as unmotivated as that of
language. The difference between *A* signs (motivated) and *B* signs
(unmotivated) will be of great importance when we take up the
analysis of what could be called the ethics of the general system
of Fashion.[18]

---

[17] Cf., above, 12.10.
[18] Cf., below, chap. 20.

II

THE
RHETORICAL
SYSTEM

16

The Analysis of the Rhetorical System

"She likes studying and surprise parties, Pascal, Mozart, and cool jazz. She wears flat heels, collects little scarves, adores her big brother's plain sweaters and those bouffant, rustling petticoats."

I. POINTS OF ANALYSIS OF THE RHETORICAL SYSTEM

16.1. *Points of analysis*

With the rhetorical system, we broach the general level of connotation. We saw that this system covered the vestimentary code in its entirety[1] since it makes the utterance of signification the simple signifier of a new signified. But as this utterance, at least in the case of A ensembles with explicit signifieds, is itself composed of a signifier (the garment), a signified (the "world"), and a sign (the union of the two), here the rhetorical system has an autonomous relation with each element of the vestimentary code, and no longer with its ensemble alone (as would be the case in language). Within the Rhetoric of Fashion, there are, we might say, three smaller rhetorical systems, distinguished by their objects: a rhetoric of the vestimentary signified, which we shall call the "poetics of clothing" (chapter 17), a rhetoric of the worldly signified, which is the representation Fashion gives to the "world" (chapter 18), and a rhetoric of the Fashion sign, which we shall call the "reason" of Fashion (chapter 19). However, these three

---

[1] Cf., above, chap. 3.

smaller rhetorical systems share the same type of signifier and the same type of signified; we shall call the former the *writing of Fashion* and the latter the *ideology of Fashion*, both of which will be dealt with immediately, in this chapter, before we turn to each of the three elements of the vestimentary code:[2]

Vestimentary Code	Rhetorical System	
	Sr	Sd
Sr: clothing	"Poetics of clothing"	
Sd: the "world"	"The world of Fashion"	
Sign of Fashion	"The reason of Fashion"	
	Writing of Fashion	Ideology of Fashion

16.2. An example

Before beginning the different analyses, we must give an example of the points through which the Fashion system may be entered. Take the following utterance: *She likes studying and surprise parties, Pascal, Mozart, and cool jazz. She wears flat heels, collects little scarves, and adores her big brother's plain sweaters and those bouffant, rustling petticoats*. It is an utterance of signification;[3] in the first place, on the level of the vestimentary code, it contains an utterance of the signifier, which is the clothing itself (*flat heels; little scarves, her big brother's plain sweaters; bouffant, rustling petticoats*); this signifier itself contains a certain number

---

[2] We shall not deal with the rhetorical sign (union of the signifier and the signified) separately, insofar as the writing and the ideology of Fashion exhaust its analysis.

[3] There is only one utterance of signification, if it is understood that the young girl wears all these vestimentary features at the same time; the intended object of signification is then implicit, it is the outfit, the final variant is that of association, expressed by a simple comma:

flat heels,		little scarf,		plain sweater,		bouffant petticoat	
V	SO	V	SO	V	SO	V	SO
S_1	V	S_2	V	S_3	V	S_4	
			O				

But it can also be understood that any one of these features is enough to determine the signified; thus, there are as many significations as there are basic matrices. Moreover, this ambiguity has no effect on rhetorical analysis.

of phraseological markings (*little, big brother's, rustling*), which functions as the rhetorical signifier of a latent signified, of an ideological or, we might say, "mythological" order, and which, in a total manner, is the vision the Fashion magazine gives of itself and of clothing, even beyond its vestimentary meaning. In the second place, the example contains an utterance of the worldly signified (*She likes studying and surprise parties, Pascal, Mozart, and cool jazz*); since here it is explicit, this utterance of the signified also includes a rhetorical signified of its own (the rapid succession of heterogeneous units, apparently without order), and a rhetorical signified which is the vision that the magazine gives of itself and wants to give of the psychological type of woman wearing the clothes. Finally, in the third place, the ensemble of the utterance (or the utterance of signification) is provided with a certain form (use of the present tense, parataxis of verbs: *likes, wears, collects, adores*), which functions as the rhetorical signifier of a final, total signified, namely the entirely consequential way in which the magazine represents itself and represents the equivalence between clothing and the world, i.e., Fashion. Such are the three rhetorical objects of Fashion; but before dealing with them in detail, we must say a word of method about the signifier and the signified of the rhetorical system in general.[4]

II: THE RHETORICAL SIGNIFIER: FASHION WRITING

16.3. *Toward a stylistics of writing*

The rhetorical signifier—whether it concerns the signifier, the signified, or the vestimentary sign—obviously derives from linguistic analysis. Nevertheless, we must here employ an analysis which, on the one hand, recognizes the existence of the phenomenon of connotation and, on the other, distinguishes writing from style; for if we reserve the term *style* to an absolutely singular speech (that of a writer, for example), and the term *writing* to a speech that is collective but not national (that of a

---

[4] Evidently, we must distinguish between *rhetorical signifier* and *rhetoric of the signifier*, for in the second case we are concerned with the signifier of the vestimentary code; the same applies to *signified* and to *sign*.

group made up of editors, for example), as we attempted to propose elsewhere,[5] it is obvious that Fashion utterances derive entirely, not from a style, but from a writing; by describing a garment and its use, the editor invests nothing of himself in his
speech, nothing of his deep psychology; he simply conforms to
a certain conventional and regulated tone (we could say an
ethos), by which, moreover, we immediately recognize a Fashion
magazine; what is more, we shall see that the rhetorical signified
of vestimentary descriptions composes a collective vision bearing
upon social models, and not on an individual thematics; furthermore, because it is entirely absorbed in a simple writing, the
Fashion utterance cannot derive from literature, however "well-
turned" it may be: it can parade literature (by copying its tone),
but precisely because literature is what it signifies, it cannot
achieve literature. What we would need, then, in order to account
for the rhetorical signifier, is, so to speak, a stylistics of writing.
This stylistics is not an elaborate one; we can simply mark its
place in the general system of Fashion and indicate, in passing,
the most common features of the rhetorical *tone*.

16.4. *Principal features of Fashion writing*

We shall make a distinction between segmental features formed
by discrete lexical units, and suprasegmental features, coextensive with several units or even with the utterance in its entirety.
In the first group, we must quite banally list all metaphors (*The
accessories dance a white ballet*), and in a more general way
all features which derive from the "value" of the word; a good
example is the word *little;* as we have seen and as we shall discuss again further on, through its denotative meaning, *little*
belongs to the terminological level (variant of size), but by its
different values, it also belongs to the rhetorical level; it then
takes on a more diffuse meaning, made of economical (*not expensive*), aesthetic (*simple*), and caritative (*what one likes*) nuances;
just as a word like *rustling* (borrowed from the example analyzed
above), beyond its denotative meaning (*which imitates the sound
produced by a rustle of leaves or fabric*), participates in a certain
stereotype of feminine erotics; *big brother*, whose denoted mean-

---

[5] *Writing Degree Zero.*

ing here is simply *masculine* (a usual semantic unit), participates
in a familial and juvenile language, etc. In a more general way,
it is what could be called the adjectival substances (a broader
notion than the *adjective* of grammars) which furnishes the essential character of these segmental connotations. As for suprasegmental features, we must list here, at the elementary level (since
they still concern units which are discrete though associated by
sound), all rhyme play, used quite frequently in certain Fashion
magazines: *on the beach, the latest and the greatest; six wardrobes you can put to good use, for any excuse; your face—gra-
cious, precious, joyous;* then certain turns of phrase that approach
the utterance of a couplet or a proverb (*A little braid makes it
look handmade*); finally, all expressive varieties of parataxis: for
example, the rapid and disordered succession of verbs (*she likes
. . . she adores . . . she wears*) and semantic units, here original
ones (*Pascal, Mozart, cool jazz*), function as the sign of a profusion of tastes and consequently of a great richness of personality. When it is a question of the worldly signified, beyond these
strictly stylistic phenomena, the simple selection of units suffices
to constitute a signifier of connotation: to speak of *a long walk
at the end of an afternoon, in the country, during a weekend in
autumn* (an utterance composed only of usual units), is to refer,
through a simple concurrence of circumstances (terminological
level), to a particular "mood," to a complex social and emotional
situation (rhetorical level). The phenomenon of composition is
then itself one of the principal forms of the rhetorical signifier,
all the more active because in the Fashion utterance the units
involved derive from a code which is ideally (if not practically)
external to language, which increases, so to speak, the connotative
force of the simplest speech. By their suprasegmental character,
all these elements play nearly the same role in the rhetorical system that intonation plays in language: moreover, intonation is
an excellent signifier of connotation.[6] Since we are dealing with
a signifier (albeit a rhetorical one), the features of Fashion writing
should be divided into classes of opposition or paradigms; this is
certainly possible for segmental features, more difficult for supra-

---

[6] To the point where, in a verbal message addressed to an animal, it is the
connotation (a tone of anger, of kindness) which is understood, not the denotation (the word's literal meaning).

segmental features (as elsewhere for linguistic intonation); here we must await the progress of structural stylistics.

III. THE RHETORICAL SIGNIFIED:
THE IDEOLOGY OF FASHION

16.5. *Implicit and latent*

On the rhetorical level, a general signified corresponds to the writing of Fashion, and this general signified is the ideology of Fashion. The rhetorical signified is subject to particular conditions of analysis, which must now be examined; these conditions depend upon the original character of the rhetorical signified: this signified is neither explicit nor implicit, it is *latent*. An example of the explicit signified is that of the vestimentary code in *A* ensembles: it is actualized, as a signified, through a material object: the word (*weekend, cocktail, evening*). The implicit signified is, for example, that of language: in this system, as we have said, signifier and signified are marked by isology;[7] it is impossible to objectify the signified apart from its signifier (unless we resort to the metalanguage of a definition), but at the same time, to isolate a signifier is immediately to affect its signified; the implicit signified is thus simultaneously discrete, invisible (as signified), and yet perfectly clear (by reason of the discontinuity of its signifier): in order to decipher a word, no knowledge other than that of the language is necessary, i.e., of the system of which it is a function; in the case of the implicit signified, the relation of signification is, one might say, necessary and sufficient: the phonic form /*winter*/ necessarily has a meaning and this meaning is enough to exhaust the signifying function of the word *winter;* the "closed" character of the relation[8] derives from the nature of the linguistic system, which is a system whose material immediately signifies. In contrast to the implicit signified, the *latent* signified (this is the case for all rhetorical signifieds) has original characteristics, derived from its place in the system

---

[7] Cf., above, 13.1.

[8] Here it is a matter of the minimum structural conditions for constituting the linguistic sign, since we note only the signification, without taking "value" into consideration, however essential it may be in the language system.

as a whole: situated at the termination of a process of connotation, it participates in its constitutive duplicity; connotation generally consists of masking the signification under a "natural" appearance, it never presents itself under the species of a system free of signification; thus, phenomenologically speaking, it does not call for a declared operation of *reading;* to consume a connotative system (in this case, the rhetorical system of Fashion) is not to consume signs, but only reasons, goals, images; it follows that the signified of connotation is, literally, *hidden* (and no longer implicit); in order to reveal it—i.e., ultimately, in order to reconstitute it—it is no longer possible to rely on immediate evidence shared by the mass of users of the system, as is the case for the "speaking mass" of the linguistic system.[9] It can be said that the sign of connotation is unnecessary, since, if it is unnoticed when read, the entire utterance remains valid by its denotation alone; and it is insufficient since there is no exact adjustment between a signifier whose extensive, suprasegmental nature we have seen, and a diffuse, total signified, penetrated by knowledge which is unequal (depending on how cultured its consumers are), steeped in a mental zone where ideas, images, and values remain as if suspended in the penumbra of a language which is uncertain since it fails to acknowledge itself as a system of signification. Thus, when the magazine speaks of *big brother's sweaters* (and not men's sweaters), or of the young girl who likes *surprise parties and Pascal, cool jazz and Mozart* all at once, the somewhat childish "homeliness" of the first utterance and the eclecticism of the second are signifieds whose very status is questionable since they are perceived in one place as the simple expression of a simple nature and in another with the distance of a critical regard which discerns the sign behind the index; we can assume that for the woman who reads Fashion there is no awareness here of a signification, yet she receives from the utterance a message structured enough for her to feel changed by it (for example, reassured and confirmed in a euphoric situation of "homeliness" or in the right to like very difficult genres which nonetheless have subtle affinities). With the rhetorical or latent signified, we thus approach the essential paradox of connoted signification: it is, one

---

[9] It goes without saying that, even in language, connotation is a factor of ambiguity: it complicates (to say the least) communication.

might say, a signification which is *received*, but which is not *read*.[10]

16.6. The *"nebulosity"* of the rhetorical signified

Before examining the effects of this paradox on the course of the analysis, we must point out another original characteristic of the rhetorical signified. Take the following utterance: *coquettish without coquetry;* its rhetorical signifier is the paradoxical relation which unites two opposites; this signifier then refers to the idea that the world aimed at by written Fashion ignores opposites, that we can be provided with two originally contradictory characteristics, between which nothing necessitates a choice; in other words, the signified is here constituted by a vision of the world which is at once syncretic and euphoric. Now, this rhetorical signified is the same for a great number of utterances (*discreet audacity, sober fantasy, casual rigor, Pascal and cool jazz*, etc.); hence, there are only a few rhetorical signifieds for many signifiers; and as each of these few signifieds is a small ideology placed, as it were, in a situation of osmosis with a much larger ideology (euphoria and syncretism necessarily refer to a general idea of nature, happiness, evil, etc.), it can be said that there is only one rhetorical signified, formed by an undefined mass of concepts, and which could be compared to a large nebula, with vague connections and contours. This "nebulosity" is not a systematic lack: the rhetorical signified is confused insofar as it depends closely on the situation of the individuals who wield the message (as has already been pointed out with regard to the highway code as taught[11]): on their knowledge, their feelings, their morals, their consciousness, and on the historical conditions of the culture in which they live. The massive imprecision of the rhetorical signified is therefore in fact an opening into the world. Through its ultimate signified, Fashion reaches the limit of its system: this is where the system, touching the entire world, comes undone. Thus, we understand that by acceding to the rhetorical level, the

---

[10] The existence of latent messages seems to be known to social psychology, as is shown by the distinction between *phenotype* (or manifest behavior) and *genotype* (or latent, hypothetical, inferred behavior) established by C. Coombs and developed by J. Stoetzel ("Les progrès méthodiques récents en sociologie," in *Actes du IVe congrès mondial de sociologie, II*, London, A.I.S., p. 267).
[11] Cf., above, 3.3.

analysis, carried along by this movement, is led to abandon its formal premises, and, itself becoming ideological, recognizes the limits simultaneously imposed on it by the historical world in which it is uttered and the existence of the world which utters it: here, by a double contrary movement, the analyst must detach himself from the system's users in order to objectify their attitude, and yet feel this distance not as the expression of a positive truth but as a particular and relative historical situation: at the same time, in order to understand terms used in diverse ways, the analyst must be both objective and committed.

16.7. *The problem of "proving" the rhetorical signified*

Objectivity here consists of defining the rhetorical signified as probable, but not as certain; we cannot "prove" the rhetorical signified by direct recourse to the mass of its users, since this mass does not *read* the message of connotation, but rather *receives* it. There is no "proof" for this signified, only "probability." This probability can, however, be submitted to a double control. First, an external control: the reading of Fashion utterances (in their rhetorical form) could be verified by submitting women who read them to non-directive interviews (this seems the best technique here, since in the end it is a matter of reconstituting an ideological totality); next, an internal control, or more precisely, one intrinsic to its object: the rhetorical signifieds collected here combine to form a general vision of the world, which is that of human society constituted by the magazine and its readers: on the one hand, the Fashion world must be entirely saturated by all rhetorical signifieds and, on the other hand, within this whole, all signifieds must be functionally linked together; in other words, if the rhetorical signified, in its unitary form, can only be a *construction*, this construction must be coherent:[12] the internal probability of the rhetorical signified is established in proportion to its coherence. Confronted with demands for a positive demonstration or for a real experiment, simple coherence may appear disappointing as a "proof"; yet we are increasingly inclined to recognize in it a law which, if not scientific, is at least heuristic; one part of modern criticism aims at reconstituting creative uni-

---

[12] Internal coherence must be obviously non-contradictory with our possible knowledge of the total society.

verses through a thematic approach (the method proper to immanent analysis), and in linguistics it is a system's coherence (and not its "use") which demonstrates its reality; and without claiming to underestimate the practical importance of Marxism and psychoanalysis in the historical life of the modern world, the list of their "effects" is far from exhausting their respective theories, which owe a decisive part of their "probability" to their systematic coherence. Thus, it would seem that in modern epistemology there is a kind of "slippage" in proofs, inevitable whenever we shift from a problematics of determinisms to a problematics of meanings, or, to put it another way, when social science deals with a reality partially transformed into language by society itself: this, moreover, is why every sociology of motivations, symbols, or communications, which cannot achieve its object except through human speech, is called upon, it seems, to collaborate with semiological analysis; furthermore: being language, sociology ultimately cannot avoid this analysis; there is, there inevitably will be, a semiology of semiologists. Thus, by acceding to the rhetorical signified, the analyst touches the termination of his task; but this termination is the very moment when he joins the historical world and, in that world, the objective place he himself occupies.[13]

---

[13] Cf., below, 20.13.

17

Rhetoric of the Signifier:
The Poetics of Clothing

"Hot boots, hot ankle boots here!"

I. POETICS

17.1. *Matter and language*

The description of a garment (i.e., the signifier of the vestimentary code) may be the site of a rhetorical connotation. This rhetoric derives its particularity from the material nature of the object being described, namely the garment; it is defined, one might say, by the coming together of matter and language: this is the situation we shall term *poetic*. Certainly, language can be imposed on an object without its being "poetry"; at least this is the case for all utterances of denotation: a machine can be described technically through a simple nomenclature of its elements and their functions; denotation is pure as long as description remains functional, produced with a view to an actual use (to construct the machine or to make use of it); but if technical description is only the spectacle of itself, as it were, and passes itself off as a signaletic copy of a genre (for example, in a parody or a novel), there is connotation and the beginnings of a "poetics" of the machine; it is perhaps the transitivity of language which is in fact the real criterion of denotation; and it is the intransitivity of language (or its false transitivity, or again its reflexivity) which is the mark of connotation; there is a poetic mutation as soon as we shift from real function to spectacle, even when this spectacle disguises itself under the appearance of a function. In short, every intransitive (unproductive) description founds the possibility of a certain poetics, even if this poetics is not fulfilled according to aesthetic values; for, by describing a material object, if it is not to construct it or to use it, we are led to link the qualities of its matter to a second meaning, to be signified through the notable which we attribute to it: every intransitive description implies an image-repertoire. What is the nature of the image-repertoire described by the Fashion magazine?

17.2. *A rare and poor rhetoric*

We can expect clothing to constitute an excellent poetic object; first, because it mobilizes with great variety all the qualities of matter: substance, form, color, tactility, movement, rigidity, luminosity; next, because touching the body and functioning simultaneously as its substitute and its mask, it is certainly the object of a very important investment; this "poetic" disposition is attested to by the frequency and the quality of vestimentary descriptions in literature. Now, if we look at the utterances the magazine devotes to clothing, we immediately note that Fashion does not honor the poetic project which affords it its object; that it furnishes no raw material to a psychoanalysis of substances; that here connotation does not refer to an exercise of the imagination. First, in a great number of cases, the signifier of the first system (i.e., the garment) is presented without rhetoric; the garment is described according to a nomenclature pure and simple, deprived of all connotation, and entirely absorbed by the denotative level, i.e., by the terminological code itself; all descriptive terms are then drawn from the previously established inventory of genera and variants; in an utterance like *sweaters and hoods: clothes for the chalet,* the garment is reduced to the assertion of two species.[1] These defective cases attest to an interesting paradox: Fashion is least literary on the level of the garment itself, as if, encountering its own reality, it tended to become ob-

---

[1] There may nevertheless remain some "rhetoric" in the utterance at the level of the signified (the world); here *chalet* (the signified) carries a social connotation, one of leisure and luxury, and the abrupt parataxis refers to a sort of peremptory evidence.

jective, and reserved the luxury of connotation for the world, i.e., for the garment's *elsewhere;* herein lies the first indication of a denotative constraint on the Fashion system: Fashion tends to denote the garment because, however utopian it may be, it does not abandon the project of a certain *activity,* i.e., of a certain transitivity of its language (it must persuade its readers to wear the garment). Next, when there is a rhetoric of clothing, this rhetoric is always poor; whereby it must be understood that the metaphors and turns of phrase which constitute the rhetorical signifier of clothing, when there are any, are determined not by a reference to the radiant qualities of matter but by stereotypes borrowed from a vulgarized literary tradition, either from rhyming games (*petticoats—creamy and dreamy*) or from commonplace comparisons (*a belt as thin as a line*); in short, this is a banal rhetoric, i.e., one weak in information. We can say that each time Fashion agrees to connote a garment, between the "poetic" metaphor (derived from an "invented" quality of matter) and the stereotypic metaphor (derived from an automatic literary response), it chooses the latter: nothing is better suited to a poetic connotation than the sensation of warmth: yet Fashion prefers to make the connotation echo the cry of a chestnut vendor (*Hot boots, hot ankle boots here!*), here assuming nothing more than the most banal "poetry" of winter.

17.3. *Denotation and connotation: mixed terms*

The rarity and the poverty of the rhetorical system at the level of the signifier are explained by a constant denotative pressure on the garment's description. The exertion of this pressure is evident each time Fashion sets itself up, as it were, between the terminological level and the rhetorical level, as if it could not choose between the two, as if it continually penetrated the rhetorical notation of a kind of regret, a terminological temptation; now, these cases are quite numerous. The imbrication of the two systems occurs at two points, on the one hand at the level of certain variants, on the other hand at the level of what have already been termed mixed adjectives.[2] In passing, we have seen that certain variants, though belonging to the denotative system,

---

[2] Cf., above, 4.3.

or at least classified in the inventory of the first code (insofar as they are linked to variations of the vestimentary meaning), had a certain rhetorical value: for example, the existence of *mark* or *regulation* depends in fact on a purely terminological expression, i.e., it would be difficult to "translate" them precisely into real (and no longer written) clothing: their verbal nature predisposes them to rhetoric, yet it does so without enabling them to leave the plane of denotation, since they possess a signified belonging to the vestimentary code. As for mixed adjectives, these are all adjectives which, within the language system, possess both a material and a non-material value simultaneously, like *little, bright, simple, strict, rustling,* etc.; by their material value, they belong to the terminological level, and by their non-material value, to the rhetorical level. In *little* (which has been analyzed elsewhere[3]), dividing the two systems is simple because the denoted value of the word takes its place directly in a paradigm belonging to the vestimentary code (variant of size); but adjectives like *nice, good (a good travel coat), strict* belong to the denoted level only by approximation: *nice* belongs to the zone of *little, good* to that of *thick, strict* to that of *plain* (without ornament).

17.4. *Signifier-signifieds*

The pressure of denotation is exerted on another point of the system. Certain terms can be considered as signifieds or signifiers simultaneously; in *a masculine sweater, masculine* is a signified insofar as the sweater signals a real masculinity (the social or worldly domain), but it is also a signifier insofar as use of the term permits defining purely and simply a certain state of the garment. Here again we encounter a diachronic phenomenon we have had occasion to note several times: certain species of clothing function as old signifieds "fossilized" into signifiers (*sport shirt, Richelieu shoes*); the mixed adjective often represents the initial stage of this process, the fragile moment when the signified is going to "take," to solidify into a signifier: *masculine* is a signified as long as masculinity is a sufficiently aberrant value of feminine clothing; but if the masculinization of this garment is

---

[3] Cf., above, 3.11; 4.3.

institutionalized (without becoming total, however, for in order for it to have a meaning, the possibility of a choice between the feminine and the masculine must subsist[4]), *masculine* will become a notation as *matte* as *sport;* it will define a certain species of clothing as a pure signifier: there is a kind of diachronic vacillation between the signified origin of the term and its gradual development into a signifier.[5] Now, to "fossilize" a signified into a signifier is inevitably to go in the direction of a certain denotation, since it means nudging a system of inert equivalence (signifier $\equiv$ signified) toward a terminological nomenclature which is then ready to be used for transitive ends (to construct the garment). By accepting the pressure of denotation on the vestimentary part of its system (or, at the very least, by preparing for a close exchange between the rhetorical and terminological levels), Fashion remembers that it must help to construct the garment, even in a utopian way. Whence the parsimony and the ruses of its rhetorical system, as soon as it affects the garment itself.

II. THE RHETORICAL SIGNIFIED OF CLOTHING: THE MODELS

17.5. *Cognitive models: "culture"*

Though poor, the rhetorical system of clothing nevertheless does exist here and there. What is its signified?[6] Since Fashion rejects a "poetics" of clothing, it is not an "imagination" of substances; it is an ensemble of social models, which can be divided into three large semantic fields.[7] The first of these fields is constituted by a network of cultural or cognitive models. The signifier of this ensemble is usually constituted by a metaphorical naming of the

---

[4] *Feminine* remains a connoted term (frequent in the Fashion vocabulary), although the Fashion garment is literally entirely feminine, because a tension subsists between the masculine and the feminine; the existence of the couple on the level of styles permits the connotation of each of its terms.

[5] Where are these signifier-signifieds to be classified? If the matrix is already saturated by a variant, the mixed term is found transferred to the worldly (social) domain (*rustling, bouffant petticoats*); but if the mixed adjective is confronted directly by the species (*rustling petticoats*), it takes on the value of a variant (fit).

[6] We speak of a single signified, since the rhetorical signified is "nebulous" (above, 16.6).

[7] We recall that, in the terminology used here, *semantic* refers to the level of content, not to the level of expression.

species: *the dress Manet would have loved to paint; this poison-pink would have charmed Toulouse-Lautrec;* a certain number of objects or styles dignified by culture thus give their name to the garment; one might say that these are formative models of the sign, with the clear understanding that the analogical relation which unites the eponymous theme to its incarnation at a given moment has an essentially rhetorical value: to place a dress under the "sign" Manet is more to display a certain culture than it is to name a form (this duplicity is proper to connotation); the cultural reference is so explicit that one then speaks of *inspiration* or *evocation.*[8] There are four great eponymous themes: nature (*flower-dress, cloud-dress, hats in bloom,* etc.); geography, acculturated under the theme of the exotic (*a Russian blouse, Cherkess ornaments, a samurai tunic, pagoda sleeve, toreador tie, California shirt, Greek summer tints*); history, which primarily provides models for an entire ensemble ("lines"), as opposed to geography, which inspires "details" (*Fashion 1900, a 1916 flavor, Empire line*); and last, art (painting, sculpture, literature, film), the richest of inspirational themes, marked in the rhetoric of Fashion by total eclecticism, provided the references themselves are familiar (*the new Tanagra line, Watteau's déshabillés, Picasso colors*[9]). Naturally—this is the characteristic of connotation—the signified of all these rhetorical signifiers is not, strictly speaking, the model, even if it is conceived in a generic manner (nature, art, etc.): it is the very idea of culture which is intended to signify, and by its own categories this culture is a "worldly" culture, i.e., ultimately, academic: history, geography, art, natural history, the divisions of a high-school girl's learning; the models Fashion proposes pell-mell are borrowed from the intellectual baggage of a young girl who is *"on the go and in the know"* (as Fashion would say), who would take courses at the Ecole du Louvre, visit a few exhibitions and museums when she travels, and would have read a few well-known novels. Moreover, the sociocultural model thus constituted and signified can be entirely projective; nothing requires that it coincide with the

[8] *"Fashion '59 has nothing and it has everything: it evokes Gigi, Manet, Vigny, and George Sand, one after the other."* Sometimes the notation is more direct: this is *borrowing,* also a literary notion.

[9] Haute Couture itself can constitute a cultural model, the chief designers serving as kinds of signifieds (*Chanel-style, the Chanel look*).

actual status of the women who read Fashion magazines; it is even likely that it simply represents a reasonable degree of social advancement.

17.6. *Affective models: "caritatism"*

The second group of models involved in the rhetorical signified includes the affective models. Here again, we must start with the signifier. Right away we note that when Fashion writing is not "cultural," sublimated, it is exactly the opposite: familiar, even intimate, a bit infantile; its language is domestic, articulated on the opposition of two principal terms: *good* and *little* (these two words are understood here in a connotative sense). *Good* (*good thick woolens*) carries a complex idea of protection, warmth, correctness, simplicity, health, etc.; *little* (which we have come across quite often) refers to values every bit as felicitous (Fashion is always euphemistic), but at the heart of this notion is an idea of seduction, more than one of protection (*pretty, nice* are part of the zone of the *little*). The opposition *good/little* can divide a terminologically homogeneous meaning (which attests to the reality and the autonomy of the rhetorical level): *gay* refers to *little*, but *happy* refers to *good;* these two poles, of course, coincide with two classic motivations of clothing, protection and adornment, warmth and graciousness; but the connotation they support is elsewhere: it conveys a certain filial tone, the complementary relation *a good mother/a nice little girl;* the garment is sometimes loving, sometimes loved: we could call this the "caritative" quality of clothing. Hence, what is being signified here is the role, simultaneously maternal and childlike, that devolves upon the garment. This role is given with all its childish resonances: the garment is intentionally dealt with in a fabulous manner (*princess gown, miracle dress, King Coat the First*); here the "caritative" quality of clothing combines with legends of royalty, the importance of which is well known, under cover of headlines, in mass culture today.

17.7. *The "seriousness" of Fashion*

Though contradictory in appearance, the cultural model and the caritative model have a common aim, for the situation in which they place the reader of Fashion is the same, at once educative and childlike; so that simple semantic analysis allows the mental age of this model reader to be determined quite precisely; it is a young girl who goes to high school but still plays with dolls at home, even if these dolls are merely knickknacks on her bookshelves. In short, vestimentary rhetoric participates in the very ambiguity of children's roles in modern society: the child is excessively childish at home and excessively serious at school; this excess must be followed to the letter; Fashion is both *too* serious and *too* frivolous at the same time, and it is in this intentionally complementary interplay of excess that it finds a solution to a fundamental contradiction which constantly threatens to destroy its fragile prestige: in point of fact, Fashion cannot be literally serious, for that would be to oppose common sense (of which it is respectful on principle), which easily deems Fashion's activity idle; conversely, Fashion cannot be ironic and put its own being in question; a garment must remain, in its own language, both essential (it gives Fashion life) and accessory (common sense considers it thus); whence a rhetoric which is sometimes sublime, giving Fashion the security of an entirely nominal culture, sometimes familiar, shifting the garment to a universe of "little things."[10] Moreover, it is probable that the juxtaposition of the excessively serious and the excessively frivolous, which is the basis for the rhetoric of Fashion,[11] merely reproduces, on the level of clothing, the mythic situation of Women in Western civilization, at once sublime and childlike.

17.8. *The vitalist model: the "detail"*

There is a third model present in the rhetoric of clothing which participates in neither Fashion's sublimity nor its frivolity, be-

---

[10] Another version of this "minimizing" language (but of a different ethical scope) is given by the theme of the "crazy" (more and more frequent, but reserved to Fashion photography). Cf. Appendix II.

[11] If it were a matter of a dialectic of the serious and the frivolous, i.e., if the frivolity of Fashion were *immediately* taken as absolutely serious, we would then have one of the most elevated forms of the literary experience: i.e., the very movement of the Mallarmean dialectic apropos of Fashion itself (Mallarmé's *La dernière mode*).

cause it doubtless corresponds quite closely to a real (economic) condition of the production of Fashion. Its signifier is constituted by all the metaphorical variations of the "detail" (which is itself a mixed term, connoted-denoted, since it also belongs to the inventory of genres[12]). The "detail" involves two constant and complementary themes: tenuousness[13] and creativity; the exemplary metaphor here is the seed, the tiny being from which an entire harvest springs: a "morsel" of "nothing," and suddenly we have an entire outfit permeated with the meaning of Fashion: *a little nothing that changes everything; those little nothings that can do everything; just a detail will change its appearance; the details insure your personality,* etc. By giving a great deal of semantic power to "nothing," Fashion is, of course, merely following its own system, whose matrices and chains are precisely responsible for radiating meaning through inert materials; structurally, the meaning of Fashion is a meaning at a distance; and within this structure it is precisely this "nothing" which is the radiant nucleus: its importance is energetic rather than extensive, there is a propagation from the detail to the ensemble, *nothing* can signify *everything*. But this vitalist imagination is not an irresponsible one; the rhetoric of the detail seems to take on an increasing extension, and the stake it has in doing so is an economic one: by becoming a mass value (through its magazines, if not through its boutiques), Fashion must elaborate meanings whose fabrication does not appear costly; this is the case of the "detail": one detail is enough to transform what is outside meaning into meaning, what is unfashionable into Fashion, and yet a "detail" is not expensive; by this particular semantic technique, Fashion departs from the luxurious and seems to enter into a clothing practice accessible to modest budgets; but at the same time, sublimated under the name *find,* this same low-priced detail participates in the dignity of the idea: likewise free, likewise glorious, the detail consecrates a democracy of budgets while respecting an aristocracy of tastes.

---

[12] Examples: *finds, complements, ideas, refinements, note, seed, accent, whim, trifle, nothing.*
[13] The "nothing" can be intensified, subtilized to the ineffable (which is the very metaphor of life): *These little dresses have belts either like this or like that. A certain Claudine collar.*

III. RHETORIC AND SOCIETY

17.9. *Rhetoric and Fashion audiences*

The rhetorical signified of description is not situated on the side of a poetics of substances, but only (when it does exist) on the side of a psycho-sociology of roles. Whereby a certain sociology of Fashion becomes possible, beginning with its semantics: since Fashion is entirely a system of signs, variations in the rhetorical signified no doubt correspond to variations in audience.[14] At the level of the corpus under study, the presence or absence of vestimentary rhetoric clearly seems to reflect different types of magazines. It seems that poor rhetoric, i.e., strong denotation, corresponds to a socially higher audience;[15] on the contrary, a strong rhetoric, developing mainly the cultural and caritative signifieds, corresponds to a more "popular" audience.[16] This opposition can be explained: we could say that the higher the standard of living, the more chances the proposed (written) garment has of being obtained, and denotation (the transitive character of which has been discussed) regains its powers; conversely, if the standard of living is lower, the garment cannot be obtained, denotation becomes vain, and it is then necessary to compensate for its uselessness with a system strong in connotation, whose role is to permit the utopian investment: it is easier to dream about *the dress Manet would have liked to paint* than to make it. This law, however, does not seem infinite: cultural investment, for example, is possible only if its image is in fact within the means of the group to which it is offered: thus, connotation is strong where there is tension (and equilibrium) between two contiguous states, one real and the other dreamed: though utopian, the dream must be near at hand; but if we descend yet another level on the socio-professional scale, the cultural image becomes poorer, the system again tends toward denotation;[17] in short, we would be dealing with a bell curve: at the top would be the system strong in con-

---

[14] Since we are not here concerned to establish a sociology of Fashion, these indications are purely approximate: however, there would be no methodological difficulty in defining sociologically the level of each Fashion magazine.

[15] Magazines such as *Jardin des Modes*, *Vogue*.

[16] Magazines such as *Elle*.

[17] Magazines such as *Echo de la Mode* (until recently, *Petit Echo de la Mode*).

notation and an audience of average status; at the two extremities, the systems strong in denotation and audiences of either inferior or superior status; but in these last two cases, the denotation is not the same; the denotation of the luxury magazines implies a rich garment with many variations, even if it is described exactly, i.e., without rhetoric; the denotation of the popular magazine is poor, for it apprehends a cheap garment which it regards as obtainable: utopia occupies, as it should, an intermediary position between the praxis of the poor and that of the rich.[18]

---

[18] This phenomenon is also found in the analysis of the rhetoric of the signified (cf. following chapter).

18

Rhetoric of the Signified: The World of Fashion

"I am a secretary, and I like to be impeccable."

I. THE REPRESENTATION OF THE WORLD

18.1. *Metaphor and parataxis: the Fashion novel*

When its signified is explicit,[1] the vestimentary code divides the world into semantic units which rhetoric apprehends in order to "dress them up," order them, and from them construct a genuine vision of the world: *evening, weekend, promenade, spring,* are erratic units which, coming from the world, do not imply any particular "world," any definite ideology, which is why, at the level of the vestimentary code, they resist classification.[2] This rhetorical construction of a world, which could be compared to a genuine cosmogony, is realized through two principal means (which have already been pointed out with regard to the rhetorical signified[3]): metaphor and parataxis. The usual role of the worldly metaphor is to transform a usual (therefore conceptual) semantic unit into an apparently original contingency (even if this contingency refers rhetorically to a stereotype); thus, in *For*

---

[1] Whenever the signified is implicit (*B* ensembles), this signified is Fashion; its rhetoric is identified with that of the sign (cf. following chapter); this chapter can treat only *A* ensembles.

[2] Cf., above, 13.9.

[3] Cf., above, 16.4.

*your walks in the country and visits to the farm, your dresses will
be full of color,* what the metaphorical redundance (*visits to the
farm*) adds to the elements of the first code (*walk • country*) is,
on the one hand, the vision of an object (the farm) which here
substitutes for the intellection of a concept (the country), and,
on the other hand, the suggestion of a fictive social situation,
stemming from a whole literature for young girls (*visiting* the
farm implies that one comes from a château, from the gentry,
from a place of leisure where this mixed essence of country and
labor will be looked upon as a rather exotic spectacle). As for
parataxis, it extends the power of metaphor by developing what
could be called an "atmosphere" from discontinuous situations
and objects; *This blazer is for the girl who's something of an
Anglophile, perhaps smitten with Proust, who spends her vacations at the shore,* vacation, shore, girl, English style, and Proust
reconstruct, by their simple narrative contiguity, a familiar literary setting: i.e., the beach in Normandy, Balbec, the troop of
"les jeunes filles en fleurs." Thus is born an ensemble of objects
and situations no longer linked to one another by a logic of uses
and signs, but by constraints of an entirely different order, i.e.,
those of narrative: rhetoric shifts the semantic units from pure
combinative discontinuity to *tableau vivant,* or, one might say,
from structure to event; it is in fact the role of rhetoric to elaborate an apparently factual order starting from structural elements
(the semantic units of the vestimentary code), and it is in this
regard that the rhetoric of Fashion is an *art* (all question of *value*
aside); actually, narrative permits simultaneously completing
and eluding the structure which inspires it: the farm confirms the
existence of the country, but it also masks its abstract (semantic)
nature, to the benefit of new values; an appearance of *the experienced* (i.e., tendentially, of the ineffable) compensates for the
pure combination of signs, without destroying it. In short, it is a
matter of a ludic equilibrium between the code and its rhetoric;
a fundamental ambiguity which up to now has allowed the novel
to be both structure and event, a collection of essential features
(roles, models, situations, characters) and a closely linked narrative. In Fashion's fictionalizing, the weight of the structure is
very strong, for the metaphors and parataxes are, informationally
speaking, banal, i.e., drawn from already familiar units and combinations; yet it is a structure placed entirely under the guarantee

of the event; we could perhaps call this degraded form of structure—or this timid form of event—a *stereotype:* it is the stereotype which founds the equilibrium of Fashion rhetoric, and which
allows for the presentation of information that is altogether reassuring and yet given a vague appearance of the *never-before-
seen* (we could say that the stereotype functions like a poorly
recalled memory). Such is the structural situation of the fictional
tone elaborated by the rhetoric of the signified: to mask the structure beneath the event.

18.2. *Principle of analysis: the notion of "work"*

What is the "subject" of this novel, or, in other words, what is
the signified of the rhetoric of Fashion when it speaks of the
"world"?[4] As has been said and will be said again,[5] it can be
named only through a new metalanguage, i.e., that of the analyst.
It seems that the notion which best explains the coherence of
the Fashion universe, or rather, which does not contradict any
of its features, is the notion of work.[6] No doubt, the most frequent
and the densest representations of Fashion rhetoric concern not
work but its opposite, leisure; but it is precisely a matter of a
complementary pair: the world of Fashion is work in reverse;
a first network of rhetorical signifieds will thus include all units
(and their metaphors or partial parataxes) which have a relation
to human activity, the things people do, even if this activity, this
doing, is tinged with a certain unreality; generally, this will be
all the functions and all the situations which imply either an
activity (even if a leisure one) or the circumstances in which we
assume this activity takes place; but since "doing" in Fashion
(and therein lies its unreality) is ultimately never anything but
the decorative attributes of being, since work is never presented
apart from a population of psychological essences and human
models, and since work, in Fashion, does not produce man, but

---

[4] We are reminded that it is possible to speak of a singular rhetorical signified
(even if it is composed of several themes) because, on the rhetorical level, the
signified is "nebulous."

[5] Cf., above, 16.5, 16.7; and, below, 20.13.

[6] A. J. Greimas has already proposed a classification of the signifieds of language in relation to this notion: on the symbolic level of language, *lexicons* would
correspond to *techniques* ("Les problèmes de la description mécanographique,"
in *Cahiers de Lexicologie,* I, 1959, p. 63).

rather follows him, the second network of rhetorical signifieds will include all the units having a relation to a certain being of mankind. Thus, the Fashion novel is organized around two equivalences; according to the first, Fashion presents the reader with an activity defined either in itself or by its circumstances of time and place (*If you want to signify what you are doing here, dress like this*); according to the second, it offers an identity to be read (*If you want to be this, you must dress like this*). In short, the woman who wears Fashion finds herself asked four questions: who? what? when? where? Her (utopian) garment always answers at least one of these questions.[7]

II. FUNCTIONS AND SITUATIONS

18.3. *Active and festive situations*

In the realm of doing, the woman of Fashion is always placed in relation to one of these three questions: what? (transitivity), when? (temporality), where? (locality). It is clear that doing must be understood in a broad sense: an action may very well be presented only in the form of the circumstances which accompany it (time and place). In fact, Fashion knows no genuine transitivity;[8] what it notes is rather the manner in which the subject makes her situation in relation to a milieu where she is supposed to act: the hunt, a ball, shopping, are forms of social, not technical, behavior. The doing involved in Fashion is, as it were, abortive: its subject is torn by a representation of essences at the moment of acting: to dress *in order* to act is, in a certain way, not to act, it is to display the being of doing, without assuming its reality. Also, transitive situations in Fashion are always *occupations*, i.e., much more a way of employing the subject's being

---

7

Who?	BEING	Essences and models
What? When? Where?	DOING	Functions and situations

[8] This is the objection the Soviets raise to Western Fashion: it does not deal with work clothes.

250/

than of effectively transforming reality. Thus immobilized, the notional field of doing is structured as a complex opposition having four terms; there are two polar terms: *active situations and festive situations;* a complex term participating in both the active and the festive, *sport;* and a neutral term (neither active nor festive), *nothing planned.* Active situations proper are scant: work is undetermined,[9] and Fashion names only very marginal activities: errands, shopping, housework, tinkering, gardening; what is essential is undefined, and the defined is accessory. Festive situations are quite rich; they are the most socialized: distraction here is largely absorbed in appearances (dance, theater, ceremony, cocktails, galas, garden parties, receptions, excursions, parties, visits). As for sport, it perhaps owes the extraordinary esteem in which Fashion holds it to its nature as compromise: on the one hand, whenever it is solidified into a signifier (*a sport shirt*), it suits all active situations (it then relates to the *practical*), and on the other hand, whenever it is signified, it achieves a luxury form of doing, a useless transitivity, it is both active and idle (hunting, walking, golfing, camping). The aimless is rare (but significant nonetheless): *for those days without plans:* in a world where one must always be or do something, the absence of occupation itself has the rank of an activity; moreover, only rhetoric can signal this negative activity.

18.4. *Temporal situations: spring, vacation, weekends*

In Fashion, festivity is tyrannical, it conquers time: Fashion time is essentially festive time. No doubt, Fashion has its own detailed calendar of seasons and pre-seasons throughout the year, and a very complete timetable of notable moments throughout the day (nine o'clock, noon, four o'clock, six o'clock, eight o'clock, midnight); there are, however, three periods of time which are privileged: with regard to the seasons, it is spring, with regard to the year, vacation, and with regard to the week, the weekend. Of course, every season has its own Fashion; however, that of spring is the most festive; why? because, as a season, spring is both pure and mythical at once: pure because it is not mixed with any other signified (summer Fashion is Fashion for vacation, that of autumn

---

[9] This is no longer the case once we turn to the being defined by his work in the form of a socioprofessional role (cf., below, 18.7).

is Fashion for the return to routine, and that of winter is Fashion for work); mythical, by virtue of the awakening of nature; Fashion takes this awakening for its own, thus giving its readers, if not its buyers, the opportunity to participate annually in a myth that has come from the beginning of time; spring Fashion, for the modern woman, is a bit like what the Great Dionysia or the Anthesteria were for the ancient Greeks. Vacations are constituted by a complex of situations: these vacations are dominated by time in its cyclic (annual recurrence) and climatic (the sun) aspects, but Fashion invests them with other circumstances and other values: nature (the season, the country, the mountains) and certain forms of activity (travel, swimming, camping, visiting museums, etc.). As for the weekend, it is a very rich value: geographically, it constitutes a field midway between city and country, i.e., it is experienced (and savored) as a relation: the weekend is a pinch of the country, hence, a refined essence of the country, miraculously apprehended in its clearest signs (walks, huge wood fires, old houses), not in its insignificant opacity (boredom, chores); temporally, it is a Sunday sublimated by its length (two or three days); the weekend, of course, carries a social connotation: it sets itself in opposition to Sunday, a trivial, popular day as shown by the discredit attached to its vestimentary version: putting on your Sunday best.[10]

18.5. *Situations of place: sojourns and travels*

This same alienation is at the heart of all notations of place. For Fashion (as for Leibnitz), to be in a particular place is to pass through it; i.e., travel is the great locus of Fashion: "sojourns" themselves are merely the poles of a single itinerant function (*city/country/sea/mountains*), and all countries always have a certain appeal. The geography of Fashion marks two "elsewheres"; a utopian "elsewhere," represented by everything that is exotic, exoticism being an acculturated geography;[11] and a real "elsewhere," which Fashion borrows from outside itself—from an

---

[10] One's Sunday best is, however, the fundamental fact of real clothing: a large part of the French population still dresses up for Sundays; a common wardrobe (that of a miner, for example) includes only two outfits: one for work (or more precisely, for going to work) and one for Sundays.

[11] Today this exoticism includes not necessarily distant countries, but the star sites, frequented by the Olympians: Capri, Monaco, Saint-Tropez.

entire economic and mythic situation of contemporary France: the Riviera.[12] Yet Fashion always experiences these places it is aimed at or passes through as absolute loci whose essence must be apprehended at a single stroke: it lives immediately immersed in a space or an element which is never anything but its goal; this is why climate—an important Fashion signifier—is always a paroxysmal element, as indicated by numerous superlatives of the *full* or *all* type: *sun-filled, full of trees, wind-filled:* Fashion is a rapid succession of absolute sites.

18.6. *The vision of "doing"*

As we see, the semantic discontinuity of the vestimentary code (since this code includes only discrete units) reappears on the rhetorical level in the form of essentially separate entities; through the connotation of its second system, Fashion divides human activity not into structural units available to a combinatory (such as the analysis of a series of technical actions might generate), but rather into gestures which carry their own transcendence within themselves; it can be said that the function of rhetoric here is to transform uses into rituals: in their connoted aspect, *weekend, spring,* and *the Riviera* are "scenes" in the sense this word could have in a liturgy, or, better still, in a theory of fantasy; for, in the end, it is a matter of absolute projections, infinitely repeated and infinitely evocative; the rhetorical activity of Fashion escapes time: it has no density, i.e., neither dilapidation nor boredom; the activity assumed by Fashion neither initiates nor exhausts itself; it no doubt constitutes a dreamed pleasure, but this pleasure is "cut short" fantastically, in an absolute instant, divested of all transitivity, since no sooner are they spoken than the weekend and the shopping no longer need "doing"; thus, we realize the double quality of the Fashion action: it is simultaneously voluptuous and intelligible. Applied to "doing," the rhetoric of Fashion appears as a "preparation" (in the chemical sense), destined to rid human activity of its major scoria (alienation, boredom, uncertainty, or more fundamentally: impossibility), while retaining its essential quality of a pleasure and the reassuring clarity of a sign: *doing the shopping* is no longer impossible,

---

[12] The eccentric is what is not the Midi: *practical on beaches everywhere, even those that aren't in the South.*

or costly, or tiring, or troublesome, or disappointing: the episode is reduced to a pure, precious sensation, simultaneously tenuous and strong, which combines unlimited buying power, the promise of beauty, the thrill of the city, and the delight of a perfectly idle super-activity.

III. ESSENCES AND MODELS

18.7. *Socioprofessional models*

"Doing" thus reduced to an array of essences, there is no breach between the (rhetorical) activity of the woman of Fashion and her socioprofessional status; in Fashion, work is only a simple reference, it provides identity, then immediately loses its reality: *secretary, librarian, press attaché, student* are all "names," actually epithets of nature, destined paradoxically to found what could be called the *being of doing;* thus, it is logical that the jobs (rare in any case) given by the rhetoric of Fashion are defined not by their technical conduct but by the situation they confer: a secretary (since she is often the subject) is not the woman who types, files, or answers the phone, but rather a privileged being who works closely with the top executive, who by contiguity participates in his superior essence (*I am a secretary, and I like to be impeccable*). Invariably, whenever Fashion grants a woman a job, this job is neither entirely noble (it is not well taken that women really compete with men) nor entirely inferior: it is always a "clean" job: secretary, decorator, bookseller; and this job always remains subject to the type of what could be called jobs of devotion (as formerly those of nurse and reader to an old lady): the woman's identity is thus established, in the service of Man (the boss), of Art, of Thought, but this submission is sublimated under the appearance of agreeable work and aestheticized under that of a "worldly" relation (appearances are always very important here, since it is a question of showing the garment). This sort of distance between the work *situation* and its technical unreality allows the woman of Fashion to be simultaneously moral (for work is a value) and idle (for work would sully her). This explains how Fashion can speak of work and leisure in the same manner; in Fashion, all work is empty, all pleasure is dynamic, voluntary, and, we could almost say, *laborious;* by exercising her right to Fashion, even through fantasies of the most improbable luxury, the woman always seems *to be doing something.* There is, moreover, a status which presents in its pure state the precious dialectic between leisure proposed as a sublime mission, provided with a very difficult task, and with an infinite vacation: i.e., the status of a "star" (frequently used in the rhetoric of Fashion): the star is a model (this status cannot be a role); she therefore takes her place in the universe of Fashion only by way of a pantheon (Dany Robin, Françoise Sagan, Colette Duval[13]), each deity of which appears both entirely idle and entirely occupied.

18.8. *Character essences: "personality"*

Psychological essences are as rich as professional models are poor: *fast, carefree, naughty, sharp, discriminating, balanced, easygoing, sassy, sophisticated, coquettish, serious, ingenue,* etc.: the woman of Fashion is a collection of tiny, separate essences rather analogous to the character parts played by actors in classical theater; this analogy is not arbitrary, since Fashion presents the woman as a representation, in such a way that a simple attribute of the person, spoken in the form of an adjective, actually absorbs this person's entire being; in *coquettish* and *ingenue,* there is a confusion of subject and predicate, of what is and of what is being spoken about. This psychological discontinuity has several advantages (since every connotation usually has the value of an alibi); first, it is familiar, since it stems from a sort of vulgate of classical culture, which we find in the psychology of horoscopes, palmistry, and elementary graphology; next, it is clear, since discontinuity and immobility are always considered more intelligible than continuity and movement; and furthermore, it permits outlining typologies of a scientific, hence authoritative and reassuring quality (*"Types A: casual; B: avant-garde; C: classic; D: work-first-of-all"*); last and most important, it makes possible a genuine combinatory of character units and, so to speak, technically prepares the illusion of a quasi-infinite richness of the person, which is precisely what in Fashion is called *personality;* the Fash-

---

[13] The star is of a royal essence, since it suffices to share her blood in order to be promoted to model status (*Françoise Sagan's mother*).

ion personality is in effect a quantitative notion, it is not defined, as elsewhere, by the obsessional force of a feature; it is essentially an original combination of common elements, the detail of which is always given; personality here is *compound*, but it is not complex; in Fashion, the individualization of the person depends on the number of elements in play, and still better, if it is possible, on their apparent opposition (*demure and determined, tender and tough, casual and cunning*): these psychological paradoxes have a nostalgic value: they give evidence of a dream of wholeness according to which the human being would be everything at once, without having to choose, i.e., without having to emphasize any feature in particular (Fashion, we know, does not like to make choices, i.e., to hurt anyone); the paradox consists then of maintaining the generality of the characteristics (which alone is compatible with the institution of Fashion) in a strictly analytical state: it is a generality of accumulation, not of synthesis: in Fashion, the *person* is thus simultaneously impossible and yet entirely known.

18.9. *Identity and otherness: the name and the game*

The accumulation of tiny psychological essences, often even opposing ones, is merely a way for Fashion to give the human person a double postulation: to confer either individuation or multiplicity, depending on whether the collection of characteristics is considered a synthesis or whether, on the contrary, we assume that this being is free to be masked behind one or the other of these units. Whence a double dream, which the rhetoric of Fashion places within a woman's reach: a dream of identity and play. The dream of identity (to be *oneself*, and to have this *self* be recognized by others) seems to be found in all mass works, and in all the activities of those who participate in it, whether we see it as the behavior of alienated classes, or we call it a compensatory action meant to react against the "depersonalization" of mass society; in any case, the dream of identity is essentially expressed by the assertion of a name, as if the name magically realized the person; in Fashion, the name cannot be directly displayed, since the reader is anonymous; but it appears that this reader dreams of her own name while delegating her identity to several personalities who complete the pantheon of

usual stars, not because they proceed from an Olympus of ac-
tresses, but precisely because they have a name: *Countess Albert
de Mun, Baroness Thierry van Zuplen;* doubtless the aristocratic
label is not free of connotation, but it is not determinant; the
name does not summarize breeding, but rather money: *Miss Non-
nie Phips* is a notable person insofar as her father owns a ranch
in Florida: to be is to have ancestors, and wealth; and if one or
the other is lacking, the name, like an empty sign which nevertheless retains its function as sign, continues to preserve identity;
such is the case for all women who wear dresses and are accom-
modatingly *named (Annie, Betty, Cathy, Daisy, Barbara, Jackie,*
etc.[14]); ultimately, there can no longer be any difference in nature between proper and common nouns: calling its subject *Miss
More-taste-than-money,* Fashion arrives at the very secret of the
anthroponymic process. The name is an excellent structural
model,[15] since it can sometimes be considered (mythically) as a
substance, sometimes (formally) as a difference; obsession with
the name refers simultaneously to a dream of identity and a dream
of otherness; thus, we see the woman of Fashion dreaming of
being at once herself and another. This second dream is an important one; we see continual evidence of it in all the games of
being that Fashion recounts (to be someone else by changing
only *this* detail); a transformational myth which seems attached
to all mythic reflection on clothing, as confirmed by so many
stories and proverbs, is quite prevalent in the literature of Fashion;[16] the multiplication of persons in a single being is always
considered by Fashion as an index of power; *You're demanding,
and you're sweet, too; with the couturiers you discover you can
be both, you can lead a double life:* herein lies the ancestral theme
of disguise, the essential attribute of gods, police, and bandits. Yet,
in the vision of Fashion, the ludic motif does not involve what
might be called a vertigo effect: it multiplies the person without

---

[14] These names are not completely empty, they display (to a French ear) a
certain anglomania; moreover, they are most probably the names of international
models and cover girls. But the cover girl tends increasingly toward stardom:
she herself becomes a model, *yet without masking her profession.*

[15] Cf. Claude Lévi-Strauss, *The Savage Mind.*

[16] Three conceptions can be distinguished here: (1) a popular and poetic conception: the garment (magically) produces the person; (2) an empirical conception: the person produces the garment, *is expressed* through it; (3) a dialectical
conception: there is a "turnstile" between person and garment (J.-P. Sartre,
Critique of Dialectical Reason).

any risk to her of losing herself, insofar as, for Fashion, clothing is not play but the *sign* of play; here once again we find the reassuring function of any semantic system; by *naming* vestimentary play (*to play the gardener; a fraudulent little hint of the Boy Scout in you*), Fashion exorcises it; the game of clothing is here no longer the game of being, the agonizing question of the tragic universe;[17] it is simply a keyboard of signs from among which an eternal person chooses one day's amusement; it is the final luxury of a personality rich enough to be multiplied, stable enough never to be lost; thus, we see Fashion "play" with the most serious theme of human consciousness (*Who am I?*); but by the semantic process to which it submits this theme, Fashion stamps it with the same futility which allows it always to disinculpate the obsession with clothing, on which Fashion thrives.

18.10. *Femininity*

To socioprofessional models and psychological essences must be added two fundamental signifieds of an anthropological order: sex and the body. Fashion understands the opposition between the feminine and the masculine quite well; reality itself requires that it do so (i.e., on the denotative level), since reality often puts features derived from men's clothing (pants, tie, jacket) in women's wardrobes; in fact, between the two kinds of clothing, differential signs are extremely rare and are always situated at the level of the detail (e.g., the way in which women's clothes are fastened): feminine clothing can absorb nearly all masculine clothing, which is content to "reject" certain features of feminine clothing (a man may not wear a skirt, while a woman may wear pants); this is because the taboo of the other sex does not have the same force in both cases: there is a social prohibition against the feminization of men,[18] there is almost none against the masculinization of women: Fashion notably acknowledges the *boyish look*. *Feminine* and *masculine* each have their own rhetori-

---

17 *Who am I? Who are you?* —The question of identity, the Sphinx's question, is at once the tragic and the ludic question par excellence, that of tragedies and that of societies' games; this does not prevent the two levels from occasionally coinciding: in the Maxims (derived from parlor games), in the Truth Game, etc.

18 Although certain forms of modern dandyism tend to feminize masculine apparel (a sweater with nothing underneath, a necklace): both sexes tend to become uniform under a single sign, as we shall see: that of *youth*.

cal version; *feminine* can refer to the idea of an emphatic, quint-
essential woman (*an exquisite femininity underneath*); when noted,
the *boyish look* itself has more a temporal than a sexual value: it
is the complementary sign of an ideal age, which assumes increasing importance in Fashion literature: the *junior*;[19] structurally,
the *junior* is presented as the complex degree of the *feminine/
masculine*: it tends toward androgyny; but what is more remarkable in this new term is that it effaces sex to the advantage of age;
this is, it seems, a profound process of Fashion: it is age which
is important, not sex; on the one hand, the model's youth is constantly asserted, defended, we might say, because it is naturally
threatened by time (whereas sex is a given), and it must constantly be recalled that youth is the standard for all measurements
of age (*still young, forever young*): its fragility creates its prestige; and on the other hand, in a homogeneous universe (since
Fashion deals only with the Woman, for women), it is to be
expected that the phenomenon of opposition should shift to where
there is perceptible, rational variation: thus, it is age which receives the values of glamor and seduction.

18.11. *The body as signified*

As for the human body, Hegel had already suggested that it was
in a relation of signification with clothing: as pure sentience, the
body cannot signify; clothing guarantees the passage from sentience to meaning;[20] it is, we might say, the signified par excellence. But which body is the Fashion garment to signify? Here
Fashion is faced, if not with a conflict, at least with a well-known
structural discontinuity: that of Language and Speech,[21] of the
institution and its actuality. Fashion resolves the passage from
the abstract body to the real body of its readers in three ways.
The first solution consists of proposing an ideal incarnate body;
i.e., that of the model, the cover girl; structurally, the cover girl
represents a rare paradox: on the one hand, her body has the

---

[19] "A sports outfit for juniors, certain parts of which might be borrowed from a big brother."
[20] "It is clothing which gives the body's attitude its relief, and for this reason it must be considered as an advantage, in the sense that it protects us from the direct view of what, as sentience, is devoid of signification" (Hegel, *Esthétique*, Paris, Aubier, 1944, vol. III, 1st part, p. 147).
[21] Cf., above, 1.14.

value of an abstract institution, and on the other hand, this body is individual, and between these two conditions, which correspond exactly to the opposition of Language and Speech, there is no *drift* (contrary to the system of language); this structural paradox defines the cover girl utterly: her essential function is not aesthetic, it is not a question of delivering a "beautiful body," subject to the canonic rules of plastic success, but a "deformed" body with a view to achieving a certain formal generality, i.e., a structure; it follows that the cover girl's body is no one's body, it is a pure form, which possesses no attribute (we cannot say it is *this* or *that*), and by a sort of tautology, it refers to the garment itself; here the garment is not responsible for signifying a full, slim, or slight body, but, through this absolute body, for signifying itself in its own generality; this first means of conciliation between the institution and its actuality is taken over by the photograph (or the Fashion drawing); if we cite this solution (in spite of the terminological rule), it is because it seems clear that the Fashion magazine feels an increasing scruple about accepting the abstraction of the cover girl as is: more and more we see the body photographed "in a situation," i.e., to unite with the pure representation of structure a rhetoric of gestures and poses meant to give a spectacularly empirical version of the body (the cover girl traveling, by the fireside, etc.[22]): more and more, the event threatens the structure. This is clearly seen in the two other ways Fashion has of dealing with the body, which are, strictly speaking, verbal. The first consists of a yearly decree that certain bodies (and not others) are in fashion. (*Do you have this year's face? You do if your face is small, if your features are fine, if your hat size is less than 55 cm., etc.*); this solution obviously represents a compromise between pure structure and literal event: on the one hand, it is clearly a structure, since the model is fixed abstractly, previously, and externally to any given reality; and on the other hand, this structure is born permeated by the event, insofar as it is seasonal and is immediately incarnated empirically in certain bodies and not in others, so that we no longer know whether the structure is inspired by or determines what is real. The third solution consists of accommodating clothing in such a way that it transforms the real body and succeeds in making it signify Fash-

---

[22] Cf., below, Appendix II.

ion's ideal body: to lengthen, fill out, reduce, enlarge, take in, refine—by these artifices,[23] Fashion asserts that it can submit any event (the real body notwithstanding) to the structure it has postulated (the year's Fashion); this solution explains a certain feeling of power: Fashion can convert any sentience into the sign it has chosen, its power of signification is unlimited.[24] We can see that these three solutions have different structural values; in the case of the cover girl, the structure is given without circumstance (a "Language" without "Speech"); in the case of the "fashionable body," there is a coincidence between structure and circumstance, but this coincidence is limited by time (one year); in the case of the "transformed body," there is complete submission of circumstance to structure by means of an art (couture). But in all three cases there is a structural constraint, the body is taken "in charge" by an intelligible system of signs, and sentience is dissolved in the signifier.[25]

IV. THE WOMAN OF FASHION

18.12. *From the reader to the model*

Such is the Woman ordinarily signified by the rhetoric of Fashion; imperatively feminine, absolutely young, endowed with a strong identity and yet with a contradictory personality, she is named Daisy or Barbara; she is often seen with the Countess de Mun and Miss Phips; an executive secretary, her work does not keep her from being present at every festive occasion throughout the year or the day; she leaves the city every weekend and travels constantly, to Capri, to the Canary Islands, to Tahiti, and each time she travels she goes to the South; she stays only in mild climates, and she likes everything all at once, from Pascal to cool jazz. In this monster we obviously recognize the permanent com-

---

[23] Cf., below, on transformation, 20.12.

[24] To the point where Fashion can transcend the law of euphemism and speak of ill-made bodies, since it is omnipotent to rectify them: *I'm not built like a model. I don't have a tiny waist. My hips are too broad. My bust is too full*, etc., say a whole procession of plaintiffs to the magazine, coming to Fashion as to a healing goddess.

[25] Nudity, for example, is nothing more in Fashion than the sign of the dressy (*The arm bare between shoulder and glove creates the dressy*).

promise which marks the relation between mass culture and its consumers: the Woman of Fashion is simultaneously what the reader is and what she dreams of being; her psychological profile is nearly that of all the stars "told" about every day by mass culture, so true is it that Fashion, by its rhetorical signified,[26] participates profoundly in this culture.

18.13. *The euphoria of Fashion*

There is, however, one point at which the Woman of Fashion differs in a decisive manner from the models of mass culture: she has no knowledge of evil, to any degree whatsoever. For, not having to deal with her defects and her difficulties, Fashion never speaks of love, it knows neither adultery nor affairs nor even flirtation: in Fashion, a woman always travels with her husband. Does she know about money? Barely; she can no doubt distinguish big budgets from average budgets; Fashion teaches how to "adapt" a garment, not how to make it last.[27] In any case, financial constraints do not weigh upon the Woman of Fashion, precisely because Fashion is omnipotent to thwart them: the high price of a garment is mentioned only to justify it as "outrageous": money problems are never invoked except insofar as Fashion can solve them. In this way, Fashion immerses the Woman about whom and to whom it speaks in a state of innocence, where everything is for the best in the best of all possible worlds: there is a law of Fashion euphoria (or of euphemia, since we are dealing here with written Fashion). Fashion's *bon ton*, which forbids it to offer anything aesthetically or morally displeasing, no doubt unites here with maternal language: it is the language of a mother who "preserves" her daughter from all contact with evil; but this systematic euphoria today seems peculiar to Fashion (it formerly belonged to all literature for young girls): it is not found in any other products of mass culture (film, magazines, popular novels), whose narratives are always dramatic, even catastrophic. The resistance to pathos is all the more notable here in that Fashion rhetoric, as we have seen, tends increasingly to the novelistic;

---

[26] And of course as a result of the tremendous circulation of its magazines.

[27] Resistance to *wearing out* is not one of Fashion's values (since what Fashion must do is in fact to accelerate the rhythm of buying), except, rarely, as the sign of a "chic" durability: *an old leather jacket.*

and if it is possible to conceive and to enumerate novels "in which nothing happens," literature does not offer a single example of a continually euphoric novel;[28] perhaps Fashion wins this wager insofar as its narrative is fragmentary, limited to citations of decor, situation, and character, and deprived of what could be called organic maturation of the anecdote; in short, Fashion would derive its euphoria from the fact that it produces a rudimentary, formless novel without temporality: time is not present in the rhetoric of Fashion: in order to rediscover time and its drama, we must abandon the rhetoric of the signified and move on to the rhetoric of the Fashion sign.

---

[28] The happy ending obviously belongs to a struggle between good and evil, i.e., to a drama.

19

Rhetoric of the Sign: The Reason of Fashion

"Every woman will shorten her skirt to just above the knee, wear pastel checks, and walk in two-tone pumps."

I. THE RHETORICAL TRANSFORMATION OF THE FASHION SIGN

19.1. *Signs and reasons*

The sign is the union of the signifier and the signified, of clothing and the world, of clothing and Fashion. Yet the Fashion magazine does not always present this sign in a declared manner; it does not necessarily say: *The accessory is the signifier of the signified spring. This year, short dresses are the sign of Fashion;* it says, in an entirely different manner: *The accessory makes the spring. This year, dresses are worn short;* by its rhetoric, the magazine can transform the relation between signifier and signified and substitute for pure equivalence the illusion of other relations (transitivity, finality, attribution, causality, etc.). In other words, precisely when Fashion constructs a very strict system of signs, it strives to give these signs the appearance of pure reasons;[1] and it is obviously because Fashion is tyrannical and its sign arbitrary that it must convert its sign into a natural fact or a rational law: connotation is not gratuitous; within the general economy of the system, it is responsible for restoring a certain *ratio*. However,

---

[1] On the general bearing of this process, cf., below, 20.II.

the bearing of this conversion differs according to whether it concerns *A* ensembles (having worldly and explicit signifieds) or *B* ensembles (having Fashion as implicit signified); in the first case, the sign takes shelter behind a use, a function, its *ratio* is empirical, natural; in the second case, the sign takes the form of an established fact or decree, its *ratio* is legal, institutional; but as in *A* ensembles, Fashion is equally present as the rhetorical signified of an intermediary system of connotation,[2] it follows that Fashion's legal *ratio* ultimately applies to all its utterances.

II. A ENSEMBLES: THE FUNCTION-SIGN

19.2. *Signs and functions in real clothing*

We might be tempted to set purely functional clothing (blue-jeans) in opposition to purely signaletic Fashion clothing, even when its signs are hidden behind functions (*a black dress for cocktails*). This would be an inexact opposition: however functional it may be, real clothing always includes a descriptive element, insofar as every function is at least a sign of itself; blue-jeans are useful for working, but they also "say" work, a raincoat protects from the rain, but it signifies rain as well. This movement of exchange between function and sign (at the level of reality) can probably be found in a large number of cultural objects: food, for example, is dependent on both a physiological need and a semantic status: foodstuffs satisfy and signify, they are at once satisfaction and communication.[3] In fact, as soon as a norm of fabrication takes over a function, this function enters with this norm into the relation between an event and a structure, and every structure implies a differential system of forms (units): the function becomes *readable*, and no longer merely transitive; thus no normalized (standardized) object is entirely exhausted by a pure *praxis:* every object is also a sign.[4] In order to find purely functional objects, it is necessary to imagine improvised objects:

---

[2] Cf., above, 3.7.

[3] The function-sign thus belongs to what can be called secondary systems, whose existence is not to be found entirely in signification.

[4] Thus, it is to be expected that the new milieu, stemming from technological society, imposes on the man who lives in it certain perceptions which are immediately penetrated by *reading,* as G. Friedman pointed out in 1942 (in *Mélanges Alexandre Koyré,* p. 178).

for example, the shapeless covering Roman soldiers threw over their shoulders to protect themselves from the rain; but once this makeshift garment has been fabricated, and, we might say, institutionalized under the name *paenula*, the protective function is taken over by a social system of communication: the paenula is set in opposition to other garments and has referred to the very idea of its use, just as a sign is set in opposition to other signs and conveys a certain meaning. This is why, as soon as real objects are standardized (and is there any other kind today?), we must speak not of functions but of function-signs. Whence it is understood that the cultural object possesses, by its social nature, a sort of semantic vocation: in itself, the sign is quite ready to separate itself from the function and operate freely on its own, the function being reduced to the rank of artifice or alibi: the *tengallon hat* (rainproof, sunproof) is nothing more than a sign of what is "Western"; the sport jacket no longer has an athletic function, but exists only as a sign, opposed to the *dressy;* blue-jeans have become the sign of leisure, etc. This process of signification grows all the stronger as society multiplies the number of its standardized objects: by enriching its differential system of forms, it likewise favors the birth of more and more complex lexicons of objects: this explains how modern, technological society can so easily separate the sign from the function and imbue the utilitarian objects it produces with various significations.

19.3. *Real functions and unreal functions*

There are times when the proposed (spoken) garment corresponds to a real function: a *dress for dancing* is used for dancing and also indicates dancing in a stable manner, readable to all;[5] there is an adaptation of form or matter to the act and constancy in the semantic relation. But in the vast majority of cases the functions Fashion attributes to clothing are far more complex: there is a tendency for the magazine to represent increasingly precise and increasingly contingent functions, and within this movement, rhetoric obviously plays a dominant role.[6] When it is determined

---

[5] It will be noticed that, in such utterances, the signified is sclerosed, so to speak, in the form of a species (cf. *sport shirt*).

[6] Rhetoric has a tendency to appear as soon as there is parataxis of semantic units (cf., above, 16.4).

that a garment *stands* for some grand circumstance of a, so to speak, anthropological order, a season or a celebration, the function of protection or adornment remains plausible (*a winter coat, a wedding gown*); but if it is asserted that this dress stands for a *young woman who lives 20 km. from a large city, takes the train every day, and often lunches with friends,* it is the very precision of the worldly term which renders the function unreal; here once again we find the paradox of novelistic art: all minutely detailed Fashion is unreal, but also, the more contingent the function, the more "natural" it seems; the literature of Fashion thus combines with the postulate of "realist" style, according to which an accumulation of minute and particular details accredits the truth of the thing represented better than a simple sketch, a highly wrought picture allegedly being "truer" than a cursorily drawn one; and within the order of popular literature, the scrupulous description of vestimentary functions coincides with the current tendency of mass media to personalize all information, to make every utterance a direct challenge, not directed at the entire mass of readers, but at each reader in particular; the function of Fashion (*living 20 km. from,* etc.) thus becomes a genuine confidence, as if the equivalence of this dress and such a precise habitat were posited for only one reader among all, as if once the 20 km. were traversed, there must by rights be a change of reader and of clothes. We can see that the reality implied by the Fashion function is in essence defined by a contingency; it is not a transitive reality, it is, once again, a reality experienced fantastically, it is the unreal reality of the novel, emphatic in proportion to its unreality.

19.4. *"Rationalization"*

Naturally, the more mythical a function (through the extravagance of its contingencies), the more it masks the sign; the more imperative its functions claim to be, the more the sign gives way to an apparently empirical use; paradoxically, it is in the most full-blown forms of Fashion rhetoric that the garment seems unable to show everything and is modestly reduced to the rank of a tool, as if this white mink bolero served only as protection against the cold in a cool church one spring wedding day. In this way, rhetoric introduces into Fashion a whole series of false functions whose purpose is obviously to give the Fashion sign the guarantee of reality: a guarantee all the more precious since, in spite of its prestige, Fashion always feels guilty of futility. This functional alibi is doubtless part of a general (perhaps modern) process, according to which every empirical *ratio*, stemming from "doing something" in the world, suffices to excuse not only any phenomenon of enjoyment, but also, in a more subtle way, any spectacle of essences: the function, asserted on the rhetorical level, is in short the world's right to regain possession of Fashion, the homage that a system of being offers to a system of doing. The transformation of an order of signs into an order of reasons[7] is known elsewhere under the name of rationalization. It could be described with regard to clothing itself (real clothing, and no longer written clothing): establishing the psychoanalysis of clothing, Flügel gave a few examples of this social conversion from symbol to reason:[8] long pointed shoes are not understood as a phallic symbol by the society which adopts them, but their use is attributed to simple hygienic reasons;[9] and if this example seems too dependent on the symbolics of psychoanalysis, here is one which is entirely historical: around 1830, the starching of cravats was justified by advantages of comfort and hygiene.[10] In both of these examples, we can even discern the appearance of a tendency, which is perhaps not accidental, to make the sign's reasons into the very opposite of its physical disposition: discomfort is turned into comfort; perhaps this inversion is of the same order as the one which affects reality and its representation in bourgeois society, if we abide by Marx's image;[11] it is a fact that the

---

[7] This transformation clearly seems to be what the neurotic imposes on his neurosis (system of signs) in the phenomenon of "secondary profit" (H. Nunberg, *Principes de psychanalyse*, Paris, P.U.F., 1957, p. 322).

[8] The word *rationalization* is found in Flügel (*Psychology of Clothes*, chaps. I and XIV). It seems to correspond to what Claude Lévi-Strauss described thus: "*The difference between linguistic phenomena and other cultural phenomena is that the former never emerge into clear consciousness, while the latter, although having the same unconscious origin, often rise to the level of conscious thought, thus giving birth to secondary reasonings and reinterpretations*" (*Structural Anthropology*, p. 26).

[9] Flügel, *Psychology of Clothes*, p. 27.

[10] *Cravatiana, ou Traité général des cravates*, 1823.

[11] "*If men and their conditions appear in all ideologies reversed as in a camera's lens, this phenomenon stems from their vital historical process, just as the reversal of objects on the retina stems from their directly physical process*" (K. Marx, *The German Ideology*).

signaletic nature of clothing was better stated and, we might say, more innocent in earlier periods than in ours; monarchical society openly presented its clothing as an ensemble of signs, not as the product of a certain number of reasons: the length of a train exactly signaled a social condition, no speech existed to convert this lexicon into a reason, to suggest that ducal dignity produced the length of the train, as the cold church produces the white mink bolero; in former ages, costume did not connive at function, it displayed the artifice of its correspondences. And thereby the correction of these correspondences remained openly normative: as a sign, the relation between the world and clothing had to be strictly in accordance with the social norm. On the contrary, in our written clothing (and precisely because it is written), the sign's correction is never presented as openly normative, but simply functional; it is an object's conformity to a function which must be honored (*a boat-neck décolleté, pleated skirts*) at a function which must be honored (*attending tea dances, showing the maturity of age*); the rule always seems to copy, henceforth, the law of nature: *Homo significans* takes the mask from *Homo faber*, i.e., from his exact opposite. We could say that, due to the rationalization which makes it convert all its signs into reasons, written Fashion[12] accomplishes this paradox: to be a spoken "doing."

III. *B* ENSEMBLES: THE LAW OF FASHION

19.5. *Noted-notified*

In *B* ensembles, whose implicit signified is exclusively Fashion, rhetoric obviously cannot transform the sign into a function, since the function must be named; more difficult still, the sign's rationalization is therefore possible only, we might say, at the cost of an operation of force. We have seen that by *noting* a vestimentary feature purely and simply, as soon as it is not a matter of fabricating it, which would escape the semantic process, Fashion offered itself as the signified of this feature: to note that (this

---

[12] Rationalization of the sign (i.e., making it into a function) is possible only through a language (it is a connotation), and this is the point of written Fashion: the phenomenon is not found in iconic language (photographs, drawings) except when the setting communicates the garment's function (cf. Appendix II).

year) *skirts are worn short* is to say that *short skirts* signify Fashion this year. The signified Fashion includes only a single pertinent variation, that of the *unfashionable;* but as the rule of
euphemia prohibits Fashion from naming what denies its very
being,[13] the true opposition is less between the *fashionable* and
the *unfashionable* than it is between the *marked* (by speech) and
the *unmarked* (silence); there is a confusion between the noted
and the Good, the unnoted and the Bad, without enabling the
assertion to be made that one term determines the other: all that
could be said is that Fashion does not note what it has initially
condemned and that it notes what glorifies it; it is still more likely
that it glorifies (as its own being) what it notes and condemns
what it does not note; by asserting itself, by naming itself (in the
tautological manner of a divinity *who is the one he is*), the being
of Fashion presents itself immediately as Law;[14] it follows that
the *noted* in Fashion is always the *notified;* in Fashion, being
and name, the mark and the Good, notation and legality coincide
absolutely: what is said is legal. Moreover (and here is the mask
of the Fashion sign in *B* ensembles), what is legal is true. This
final transformation (which shall be dealt with in a moment) is
symmetrical in relation to what converts the sign into a function
in *A* ensembles: just as the explicit sign needed the mask of a
reason, so the Law of Fashion needs the mask of a nature: thus,
we shall see all Fashion rhetoric used to justify its decrees, either
by distancing them under the species of a spectacle or by converting them into pure observations-of-fact external to its own
will.

19.6. *Law as spectacle*

To proclaim the Law with rhetorical emphasis is in fact a way of
distancing it and, so to speak, of playing with it in the manner
of an excessive spectacle: to issue an edict called *the Skier's Ten
Commandments* is to justify the arbitrariness of Fashion in a
joking guise, the way a man jokes exaggeratedly about his faults

---

[13] Allusion is made to the *unfashionable* only in order to crush it beneath the
blow of the new Fashion.
[14] Behind this law there is an authority external to Fashion: this is the *fashion
group* and its economic "reasons," but here we remain on the level of an immanent
analysis of the system.

in order to acknowledge them without renouncing them; each time Fashion acknowledges the arbitrariness of its decisions, it does so in an emphatic tone, as if showing off a caprice were the same as attenuating it, as if acting an order were thereby making it unreal:[15] Fashion inoculates the rhetoric of its decisions with a little arbitrariness the better to excuse itself for the arbitrariness which founds them. Its playful metaphors sometimes connect it to political power (Fashion is a monarch whose realm is hereditary, it is a Parliament which renders femininity obligatory, like public education or military service), sometimes to religious Law: from the decree it then shifts to the prescription (*every woman will shorten her skirts to just above the knee*, etc.); blending obligation and premonition, since here to foresee suffices to impose, it prefers to use the moral tense par excellence, that of the Decalogue, the future: *This summer, hats will surprise, they'll be both amusing and serious;* it is difficult to boil the Fashion decision down any further, since without in any way suggesting it might have a cause (for example, the *fashion group*), it is reduced to a pure effect, i.e., to a necessary event, in the physical and moral sense of the term: *This summer, dresses will be made of raw silk:* raw silk is what must happen to dress, both through natural causality and by legal prescription.

19.7. *From Law to Fact*

With these obligation-filled futures, so frequent in Fashion, we approach the decisive rationalization of *B* ensembles, which is the conversion of Law into Fact: what is decided on, imposed, finally appears as necessary, neutral in the manner of a pure and simple fact: for this to take place, it is enough to keep the Fashion decision secret; who will make it obligatory that this summer's dresses be made of raw silk? By its silence, Fashion transforms raw silk into an event half-real, half-normative, in a word, *fatal.* For there is a fatality of Fashion: the magazine is nothing but the chronicle of a somewhat barbarous period when men are slaves of the fatality of events and passions: play (*Colors are for*

---

[15] Naturally, if the seriousness of these metaphors seems to expose itself as a joke thanks to ironically emphatic forms, it does so with the ambiguity of false mockery: we only play at what we dare not be: socially condemned to a certain futility, Fashion can only play at being serious.

you to play with[16]), madness (we do not resist Fashion, it illuminates and possesses), war (*pastel tones on the attack, the war on knees, honor to ribbons*), these strong passions place Fashion outside humanity, as it were, and constitute it as a malign contingency: Fashion places itself at the crossroads of chance and divine decrees: its decision becomes an obvious fact. All that then remains for Fashion to do is to practice a rhetoric of pure observation-of-fact (*loose dresses are in*), and the magazine's sole function is to report *what is* (*We note the reappearance of camel's hair sweaters*), even if, in the manner of a sagacious historian, the magazine can discern in a simple event the main lines of a development (*The fashion for black-dyed mink is mounting*).[17] By thus constituting Fashion as an inevitable force, the magazine leaves it all the ambiguity of an object without cause, but not without will: sometimes the feature is given the appearance of a phenomenon so natural that it would be incongruous to justify it (*black, in any case, your cocktail dress, and of course you'll add the white note of your kid gloves*); or again, the better to separate Fashion from its creator gods, it is imputed not to its producers, but to its consumers (*They love striped swimsuits. They wear their swimsuits high in front*); or last, the feature will be made the subject of its appearance (*This year, nightgowns come in three lengths*): no more designers, or buyers, Fashion has driven people away, it becomes an autarchic universe, where ensembles choose their jackets themselves and nightgowns their length. Thus, it is to be expected that, all things considered, this universe secrete its own wisdom, elaborate its rules no longer as proud ukases coming from an upstart couture but as the ancestral law of a reign of pure nature: Fashion can be spoken in proverbs, and thus be placed no longer under the law of men but under the laws of things, as it appears to the peasant, the oldest man in human history, to whom nature speaks by its repetitions: *with dashing coats, white dress; with delicate fabrics, light accessories.* This wisdom of Fashion implies an audacious confusion between the past and the future, between what has been

---

[16] And again, "*Tweed is to fabrics what Royal Dutch is to the Stock Exchange: a safe investment.*"

[17] There is no distinction if the magazine decrees its own Fashion or if it limits itself to conveying the Fashion that comes from the *fashion group:* in all cases of magazine rhetoric, every instance is absent.

decided upon and what is going to happen: a Fashion is recorded at the very moment it is announced, at the very moment it is prescribed. All Fashion rhetoric is contained in this foreshortening: to remark what is imposed; to produce Fashion; then to see it only an effect without a named cause; then, of this effect to retain only the phenomenon; last, to allow this phenomenon to be developed as if it owed its life to itself alone: such is the trajectory Fashion follows in order to transform into fact at once its cause, its law, and its signs. Between the (real) law and the (mythical) fact, we witness a curious interchange of means and ends: Fashion's reality is essentially the arbitrariness which establishes it: here we cannot logically transform a law into a fact except metaphorically; now, what does Fashion say? When it does acknowledge its law, it is as metaphor, and when it takes shelter behind the fact, it is as if it were literal; it metaphorizes the Skier's Ten Commandments (which is its reality), it observes the fact that *this year, blue is the fashion* (which is pure metaphor); it gives its reality the rhetorical emphasis of a deliberate metaphor, and its metaphors the simplicity of an observation-of-fact; it assumes the panache of connotation where it is merely denotative, and the humble figure of denotation when it deploys its purest rhetoric. Here again, there is the exact inversion of reality and its image.

IV. RHETORIC AND TENSE

19.8. *The reason of Fashion and the time of Fashion*

The rhetorical transformation from sign to reason (functional, legal, or natural) is doubtless common to all cultural objects, whenever they are apprehended within a process of communication; it is the price the "world" pays for the sign. But in Fashion this transformation, it seems, is justified in a particular and even more imperious manner. If Fashion's tyranny is identified with its being, this being itself is ultimately no more than a certain passion of tenses. As soon as the signified *Fashion* encounters a signifier (such and such a garment), the sign becomes the year's Fashion, but thereby this Fashion dogmatically rejects the Fashion which preceded it, i.e., its own past;[18] every new Fashion is a refusal to inherit, a subversion against the oppression of the preceding Fashion; Fashion experiences itself as a Right, the natural right of the present over the past; defined by its very infidelity, Fashion nevertheless lives in a world it wants to be, and sees as, ideally stable, completely penetrated by conformist glances.[19] Rhetoric, and particularly the rationalization of the sign, allows this contradiction to be resolved: it is because the vindictive present which defines it is barely tenable, difficult to acknowledge, that Fashion is concerned to elaborate a fictive temporality of a more dialectical appearance, a temporality which has an order, bearing, and maturity which are empirical on the level of functions, institutional on the level of Law, organic on the level of fact; Fashion's aggressiveness, whose rhythm is the same as that of vendettas, is thus disarmed by a more patient image of time; in that absolute, dogmatic, vengeful present tense in which Fashion speaks, the rhetorical system possesses reasons which seem to reconnect it to a more manageable, more distant time, and which are the politeness or—the regret—of the murder it commits of its own past, as if it vaguely heard that possessive voice of the slain year saying to it: *Yesterday I was what you are, tomorrow you will be what I am.*[20]

---

[18] We have seen that, by euphemia, Fashion very rarely speaks of the unfashionable; if it does, it is always in the name of the present, as a countervalue; without scruples it calls *angles and breaks* what yesterday were *boldly drawn lines. This year,* it says, *suits will be youthful and supple:* then were they old and stiff last year?

[19] We are now better able to define Fashion's *futility:* it is infidelity, a powerfully inculpating sentiment.

[20] Read on a gravestone.

CONCLUSION

20

Economy of the System

I. ORIGINALITY OF THE FASHION SYSTEM

20.1. *Language, guardian of meaning and gateway to the world*

We have several times had occasion to remark how much the mass distribution of Fashion magazines, which may be considered truly popular magazines, had modified the Fashion phenomenon and shifted its sociological meaning: by passing through written communication, Fashion becomes an autonomous cultural object, with its own original structure and, probably, with a new finality; other functions are substituted for or added to the social functions usually acknowledged by vestimentary Fashion;[1] these functions are analogous to those found in all literature and can be summarized by saying that, through the language which henceforth takes charge of it, Fashion becomes *narrative*. The action of language occurs on two levels, that of denotation and that of connotation. On the denoted level, language acts as both the producer and the guardian of meaning; it accentuates Fashion's semantic nature, since by the discontinuity of its nomenclatures it multiplies its signs precisely where reality, proposing only a continuous substance,[2] would have difficulty signifying with any precision; this multiplication of meanings can be clearly seen in the assertion of species: when (written) Fashion makes *linen* signify, it considerably improves upon the semantic possibilities of the real garment; this garment can in fact give meaning only to *light fabrics* in relation to *heavy fabrics*; language shatters this

---

[1] The dialectic of novation and imitation analyzed by sociology since Spencer.
[2] This is notably valid in relation to photography.

rudimentary structure into a thousand significant species, thus
building a system whose justification is no longer utilitarian (to
oppose *light* to *heavy*, as *cool* to *warm*), but only semantic: it
thus constitutes meaning as a true luxury of the mind. And further,
with the signs thus multiplied, language intervenes anew, but
this time in order to give them the *bearing* of a structure; by the
very stability of the name (relative though this stability may
be, since names, too, pass away), language resists the mobility of
the real; this can be clearly seen in the system's logic; the taboos
which prevent such and such a genre from encountering such
and such a variant are in fact quite relative; none is eternal;
Fashion's prohibitions are nonetheless absolute and therefore
meaning is imperative,[3] not only at the level of synchrony, but
more deeply, at the level of nomenclature; wearing two blouses
at once would perhaps not be impossible, if one had the right
to change the name of the second blouse; but when language
denies this right (at least on the scale of its own synchrony),
Fashion can constitute itself as logic, or we might say, an exact
system. Thus, on the denotative level, language assumes a regu-
lative role, entirely subject to semantic ends: we could say that
Fashion speaks just to the degree it wants to be a system of signs.
However, on the connotative level, its role appears to be entirely
different: rhetoric opens Fashion to the world; through it, the
world is present in Fashion, no longer only as human productive
power in an abstract sense, but as an ensemble of "reasons," i.e.,
as an ideology; through rhetorical language, Fashion communicates with the world, it participates in a certain alienation and in
a certain reason of humanity; but also, as we have seen, in that
movement *toward* the world, which is the movement of its connotative system, Fashion loses much of its semantic existence (its
signs become reasons, its signifier ceases to be finely discontinuous, and its signified becomes indefinite and latent), so that language possesses two almost contradictory functions, depending
on whether it intervenes on the system's denotative or connotative
level; and (as we shall soon see more clearly) it is obviously in
this divergence of roles (whether it be pure opposition or the

---

[3] We recall that meaning is a supervised freedom, in which the limit is as constitutive as the choice.

stirrings of a dialectical movement) that the system's profound economy resides.

20.2. *Classificatory activity*

Although, in a certain manner, rhetoric undoes the system of signs elaborated outside it (on the denotative level), and although it can thus be said that the world begins where meaning ends, it is nonetheless reality (but not, it is true, "the world") which founds the signification in the very moment when it proposes its limits: reality signifies insofar as it is finite, as shown by the classificatory economy of the denotative system. This economy rests upon a gradual elimination of substance (in the sense given this word by Hjelmslev). From the outset, we might say, reality, in the form of physical, aesthetic, or moral constraints, denies certain objects certain significations by preventing them from varying or, on the contrary, by imposing on them an infinite variation. It is this regime of initial exclusions which provokes a vast *dispatching* of meaning through objects and qualities, genera and supports, according to pathways which are sometimes closed (*excluded*), sometimes wide open (*typical associations*). It is this same reticular movement which founds meaning on the level of the utterance: a unitary meaning emerges from a dust of meanings, filtered at the behest of successive matrices, in such a way that ultimately each utterance, however tangled its chains of units, has only one object aimed at by signification. This homographic composition permits a certain hierarchy to be distributed among vestimentary objects, but this hierarchy no longer takes the material importance of its elements into account; the construction of meaning now appears as a counternature; it promotes minor elements and shies away from important elements, as if the intelligible were responsible for compensating for matter's *given;* thus, meaning is distributed according to a kind of revolutionary grace; its power becomes so autonomous that it can act at a distance and in the end dissolve substance itself: it is not the cape which signifies, it is its assertion: meaning denies substances all intrinsic value. This denial is perhaps the most profound function of the Fashion system; contrary to language, this system on the one hand must in fact deal with substances (clothing) encumbered by extra-semantic uses, and on the other hand it has absolutely no need to make use of a combinative relay, like that of the double articulation,[4] since its signifieds are in fact very few in number. This constraint and this liberty generate a particular classification, which rests on two principles: on the one hand, each unit (i.e., each matrix) is like the foreshortening which leads the inert substance toward the point where it can be impregnated with meaning, so that at each instant the consumer of the system experiences the action that meaning imposes on a matter whose original being (contrary to language) is not to signify; and on the other hand, the anarchy that risks attacking a system with numerous signifiers and few signifieds is here opposed by a strongly hierarchical distribution, whose articulations are not linear, contrary to those of language (though sustained by language), but, we might say, concerted: the poverty of the signified (whether worldly or of Fashion) is thus redeemed by an "intelligent" construction of the signifier which receives the essence of the semantic power and enters into almost no relation with its signifieds. Fashion thus appears essentially—and this is the final definition of its economy—as a system of signifiers, a classificatory activity, much more a semiological than a semantic order.

20.3. *Open system and closed system*

However, this semiological order, which tends toward the void by subtly and strongly arming itself in order to "dissolve" substance, encounters the world under the general species of a certain signified; and as this signified is different in A and B ensembles, the general economy of the Fashion system is variously inflected within each of these ensembles, and here the analysis must be pursued along two different lines. Moreover, the difference between the two types of ensembles has to do not only with the qualitative difference in their signifieds, in the one case multiple and in the other binary, but much more with its place in the superimposition of disconnected systems which constitutes every Fashion utterance. We have not referred to this architecture since

---

[4] We cannot speak of a double articulation in the Fashion system as it has just been described, for elements of the matrix, all interdependent, cannot be identified with the distinctive signs or phonemes of language; the matrices can combine with each other, but this is the system's sole combinatory.

it was analyzed,[5] but it is time to take up once again the essential role it plays in the economy of the Fashion system. We recall that, in *B* ensembles, Fashion is the implicit and direct signified of vestimentary features: thus, it constitutes a signified of simple denotation; on the contrary, in *A* ensembles, making the worldly signified explicit displaces Fashion, which finds itself raised a notch, as it were, and shifted to the rank of second signified—the signified of connotation. Ultimately then, it is Fashion which constitutes the stake of the divergent economy of the two systems *A* and *B*; denoting here (*B*) and connoting there (*A*), it is involved in two different ethics, since all connotation, on the one hand, involves a transformation of the sign into a reason but, on the other hand, opens the lower system to the ideology of the world. Denoting, Fashion participates directly in a system *closed* over its signifiers and which communicates with the world only by the intelligible which every sign system represents;[6] connoting, Fashion participates indirectly in an *open* system, which communicates with the world by the explicit nomenclature of worldly signifieds. The two economies thus seem to exchange their defects and their virtues: *A* ensembles are open to the world, but because of this they participate in the inversions which ideology imposes on reality; *B* ensembles retain the poverty and, we might say, the formal probity of all denotation, but at the cost of an abstraction which appears as a way of being closed to the world. It is this symmetrical ambiguity of its ensembles which marks the Fashion system.

II. A Ensembles: Alienation and Utopia

20.4. *Nomination of the signified*

A ensembles are open to the world for three reasons: first, because their signifieds are named, taken over by a nomenclature stemming from language (it is this very absence of isology which defines them); next, because in them Fashion shifts to the state of a connoted system, i.e., assumes the mask of a reason or a

---

[5] Cf., above, 3.II.

[6] We recall, however, that, even in *B* ensembles, Fashion can communicate with the world when subjected to a rhetoric.

nature; last, because Fashion and signifieds are organized by rhetoric and form a representation of the world which itself combines with a general ideology. However, by opening itself to the world, Fashion is led to support it, so to speak, i.e., to participate in a certain conversion of reality which is customarily described under the name of ideological alienation; the moments when the system "opens" translate or, we might say, define this alienation. The nomination of the signified, which is exceptional in relation to the systems of signification we are familiar with, leads to making these worldly signifieds into immobile essences of a sort: once named, *spring, weekend, cocktails* become divinities which seem to produce the garment naturally, instead of remaining with it in an arbitrary relation of signification; according to a familiar anthropological process, the word transforms the object into a force, the word itself becomes a force; what is more, to develop a semantic relation between two distinct and separate objects, the signifier on the one hand, and the signified on the other, is considerably to reduce the system's functional structure and to attach meanings to units by a kind of segmented and immobile correspondence, we might say it is to restore the body of significations to a lexicon (*raw silk = summer*). Doubtless, these significations are in fact labile, since the Fashion lexicon is remade each year; but the signs here are not transformed from within, as in the diachrony of language; their change is arbitrary, and yet making the signified explicit gives it the very weight of things attached to each other by what might be called a public affinity: the sign is no longer mobile,[7] but only dead and renascent, ephemeral and eternal, capricious and reasonable; by naming its signifieds, Fashion thus proceeds to a kind of immediate sacralization of the sign: the signified is separated from its signifier and yet seems to adhere to it by natural and imprescriptible right.

20.5. *Fashion masked*

The second alienation which affects *A* ensembles (at the very moment when it opens them a second time to the world) con-

---

[7] Bergson has said: "*What characterizes the signs of human language is not so much their generality as their mobility. The instinctive sign is an adherent sign, the intelligent sign is a mobile sign.*" (*Evolution créatrice*, 3rd ed., Paris, Alean, 1907, p. 172).

cerns Fashion's place in the structure of these ensembles. In an utterance such as: *Prints are winning at the races*, the worldly signified (the races) drives out, as it were, the signified-Fashion and relegates it to the (literally) improbable zone of connotation; nothing indicates de jure that the equivalence of prints and races be subject to the value of Fashion, yet, de facto, the equivalence itself is always and only the signifier of the signified-Fashion: prints are the sign of the races only under the sanction of Fashion (next year the sign will be unmade); in this kind of formal "bad faith" we recognize the very definition of connotation: Fashion, avoided as a real sign, is nonetheless present as a hidden order, a silent terror, for not to respect the equivalence between prints and the races (this year) would be to fall into the "fault" of the unfashionable; the difference which sets in opposition the implicit signified of denotative systems and the latent signified of connotative systems can thus be seen to manifest itself once again;[8] in effect, the alienation here consists, quite precisely, of rendering an implicit signified latent; Fashion hides itself in the manner of a god: omnipotent and yet pretending to give prints complete freedom to signify the races *naturally*. In short, Fashion here treats itself as a shameful and tyrannical value, which hushes up its identity, no longer by depriving it purely and simply of its terminological expression (as in denotative ensembles), but by substituting for it the name of an entirely human causality (the semantic units of the worldly signified). Connotation then unites with a more general alienation which consists of giving an arbitrary determinant the mask of an inevitable nature.

20.6. *Utopian reality and real utopia*

The final point of opening onto the world (in A ensembles) is constituted by the same rhetoric which simultaneously "heads" both the terminological system and the connotation of Fashion. Rhetoric corresponds to a process of ideologically inverting reality into its contrary image: the function of the rhetorical system is to mask the systematic and semantic nature of the utterances submitted to it by transforming equivalence into reason; though

---

[8] Cf., above, 16.5.

a system itself, rhetorical activity is anti-systematic, for it deprives Fashion utterances of all semiological appearance: it makes the conjunction of the world and clothing the object of an *ordinary* discourse, mobilizing causes, effects, affinities, in short, pseudo-logical relations of all kinds. This activity of conversion can be roughly compared to the activity of the *psyche* in dreams: the dream also mobilizes crude symbols, i.e., the elements of a primary semantic system; but it links these elements in the form of a narrative in which the syntagmatic force eclipses (or masks) the systematic depth. Here, however, we observe an ethical reversal: to the extent that Fashion rhetoric affabulates, it recaptures a certain reality of the world *against* its terminological system, which itself remains (literally) improbable: here a curious interchange occurs between the real and the imaginary, the possible and the utopian. On the terminological level, semantic units (*weekend, evening, shopping*) are once more fragments of the real world, but these fragments are already transitory and illusory, for the world does not give any worldly sanction to the relation between *this sweater* and *the weekend:* it does not actualize it at the heart of a real system; thus, on its literal level, what is real in Fashion is purely assertive (what we mean by improbable). Confronted with this "unreality" on the terminological level, Fashion rhetoric is paradoxically more "real" insofar as it is absorbed by a coherent ideology, dependent on an entire social reality; to say on the terminological level that *this sweater is good for weekends* is merely an assertion, unalienated insofar as it is *matte;* to say, on the contrary, that *this sweater is a must if you're going to the Touraine for a weekend at the country home of your husband's boss* is to link the garment to an entire situation, simultaneously imaginary and true, with that same profound truth as that of a novel or a dream: it is to this extent that we can say that the terminological (denotative) level is that of a utopian reality (for the real world does not actually consist of any vestimentary lexicon, though its elements—here world and there clothing—may be really given), whereas the rhetorical level is that of a real utopia (for the totality of the rhetorical situation stems directly from a real story). We could say in another manner that Fashion has no *content* except on the rhetorical level: the very moment the Fashion system is unmade, it opens itself to the world, fills itself with reality, becomes alienated and "human," thus acting out in a symbolic manner the fundamental ambiguity of any intelligence of reality: it is not possible to *speak* about reality without being alienated from it: to understand is to be an accomplice.

20.7. *The naturalization of signs*

The interchange of denoted unreality and connoted reality corresponds to the conversion of the sign into a reason, which appears as the fundamental process of *A* ensembles: it is because these ensembles establish a "naturalistic" vision of clothing and the world that they unite in their own manner (simultaneously utopian and real) with the society which produces them, whereas a system of pure and declared signs never represents anything but the effort human beings put forth to produce "meaning," apart from all content. Thus, the general value of all conversions of signs into reasons can be understood well beyond the Fashion system itself. *A* ensembles are in effect evidence of what could be called the semiological paradox: on the one hand, it seems that all societies deploy tireless activity in order to penetrate the reality of signification and to constitute strongly and subtly organized semiological systems by converting things into signs, the perceptible into the signifying; and on the other hand, once these systems are constituted (or, more precisely, as they are being constituted), human beings display an equal activity in masking their systematic nature, reconverting the semantic relation into a natural or rational one; therein lies a double process, simultaneously contradictory and complementary: of signification and of rationalization. This, at least, is what happens, it seems, in our societies, for it is not certain that the applicability of the semiological paradox has a universal bearing, of an anthropological order; certain archaic types of societies allow the intelligible they elaborate to keep the form of an ensemble of declared signs; man does not assign himself the task of converting nature and the supernatural into a reason, but simply that of deciphering them: the world is not "explained," it is read, philosophy is a *manteia*,[9]

---

[9] G. W. F. Hegel, *Lectures on the Philosophy of History*.

and it seems, conversely, a particular characteristic of our societies—and particularly of our mass society—to naturalize or rationalize the sign through the original process described here under the name of *connotation;* this explains why the cultural objects elaborated by our society are arbitrary (as systems of signs) and yet well-founded (as rational processes); we can then imagine defining human societies according to the degree of "frankness" of their semantic systems and according to whether the intelligibility they infallibly assign to things is frankly signifying or allegedly rational; or again: according to their power of connotation.

III. *B* ENSEMBLES: THE DISAPPOINTMENT OF MEANING

20.8. *The infinite metaphor*

Compared with *A* ensembles, which are open and alienated, *B* ensembles appear partially pure; they do not in fact experience the "reifying" nomination of the signified, and in them Fashion remains a denoted value; they become alienated from the world only by the rhetoric of clothing (which, moreover, is a poor one, as we have seen[10]) and by the rhetoric of signification (which transforms the Fashion decision into Law or into Fact); furthermore, these conversions are not constant, they remain contingent upon such and such an utterance. In other words, *B* ensembles do not "lie": in them the garment signifies Fashion openly. This purity—or frankness—stems from two conditions. The first is constituted by the extreme disproportion which the denotation of Fashion introduces between the number of its signifiers and that of its signifieds: in *B* ensembles, the signified is positively singular:[11] it is always and everywhere Fashion; the signifiers are quite numerous, they include all variations of the garment, the plethora of Fashion features; here we recognize the economy of an infinite metaphor, which freely varies the signifiers of one

---

[10] Cf., above, 17.2.
[11] Structurally, the signified is double: *fashionable/unfashionable* (otherwise, it could have no meaning), but the second term is canceled out, rejected in the diachrony.

and the same signified.[12] Naturally, it is not a matter of indifference that the disproportion be established to the advantage of
the signifier: any system which consists of a large number of
signifieds for a restricted number of signifiers generates anxiety,
since each sign can be read in several ways; on the contrary,
any inverse system (with a large number of signifiers and a reduced number of signifieds) is a system which makes for euphoria;
and the more a disproportion of this type is accentuated, the more
the euphoria is reinforced: this is the case of metaphorical lists
having only one signified, which establish a poetry of solace (in
litanies, for example); metaphor thus appears as a kind of "tran-
quilizing" operator, by virtue of its very semiological structure,
and it is because it is metaphorical that Fashion, in *B* ensembles,
is a euphoric object, despite the combinatory character of the
arbitrary law which founds it.

20.9. *The disappointment of meaning*

The metaphorical process (here a radical one, since the signified
is unique) is only a first condition of this "purity" of *B* ensembles,
just discussed. The second condition concerns the very nature
of the signified which is at the heart of all Fashion utterances
when they speak only of clothing (this is the case of *B* ensembles); this signified is in fact tautological: Fashion can be defined
only by itself, for Fashion is merely a garment and the Fashion
garment is never anything but what Fashion decides it is; thus,
from signifiers to signified, a purely reflexive process is established,
in the course of which the signified is emptied, as it were, of all
content, without, however, losing anything of its power to designate: this process constitutes the garment as a signifier of something which is yet nothing other than this very constitution. Or,
to describe this phenomenon still more precisely, the signifier
(i.e., the Fashion utterance) ceaselessly continues to disseminate
meaning through a structure of signification (objects, supports,
variants, and hierarchies of matrices), but this meaning is finally
nothing more than the signifier itself. Fashion thus proposes this
precious paradox of a *semantic system whose only goal is to dis-
appoint the meaning it luxuriantly elaborates:* the system then

---

12 Same tendency (but here it is only a tendency) in A ensembles, by pansemy.
(Cf., above, 14.7 and 8.)

abandons the meaning yet does so without giving up any of the spectacle of signification.[13] This reflexive activity has a mental model: formal logic. Like logic, Fashion is defined by the infinite variation of a single tautology; like logic, Fashion seeks equivalences, validities, not truths; and like logic, Fashion is stripped of content, but not of meaning. A kind of machine for maintaining meaning without ever fixing it, it is forever a disappointed meaning, but it is nevertheless a meaning: without content, it then becomes the spectacle human beings grant themselves of their power to make the insignificant signify; Fashion then appears as an exemplary form of the general act of signification, thus rejoining the very being of literature, which is to offer to read not the meaning of things but their signification:[14] hence it becomes the sign of the "properly human." This essential status is in no way disembodied: at the moment it unveils its most formal nature, the system of written Fashion unites with its profoundest economic condition: it is the active process of a (nonetheless empty) signification which makes the Fashion magazine a durable institution; since, for such a magazine, to speak is to note, and to note is to make signify, the magazine's speech is a sufficient social act, whatever its contents: it is a speech which can be infinite because it is empty and yet signifying; for, if the magazine did have *something* to say, it would enter into an order whose very goal would be to exhaust that something; on the contrary, by making of its speech a signification pure of all argument, the magazine launches one of those processes of pure maintenance which create enterprises that are theoretically infinite.[15]

20.10. *The Fashion present tense*

The formal purity and closure of B ensembles is sustained by the very special temporality of Fashion. Of course, in A ensembles,

---

[13] Mallarmé seems to have understood this: *La dernière mode* contains no full signified, so to speak, only signifiers of Fashion; by reinstituting the pure immanence of the "knickknack," Mallarmé aimed at humanly elaborating a purely reflexive semantic system: the world signifies, but it signifies "nothing": empty, but not absurd.

[14] We have already seen that *signification* is a process (as opposed to *meaning*).

[15] Press or Fashion, we are confronted here with cultural objects having stable form and unstable content, relatively unexamined from this point of view: we could give these objects the symbol of the ship Argo, of which each piece was gradually replaced, and which nonetheless remained the Argo: actuality is a *form*, it is thus a privileged material for semiological analysis.

the equivalence between garment and world is also subject to Fashion, i.e., to a vengeful present which each year sacrifices the signs of the preceding year: it is only *today* that prints stand for the Races; yet, by opening its signs to the world in the form of functions and reasons, Fashion seems to subject time to a more natural order: in it the present becomes mute and somewhat shameful, carried within connotation along with Fashion itself. All naturalistic alibis disappearing from *B* ensembles, the Fashion present tense thereby guarantees the declared arbitrariness of the system: this system is all the more closed over its synchrony in that each year it reverses entirely and at a single stroke collapses into the nothingness of the past: reason or nature no longer supervising the signs, everything is granted to the system, beginning with the declared murder of the past. *B* ensembles, or, one might say, logical Fashion, thus sanction an exemplary confusion of present and structure; on the one hand, the Fashion's *today* is pure, it destroys everything around it, disavows the past with violence, censures the future, as soon as this future exceeds the season; and on the other hand, each of these *todays* is a triumphant structure, whose order is extensive with (or alien to) time,[16] in such a way that Fashion tames the new even before producing it and achieves that paradox of an unforeseeable and yet legislated "new"; in short, we can say that Fashion domesticates the unforeseen without, however, stripping it of its unforeseen character: each Fashion is simultaneously inexplicable and regular. Long-term memory thus abolished, time reduced to the couple of what is driven out and what is inaugurated, pure Fashion, logical Fashion (that of *B* ensembles) is never anything but an amnesiac substitution of the present for the past.[17] We could almost speak of a Fashion neurosis, but this neurosis is incorporated into a gradual passion, the fabrication of meaning: Fashion is unfaithful only insofar as it *acts out* meaning, *plays* meaning.

---

[16] As we have said, Fashion is systematically unfaithful. Now fidelity (like paralysis within the past) and infidelity (like the destruction of this same past) are equally neurotic, once they assume a form, the former of a legal or religious duty (of the Erinys type), the latter of a natural right to "life."

[17] In fact, Fashion postulates an achrony, a time which does not exist; here the past is shameful and the present constantly "eaten up" by the Fashion being heralded.

IV. THE DOUBLE SYSTEM OF FASHION

20.11. *The ethical ambiguity of Fashion*

A semantically perfect system is a closed, empty, and reflexive system: this is the case with *B* ensembles (at least when they do not mythify the Fashion decision). The system breaks down when it opens itself to the world through paths of connotation. The double system of Fashion (*A* and *B*) thus appears as a mirror in which modern man's ethical dilemma can be read: every system of signs is forced to load itself down, to convert and to corrupt itself as soon as the world "fills" it: in order to open itself to the world, it must become alienated; in order to comprehend the world, it must withdraw from it; a profound antinomy separates the model for productive behavior and that for reflexive behavior, systems of actions and systems of meanings. Through the divergence of its *A* and *B* ensembles, Fashion experiences this double postulation: sometimes it fills its signified with fragments of the world and transforms it into a dream of uses, functions, reasons; sometimes it empties this signified and is reduced to the rank of a structure rid of all ideological substance. A "naturalistic" system (in *A* ensembles) or a "logical" system (in *B* ensembles), Fashion thus travels from one dream to the other, depending on whether the magazine multiplies or on the contrary disappoints the worldly signifieds; it seems that the press having a widespread popular readership practices a naturalized Fashion, rich in function-signs, and that the more "aristocratic" press prefers to practice "pure" Fashion. This oscillation corresponds to a historical situation: originally, Fashion is an aristocratic model, but this model is currently subject to powerful forces of democratization: in the West, Fashion tends to become a mass phenomenon, precisely insofar as it is consumed by means of a mass-circulation press (whence the importance and, as it were, the autonomy of written Fashion); the maturity of the system (in this case, its "gratuitousness") is thus adopted by mass society according to a compromise: Fashion must project the aristocratic model, the source of its prestige: this is pure Fashion; but at the same time it must represent, in a euphoric manner, the world of its consumers by transforming intra-worldly functions into signs (work, sport, vacations, seasons, ceremonies): this is naturalized Fashion, whose signifieds are named. Whence its ambiguous status: it signifies the world and signifies itself, it constructs itself here as a program of behavior, and there as a luxurious spectacle.

20.12. *The transformation*

There is, however, one point in the general system of Fashion where the structure is penetrated by a "doing" *which remains included in it* (therein lies its importance); this point is what Fashion calls the *transformation* (*the summer dustcoat which will become the autumn raincoat*); a rather modest notion, but one to which we shall attach an exemplary value insofar as it represents a certain solution to the conflict which constantly sets the order of transitive behavior in opposition to that of signs. In effect, transformation is found on the frontiers of the system, without ever transgressing it; on the one hand, it remains dependent on the structure, since the utterance always unites a constant (which, in the signifier, does not change and which generally remains the object aimed at by the successive significations of the transformed garment) and a variation (the transformation itself[18]); but, on the other hand, the variation ceases to be potential (i.e., synchronic), in order to become diachronic; through transformation, diachrony is introduced into the system, no longer as a vengeful present which abolishes all signs of the past at a single stroke, but rather, we might say, in a solaced manner (precisely because it is acknowledged, absorbed by the system itself). Thus, a reconciled time (the past is no longer liquidated, it is utilized), a new "doing" (the language of Fashion becomes a true fabricator), and the expression of a system of signs (the fabricated object still conforms to a regular structure) unite in the transformation. Here, in short, is the dialectical solution proposed by Fashion to the conflict between past and present, event and structure, "doing" and sign, and it is not surprising that this solution rejoins economic reality: the transformation is

---

18 Examples: *reversible coats, spring dresses that can become summer dresses by adding an organza collar and belt.*

practically possible (it costs little), while remaining spectacularly ingenious: Fashion increasingly incorporates it into its utterances.

V. THE ANALYST CONFRONTS THE SYSTEM

20.13. *Fugitive analysis*

There remains a word to be said about the situation of the analyst confronted with or, rather, *within* the systematic universe he has just dealt with; not only because it would be something akin to bad faith to consider the analyst as alien to this universe, but also because the semiological project provides the analyst with the formal means to incorporate himself into the system he reconstitutes; more important, it forces him to do so, it is within this obligation that he finds, we might say, his ultimate philosophy, the guarantee that he both participates in the game of history, a certain moment of which he has immobilized, and that he rejoins this present tense which must carry him off to the benefit of other languages and other sciences. In order to apprehend this movement in formal terms (we can have no other project here), we must return to the rhetorical system.[19] We have seen that the signified of this system was not easily controlled on the level of the system's users: latent, general, it cannot be *named* in a uniform manner by those who receive the connoted message: it does not have an assured terminological existence, except on the level of the analyst, whose proper function is precisely to superimpose a nomenclature on latent signifieds, which he alone has the power to bring to light; if he names such and such rhetorical signifieds *syncretism* or *euphoria*[20] he is well aware that these concepts are not in use among the readers of Fashion, and that in order to manipulate them he must resort to a closed intellectual language, in short to a *writing*; now, this writing will function in relation to the system-object of Fashion like a new metalanguage. If then we want to represent the Fashion system, no longer as it is in itself (as we have pretended, of necessity, to consider it up to now), but as it is necessarily exposed in the course of the analysis, i.e., entrusted to a parasitical speech, we

---

[19] Cf., above, 16.III.
[20] Cf., above, 16.6.

must complete the schema of simultaneous systems in the following manner:[21]

4. The analyst's metalanguage	E	C		
3. Rhetorical system		E		C
2. Terminological system	E	C		
1. Vestimentary code		E	C	

It is obvious that, although it is an "operation" and not a "connotation,"[22] the analyst's metalanguage cannot help being "committed"; first, in the categories of his language (here French), for language is not reality; next, in his own historical situation and in his own existence, since a writing is never neutral;[23] for example, to speak of Fashion in terms of structure[24] is to signify a certain choice, itself dependent on a certain historical state of research and a certain discourse on the subject. We thereby understand that the relation between semiological analysis and rhetorical utterance is not at all the same as that between a truth and a lie: it is never a matter of "demystifying" the reader of Fashion; this relation is complementary, internal to the infinite (though temporarily finite) system to which Fashion and its analysis belong; when the rhetoric of Fashion proposes the idea of a certain nature (that of a world where *audacity* and *discretion* would be "true" psychological essences by law), the analyst reestablishes the idea of a certain *culture* (audacity and discretion correspond to a committed segmentation of the world, their conjunction forms the alibi of an artificial intention of euphoria); yet the system is in no way closed at the threshold of this deciphering, the opposition between nature and culture is part of a certain metalanguage, i.e., of a certain state of history; it is a transitory antinomy which other men were not (or will not be) able to speak. The relation between the system-object and the analyst's

---

[21] Schema given above, 3.2. We take the simplest ensemble as an example, i.e., the *B* ensemble with three systems (E: level of expression; C: level of content).

[22] Hjemslev, *Prolegomena*, pp. 114–25.

[23] The taxonomical imagination, which is that of the semiologist, is both psychoanalyzable and subject to historical criticism.

[24] The analyst *speaks about Fashion*, he does not *speak Fashion;* he is condemned to depart from a *praxis* in order to enter into a *logos*. To speak Fashion would be to create it.

metalanguage does not therefore imply any "real" substance to be credited to the analyst, but only a formal validity; it is a relation at once ephemeral and necessary, for human knowledge cannot participate in the world's becoming except through a series of successive metalanguages, each of which is alienated in the moment which determines it. This dialectic can again be expressed in formal terms: speaking of the rhetorical signified in his own metalanguage, the analyst inaugurates (or adopts) an infinite science: for if it happens that someone (someone else or himself later on) undertakes the analysis of his writing and attempts to reveal its content, that someone will have to resort to a new metalanguage, which will signal him in its turn: a day will inevitably come when structural analysis will pass to the rank of language-object and will be apprehended within a superior system which will in its turn explain it. This infinite construction is not a sophistry: it accounts for the transitory and, as it were, suspended objectivity of research and confirms what could be called the Heraclitean nature of human knowledge, each time it is condemned by its object to unite truth and language. Herein is a necessity which is precisely what structuralism tries to comprehend, i.e., to speak: the semiologist is a man who expresses his future death in the very terms in which he has named and understood the world.

APPENDIXES

1. HISTORY AND DIACHRONY OF FASHION

Changes in Fashion appear regular if we consider a relatively long historical duration, and irregular if we reduce this duration to the few years preceding the time at which we place ourselves; regular from afar and anarchic up close, Fashion thus seems to possess two durations: one strictly historical, the other what could be called *memorable*, because it puts into play the memory a woman can have of the Fashions which have preceded the Fashion of a given year.

The first or historical duration has been studied in part by Kroeber.[1] This author chose certain features of women's evening wear and measured variations in them over a long period of time. These features are: (1) the length of the skirt; (2) the height of the waistline; (3) the depth of the neckline; (4) the width of the skirt; (5) the width of the waist; (6) the width of the neckline. The features chosen by Kroeber correspond to certain features of the system which has just been described.[2] The difference is that, working on drawings and not on a language, Kroeber could proceed to real measurements, taking the stature of the human body as principal referent (from neck to toe). Kroeber demonstrated two things: on the one hand, that history does not intervene in the Fashion process, except to hasten certain changes in a slight way, in cases of major historical upheavals; in any case, history does not produce forms, a state of Fashion can never be explained analytically, there is no analogical relation between the Napoleonic period and high waistlines; and on the other hand, Kroeber demonstrated not only that the rhythm of changes in

---

[1] A. L. Kroeber and J. Richardson, *Three Centuries of Women's Dress Fashions*, Berkeley and Los Angeles: University of California Press, 1940.

[2] (1) Dress + length; (2) waist + vertical position; (3) neckline + length; (4) skirt + width; (5) waist + fit; (6) neckline + width.

296/   *Appendixes*

Fashion was regular (the amplitude is around half a century;
the complete oscillation, a century), but also that it tends to make
forms alternate according to a rational order: for example, the
width of the skirt and the width of the waist are always in inverse
relation to each other: when the one is narrow, the other is wide.
In short, on the scale of a period of shorter duration, Fashion is
an orderly phenomenon, and this order is derived from Fashion
itself: its evolution is on the one hand discontinuous, it proceeds
only by distinct thresholds;[3] and on the other hand it is endogenous, since it cannot be said that there is a genetic relation between a form and its historical context.[4]

That is what Kroeber demonstrated. Is this to say that history
has no control over the Fashion process? History cannot act on
forms analogically, but it can certainly act on the rhythm of
forms, to disturb or to change it. It follows that, paradoxically,
Fashion can know only a very long history or no history at all;
for, as long as its rhythm remains regular, Fashion remains outside history; it changes, but its changes are alternative, purely
endogenous: it is no more than a question of simple diachrony;[5]
in order for history to intervene in Fashion, it must modify its
rhythm, which seems possible only with a history of very long
duration.[6] For example, if Kroeber's calculations are correct, our
society practices the same Fashion rhythm over several centuries:
*it is only when this rhythm changes that a historical explanation
may intervene;* and since the rhythm depends on the system
(which Kroeber himself outlined), historical analysis must inevitably proceed by a systematic analysis. We can imagine, for

---

[3] This discontinuity matches the semiological nature of Fashion (*"Language can
only be born suddenly. Things can only come to signify gradually."* Claude Lévi-
Strauss, Introduction to M. Mauss, *Sociologie et anthropologie,* Paris, P.U.F.,
1950, p. xlvii).

[4] Certain historians of costume endeavor nonetheless to establish an analogic
relation between an epoch's form of clothing and the style of its architecture
(notably, H. H. Hansen, *Histoire du costume,* Paris, Flammarion, 1956, and
J. Laver, *Style in Costume,* London, Oxford University Press, 1949).

[5] The word *diachrony* may shock historians; nevertheless, there must be a special term to designate a process both temporal and ahistorical; we could even
speak, as do the Bloomfieldians, of a meta-chrony, to mark a discontinuous process (cf. A. Martinet, *Economie,* p. 15).

[6] The rhythm is subject to history, but this history is a long one; as a cultural
object, clothing belongs to the *long duration* analyzed by Ferdinand Braudel ("Histoire et sciences sociales: la longue durée," in *Annales,* 13th year, no. 4, Oct.–Dec.
1958, pp. 725–53).

example—but this is merely a demonstrative supposition, since it is a question of the future of clothing—that the Fashion rhythm (the one we have known for centuries) might be blocked, and that, except for minor seasonal variation, clothing will not change for a long time; history must then account not for the system itself but for its new permanence; perhaps it would then be discovered that this change in rhythm is the sign of a new society, defined by both its economy and its ideology ("worldwide" society, for example), impervious to the large historical rhythms of clothing precisely to the extent that it will have solidly institutionalized annual Fashion; to actually rather modest variations, since they do not alter the "basic type" of our Occidental clothing. Here is another possible example: that of ancient African societies in the process of development: these societies are well able to maintain their traditional costume and submit it nonetheless to variations in Fashion (yearly changes of fabrics, prints, etc.): a new rhythm is then born.

As we have said, to this historical duration, consisting of a stable rhythm, we must set in opposition a much shorter duration, that of the latest seasonal variations of Fashion, and what could be called a micro-diachrony. This second duration (which is, of course, contained within the first) derives its individuality from Fashion's yearly character; its appearance is thus marked by an intense variability. There is no secret about the economic implications of this variability, which moreover could not exhaust its explanation: Fashion is sustained by certain producer groups in order to precipitate the renewal of clothing, which would be too slow if it depended on wear and tear alone; in the United States, these groups are aptly called *accelerators*.[7] As for clothing worn (as opposed to written), Fashion can in fact be defined by the relation of two rhythms: a rhythm of dilapidation (d), constituted by the natural replacement time of a garment or wardrobe, on the exclusive level of material needs;[8] and a rhythm of purchase (p), constituted by the time which separates two purchases of the same garment or wardrobe. (Real) Fashion, we

---

[7] Contrary to the myth elaborated around Haute Couture, it is quite possible that it is average ready-to-wear clothing which plays a determining part in the real acceleration of vestimentary purchases.

[8] Obviously, an entirely abstract hypothesis: there is no "pure," notably abstract need of an intention to communicate.

might say, is p/d. If d = p, if the garment is replaced as soon as it is worn out, there is no Fashion; if d > p, if the garment is worn beyond its natural replacement time, there is pauperization; if p > d, if a person buys more than he wears, there is Fashion, and the more the rhythm of purchase exceeds the rhythm of dilapidation, the stronger the submission to Fashion.[9]

Whatever it may be for real clothing, the rhythm of written clothing is itself implacably annual,[10] and the renewal of forms from one year to the next seems to take place in an anarchic manner. What is the source of this anarchy? Most notably this: the Fashion system far exceeds human memory. Even—and above all—within a micro-diachrony, no law of change is perceptible. Fashion can of course proceed by oppositions from one year to the next by alternating the simple terms of a single variant: *soft silk crêpe* replaces *stiff taffetas:* the terms of the variant of suppleness are "turned around." But beyond this privileged case, the regularity of these "turnabouts" tends to become confused as a result of two principal causes: one arising from rhetoric, the other from the system itself.

In written Fashion, skirt length, for example—the feature which common sense takes as the very symbol of change in Fashion—is constantly obscured by phraseology; in addition to the fact that the leaders of Haute Couture often propose different lengths for the same year, rhetoric constantly mixes verbal appraisals (*long, longer*) and measurements in terms of centimeters; for if, on the synchronic level, language facilitates the process of signification by permitting a signifying change in the cut of a garment, on the diachronic level it deprives comparisons of their rigor: it is easier to compare measurements (as Kroeber did) than words. On the other hand, on the systematic level, Fashion can quite easily abandon a simple paradigmatic variation (*supple/ stiff*), and shift, as the year passes, to the notation of another variant; a synchrony is in fact never more than an ensemble of

---

[9] At times, written Fashion can make a value out of wear itself (i.e., a signified): "*The appeal of clothes made of leather increases with age, like the value of wine*" (*Vogue*).

[10] Why is the rhythm of women's Fashion much more rapid than that of men's? "*Men's clothing, made to be uniform, does not readily indicate one's financial standing. This role falls to women's clothing, due to the Fashion through which a man expresses his economic status in an indirect manner*" (K. Young, *Handbook of Social Psychology,* London, Routledge and Kegan Paul, 4th ed., 1951, p. 420).

chosen features;[11] the suppleness of a support can be noted and its variant changed: this is all that is needed to produce a new Fashion. Numerically, the combinations of a support and the variants to which it can apply depend on the richness of the support: if we grant that a support can apply on the average to seventeen variants, there are already more than several hundred possible systematic variations for each Fashion, since we have identified some sixty genera-supports. Added to internal variations of the same variant, the freedom to combine supports and variants is so great that it makes all Fashion forecasting difficult.

Actually, this matters little. What is interesting is that if Fashion forecasting is illusory, its structuration is not.[12] It must be remembered here that the more generalized a garment is, the more readable its changes appear to be: a temporal generalization which makes a long duration (like Kroeber's) seem much better organized than the micro-diachronies in which we live; a formal generalization also, since, if we were able to compare silhouettes (which written Fashion does not permit), we could readily grasp the "turnabout" in Fashion features,[13] whose actualization is risky, but whose reservoir is entirely structured. In other words, Fashion is structured at the level of its history: it is destructured at the only level at which it is perceived: actuality.

Thus, the confusion of Fashion does not stem from its status but from the limits of our memory; the number of Fashion features is high, it is not infinite: we could very well conceive of a Fashion-making machine. Naturally, Fashion's combinative struc-

---

[11] An example of features chosen for the "soft look" 1958: "*A blousy chemise, a cardigan, and a supple skirt, cuffs showing below the jacket sleeves, collar folded down and open wide to show necklaces, a casual waistline marked by a soft belt, a heavy knit cloche worn back on the head.*" Here are the features mobilized by this utterance: blouse + flection + closure; vest + species; skirt + suppleness; collar, necklace + emergence; necklace + multiplication; waist + mark; belt + suppleness; hairstyle + species + orientation; substance + species.

[12] Same problem for language, simpler because of the reduced number of differentiated units, also more complex because of the double articulation. South American Spanish is comprised of only twenty-one differentiated units, but a dictionary of this same language contains a hundred thousand different signifying elements. It would be a mistake to believe that the system excludes the aleatory; on the contrary, the aleatory is an essential factor of any system of signs (cf. R. Jakobson, *Essais*, p. 90).

[13] This is what was done by N. Truman (*Historic Costuming*), an excellent historian of costume. This generalization corresponds to Kroeber's *basic pattern* (or *fundamental inspiration*, to use J. Stoetzel's expression), which follows clothing during a certain period.

ture is mythically transformed into a pleasing phenomenon, an intuitive creation, an irrepressible, hence vital, expansion of new forms: Fashion, we are told, abhors system. Once more, the myth inverts reality: Fashion is an order made into a disorder. How does this conversion of reality into myth take place? By the rhetoric of Fashion. One function of this rhetoric is to blur the memory of past Fashions, so as to censure the number and the return of forms; in order to do this, rhetoric constantly gives the Fashion sign the alibi of a function (which seems to extract Fashion from the systematics of a language), it discredits the terms of past Fashion, making those of current Fashion euphoric, it plays on synonyms, pretending to take them for different meanings,[14] it multiplies the signifieds of a single signifier and the signifiers of a single signified.[15] In short, the system is drowned under literature, the Fashion consumer is plunged into a disorder which is soon an oblivion, since it causes the present to be perceived in the form of a new absolute. Fashion doubtless belongs to all the phenomena of *neomania* which probably appeared in our civilization with the birth of capitalism:[16] in an entirely institutional manner, the new is a purchased value.[17] But, in our society, what is new in Fashion seems to have a well-defined anthropological function, one which derives from its ambiguity: simultaneously unpredictable and systematic, regular and unknown, aleatory and structured, it fantastically conjoins the intelligible without which men could not live and the unpredictability attached to the myth of life.[18]

2. Fashion Photography

Photographing the Fashion signifier (i.e., the garment) poses problems of method which were set aside at the outset of the

---

[14] "In 1951, furry woolens were being promoted; in 1952, fuzzy woolens." [?]

[15] *"Satin triumphs, but so do velour, brocade, faille, and ribbons."*

[16] In the Renaissance, as soon as one got a new costume, one had a new portrait done.

[17] Fashion is one of those phenomena of psychic nutrition which R. Ruyer has analyzed ("La nutrition psychologique et l'économie," in *Cahiers de l'Institut de Science Economique Appliquée,* 55, pp. 1–10.

[18] Conjoining the desire for community and the desire for isolation, Fashion is, in Stoetzel's terms, *adventure without risk* (*Psychologie sociale,* p. 247).

analysis.[19] Yet Fashion (and this is increasingly the case) photographs not only its signifiers, but its signifieds as well, at least insofar as they are drawn from the "world" (*A* ensembles). Here we shall say a word about photographing Fashion's worldly signifieds, in order to complete the observations relating to the rhetoric of the signified.[20]

In Fashion photography, the world is usually photographed as a decor, a background or a scene, in short, as a theater. The theater of Fashion is always thematic: an idea (or, more precisely, a word) is varied through a series of examples or analogies. For example, using *Ivanhoe* as theme, the decor develops Scottish, romantic, and medieval variations: the branches of naked shrubs, the wall of an ancient, a ruined castle, a postern gate and a moat: this is the tartan skirt. The travel cloak for countries where the cold is misty and damp? The Gare du Nord, the Flèche d'Or, the docks, slag heaps, a ferryboat. Recourse to these signifying ensembles is a very rudimentary process: the association of ideas. *The sun* evokes *cactuses, dark night* evokes *bronze statues, mohair* evokes *sheep, fur* evokes *wild beasts* and *wild beasts* evoke *a cage:* we'll show a woman in fur behind heavy bars. And what about *reversible* clothes? *Playing cards,* etc.

The theater of meaning can assume two different tones here: it can aim at the "poetic," insofar as the "poetic" is an association of ideas; Fashion thus tries to present associations of substances, to establish plastic or coenesthetic equivalences: for example, it will associate knitwear, autumn, flocks of sheep, and the wood of a farm cart; in these poetic chains, the signified is always present (autumn, the country weekend), but it is diffused through a homogeneous substance, consisting of wool, wood, and chilliness—concepts and materials mixed together; it could be said that Fashion aims at recapturing a certain homochrony of objects and ideas, that wool is made into wood, and wood into comfort, just as the Sunda Islands kallima hanging from a stem takes on the form and color of a dried leaf. At other times (and perhaps increasingly often), the associative tone becomes humorous, the association of ideas turns into simple wordplay: for the "Trapeze" line, models are put on trapezes, etc. Once again, within this

[19] Cf., above, chap. 1.
[20] Cf., above, chap. 18.

style, we find the main opposition in Fashion between the serious (winter, autumn) and the gay (spring, summer).[21]

Within this signifying decor, a woman seems to live: the wearer of the garment. Increasingly, the magazine substitutes a garment-in-action for the inert presentation of the signifier:[22] the subject is provided with a certain transitive attitude; at least the subject displays the more spectacular signs of a certain transitivity: this is the "scene." Here Fashion has three styles at its disposal. One is objective, literal; travel is a woman bending over a road map; to visit France is to rest your elbows on an old stone wall in front of the gardens of Albi; motherhood is picking up a little girl and hugging her. The second style is romantic, it turns the scene into a painted tableau; the "festival of white" is a woman in white in front of a lake bordered by green lawns, on which float two white swans (*"Poetic apparition"*); night is a woman in a white evening gown clasping a bronze statue in her arms. Here life receives the guarantee of Art, of a noble art sufficiently rhetorical to let it be understood that it is acting out beauty or dreams. The third style of the experienced scene is mockery; the woman is caught in an amusing attitude, or better still, a comic one; her pose, her expression are excessive, caricatural; she spreads her legs exaggeratedly, miming astonishment to the point of childishness, plays with outmoded accessories (an old car), hoisting herself up onto a pedestal like a statue, six hats stacked on her head, etc.: in short, she makes herself unreal by dint of mockery; this is the "mad," the "outrageous."[23]

What is the point of these protocols (poetic, romantic, or "outrageous")? Probably, and by a paradox which is merely apparent, to make Fashion's signifieds unreal. The province of these styles is always, in fact, a certain rhetoric: by putting its signifieds in

---

[21] What must be recovered (but who will teach it to us?) is the moment when winter became an ambiguous value, converted at times into a euphoric myth of home, of sweetness, and of comfort.

[22] Actually, and this is what is strangest about Fashion photography, it is the woman who is "in action," not the garment; by a curious, entirely unreal distortion, the woman is caught at the climax of a movement, but the garment she wears remains motionless.

[23] We were not able, within the framework of this study, to date the appearance of the "outrageous" in Fashion (which perhaps owes a good deal to a certain cinema). But it is certain that there is something revolutionary about it, insofar as it upsets the traditional Fashion taboos: Art and Woman (Woman is not a comic object).

quotation marks, so to speak, Fashion keeps its distance with regard to its own lexicon;[24] and thereby, by making its signified
unreal, Fashion makes all the more real its signifier, i.e., the
garment; through this compensatory economy, Fashion shifts the
accommodation of its reader from an excessively but uselessly
signifying background to the reality of the model, without, however, paralyzing that model in the rhetoric which it freezes on
the margins of the scene. Here are two young women sharing a
confidence; Fashion *signs* this signified (the sentimental, romantic young girl), by endowing one of the girls with a huge daisy;
but thereby the signified, the world, *everything which is not the
garment*, is exorcised, rid of all naturalism: nothing plausible remains but the garment. This exorcism is particularly active in the
case of the "outrageous" style: here Fashion ultimately achieves
that *disappointment* of meaning which we have seen defined in
the world of B ensembles; [25] the rhetoric is a distance, almost as
much as denial is; Fashion effects that sort of shock to consciousness which suddenly gives the reader of signs the feeling of the
mystery it deciphers; Fashion dissolves the myth of innocent
signifieds, at the very moment it produces them; it attempts to
substitute its artifice, i.e., its culture, for the false nature of things;
it does not suppress meaning; it points to it with its finger.

---

[24] This deliberate rhetoric is served by certain techniques: the excessive vague-
ness of a decor (as opposed to the clarity of the garment), enlarged like a photogenic dream; the improbable character of a movement (a leap frozen at its
climax); the frontality of the model, who, in contempt of the conventions of the
photographic pose, looks right in your eyes.

[25] Cf., above, 20.9.